Anticipate the School You Want

Futurizing K–12 Education

Arthur B. Shostak

ROWMAN & LITTLEFIELD EDUCATION
Lanham • New York • Toronto • Plymouth, UK

Published in the United States of America
by Rowman & Littlefield Education
A Division of Rowman & Littlefield Publishers, Inc.
A wholly owned subsidiary of The Rowman & Littlefield Publishing Group, Inc.
4501 Forbes Boulevard, Suite 200, Lanham, Maryland 20706
www.rowmaneducation.com

Estover Road
Plymouth PL6 7PY
United Kingdom

British Library Cataloguing in Publication Information Available

Library of Congress Cataloging-in-Publication Data

Shostak, Arthur B.
  Anticipate the school you want: futurizing K-12 education / Arthur Shostak.
    p. cm.
  ISBN-13: 978-1-57886-854-4 (cloth: alk. paper)
  ISBN-10: 1-57886-854-8 (cloth: alk. paper)
  ISBN-13: 978-1-57886-855-1 (pbk.: alk. paper)
  ISBN-10: 1-57886-855-6 (pbk.: alk. paper)
  eISBN-13: 978-1-57886-908-4
  eISBN-10: 1-57886-908-0
  1. Education—United States—Forecasting. 2. Educational change—United
States. I. Shostak, Arthur B. II. Title.
  LA217.2.S574 2008
  370.973—dc22

                                                                2008016688

♾™ The paper used in this publication meets the minimum requirements of
American National Standard for Information Sciences—Permanence of
Paper for Printed Library Materials, ANSI/NISO Z39.48-1992.
Manufactured in the United States of America.

Dedicated with deep appreciation to
Educational Activists:

Yvonne Chan, Principal, Vaughn Next Century Learning Center, LA
John Chubb, Edison Learning Institute, NYC
Joe Klein, Chancellor in New York City
Bob Peterson, Editor of the Rethinking Schools Web site
Michelle Rhee, Chancellor in Washington, D.C.
Jason Smith, Superintendent, Melissa, Texas, who founded TeacherTube
Samuel B. Stewart, Interim Superintendent of Schools, Skillman, New Jersey
Paul Vallas, Superintendent in New Orleans
Tony Wagner, Creator of the "New Village Schools" Movement
Shimon Waronker, Principal in Junior High School 22, South Bronx, NYC

And to Howard Gardner, Herbert Kohl, Jonathan Kozol, and Marsha Lynne
Rhea, along with hundreds of thousands of unsung heroes and heroines in
the classroom, all of whom who are busy "futurizing" education, *by whatever name.*

Contents

Foreword   vii

Preface: Education 2.0   ix
32 Cautious Forecasts   xix

Introduction: The Time is Now!   xxiii
Great Expectations for the Future: Bridging Dickens to Dreams   xxxv
    by Alison J. George

Part I: **"Lift Off!"**   1

1   Futuristics: Shaping Tomorrow   7
Future Problem Solving Program International   21

2   Futures Committee: Showing the Way   35
Schooling in 2015: Beckoning Possibilities   48

3   Futuristic Schooling: Moving Parts   53
Design a City: An Individual Renewable Energy/Resource Recycling Project,   69
    by Katherine Spalding and Kelly Smith

Part II: **Jewel in the Crown**   71

4   High Schools of the Future: "Boot Camp"   73

5   Required Courses: Fundamentals   83

6   High Schools of the Future: Learning Aids   103

Part III: Educational Futures "GPS"   117

7   Futures Fair: Come, Let Us Celebrate!   119

8   Future Possibilities: World 3.0   125

Epilogue: Getting On With It   135

Selected Resources   143

Acknowledgments   151

About the Author   153

Foreword

Everyone wants to improve education. The problem is not a willingness to improve, but rather direction. *Anticipate the School You Want: Futurizing K–12 Education* is *not* another book bashing the education system. In fact educators, parents and futurists will see it as an upbeat and practical vision for the value in and processes of futurizing. We can all chant the emerging mantra—"globalization, high tech, accelerated change, greening, creativity and innovative society" and so forth. *But how can we get beyond the "little red schoolhouse" metaphor and really unlock human potential for the 21st century?*

In *Anticipate the School You Want* Art Shostak brings over four decades of futures thinking and insight to a generative work that sets us thinking and acting to transform learning through a "futurizing" model. He skillfully weaves his renowned futures insight into a compilation of examples, scenarios and practical processes that stimulate imagination.

For Shostak futurizing really comes from a verb "to future" *and* from a noun "future." For him futures are made. Hence, futurizing an academic system requires skillfully honed, practiced and encouraged skills, abilities, and tools for thinking and doing the future. On the other hand, the future (a noun) can be a constructed place, a visionary place that can be a vantage point for looking backward toward one's present. Building future visions as magnets for present action gives significant value to the present and past.

Futurizing helps give current action meaning. It connects past and present actions in a continuous link to another state. Far from an end in themselves Shostak's scenarios and case studies are fuel for synergy. Futuring is reality construction, creating worlds that have yet to be and then preparing people to live in those worlds. In this view "the future" is more likely *created* than *discovered*.

Anticipate the School You Want operates at multiple levels and appeals to many audiences. The title is a little deceptive. It suggests that modern educators may be the only audience for this work. In reality a much broader group will benefit from Art Shostak's work. This multidimensionality is revealed in the content and the processes. If you're looking for a challenging summary of some key forecasts for the future and some examples of futures building, futurists will clearly enjoy this book. If you're an educator at any level—primary, secondary, or college levels—you are bound to find some exciting and challenging examples of ways to bring the future to life in your programs, courses, and classes. Parents can gain insight on some learning options. And, for thinking about futuring for the first time you'll find some thoughtful and challenging ideas that will foster new thinking on your part and act as a primer.

In many ways *Anticipate the School You Want: Futurizing K–12 Education* is purely a vehicle for introducing anyone to the principles of future thinking. While some of the specific examples may lose their meaning with the passing of time, the work maintains a transcending quality. One could imagine extracting it from a time capsule in 2060 and be able to find reasons to be inspired. In short, it will provide new insight whenever it is removed from the shelf.

In *Anticipate the School You Want: Futurizing K–12 Education*, Art Shostak inspires our imagination for creating what a learning system can be without, as futurist John Naisbitt says in *Mind Sets*, "get(ting) so far ahead of the parade that people don't know you're in it!"

Stephen F. Steele, PhD
Professor of Sociology and Futures Studies
Institute for the Future @ AACC
Anne Arundel Community College

Preface:
Education 2.0

Like you, I weatherize my home, winterize my car, and in other like ways, try to turn the future to advantage. Which brings me to my purpose in writing this book. Quite frankly, I hope to persuade you to join me in a long-term campaign to help *futurize* K–12 schooling . . . that is, *to bring more of the art of futuristics into the art of education.*

I want to help youngsters secure a new skill set, one that should boost their confidence about the future, and their ability to help make good on that confidence. Together we can encourage the employ by teachers of more of the future in general, and possibly even get a magnet high school developed for teenagers eager to specialize in the subject.

BACKGROUND

Over my 42-year career as a college teacher (1961–2003) I took a similar tack concerning the sociology courses I taught and the university where I enjoyed sharing ideas. I tried to *futurize* them. Which is to say, I tried to apply one of my favorite subjects, futuristics, to my favorite day job, teaching and learning. From the front of the classroom, and as a longtime member of the faculty senate, I tried to promote a finer future on and off campus.

As my teaching career began in the early 1960s *BC* (Before Computers), I struggled to computerize my courses (student mentoring was indispensable). I introduced credit courses in futuristics, both on campus and on the Internet. I drew on educational simulations, both role-plays and virtual exercises (far more enjoyable). I surprised myself (and everyone else) by actually bringing virtual guests into class via teleconferences.

When not teaching I helped promote campus-wide science fiction film festivals, and created a local cable TV series of interviews with futurists. I edited several volumes of previously unpublished essays by leading forecasters, some for high schoolers, others for collegians. And, as a moonlighting futurist I helped many colleges and universities forecast enrollment out ten years or so. We then weighed changes possibly worth making in present-day and prospective curriculum.

As for my experience with K–12 schooling, in my lifelong effort to boost my moxie in these vital matters, I often shared ideas as a consultant on educational futures. I learned with and from public school superintendents, private school administrators, principals, teachers, and locals of teachers unions coast-to-coast. On many in-service days, especially at the start of a new school year, I gave auditorium talks about the near future in K–12 education. I made a point to tour any school where I was speaking, and learned much of value listening to whatever staff and students had on their mind. As often as possible I made daylong study visits to schools of every type.

In the 1960s, as cochair of the Board of a progressive K–6 school my two sons attended, I helped plan and guide its future. I also cooperated with a Philadelphia chapter of the National Urban League in an ill-fated effort to get voter approval for bonds to pay for urban Educational Parks (one of my favorite futurizing ideas, a project that could have thoroughly transformed schooling). In the 1970s I assisted a local organization (Citizens Concerned with Public Education) as an assessor of area school quality. I also aided short-lived, if also inspiring, forerunners of today's minority-led charter schools. (See also Notes on the Author).

WHY BOTHER?

We both know some attention *is* paid to tomorrow in today's classroom, as when current events get their just due. But we also know this plays second fiddle to everything else, and can be vastly improved. Indeed, it tells us something about the educational scene that we even need a separate term like "educational futuristics." I have some ideas about how we can improve the situation, and I suspect from your readership, you do also. Pooling our ideas, and joining forces with many others coast-to-coast, we may yet help improve K–12 education in valuable ways.

Soaring rhetoric and good intentions to one side, a reasonable question haunts the scene: namely, *why bother?* Some of you must be thinking, "My plate is full. The demands on me are already unreasonable. Resources [time, energy, commitment] are stretched to the limit. Why should I take on still another responsibility?"

In part, because you respect the yearning youngsters that have to learn about tomorrow, to "search out the new, the exciting, the source of energy that will release us from the bonds of the ordinary, the expected, the known."[1] And in part, because you want youngsters able to distinguish good from poor or even dangerous forecasts. You want students to appreciate the seamless web that connects us to one another, and requires us to care for one another. And, you want to promote creativity, initiative, and pizzazz, the better to be able to create value—the real measure of education.

Above all, we—you and I—might shoulder this new teaching responsibility because we want youngsters to know people *are* changing things for the better. Indeed, as I wrote these words during primary contest time (January through March, 2008), we had "a woman, a black, and a creationist . . . in the race [for president]: some U.S. taboos are falling."[2] Likewise, "the role of spouses in presidential politics is evolving, from one of smiling wife to equal and visible partner."[3] On Super Tuesday, February 5, turnout among that supposedly disengaged demographic aged 18 to 29 doubled in Massachusetts, tripled in Georgia, Missouri, and Oklahoma, and quadrupled in Tennessee."[4]

And by mid-February, a blogger became one of the Obama campaign's more prolific fund-raising bundlers, raising many thousands of dollars from hundreds of friends and strangers—albeit Karl was only 14 years old. An activist wrote—"Those of us who care about the influence of big money on politics don't really need more laws. We need more Karls."[5] The air at primary time crackled with excitement, as calls for change were heard, and evidence of change was clear. Life evolved so fast the present felt like the future.

EDUCATIONAL GAINS

Where K–12 students are directly concerned, many positive changes mark the scene; for instance, since 1991 (a peak year), the birth rate for teenagers 15 to 19 has decreased by 35 percent. In 1980, daily cigarette smoking among 12th graders was about 21 percent; by 2006, it had fallen to about 12 percent. Teen use nationwide of alcohol has fallen off sharply since 1996, and binge drinking has dropped to the lowest levels ever recorded. Teen drug use dropped 23 percent between 1999 and 2005, and for specific drugs, the decline was even more (ecstasy use fell over 50 percent; methadone, almost as much).[6] Thanks in large part to your efforts, the high school dropout rate (around 10 percent) is the lowest in the last thirty years. SAT math scores continue a climb begun in 1980, and scores on advanced placement tests are up, with black and Hispanic students making especially broad gains (although unacceptable gaps with whites persist).[7] Nearly 30 percent more U.S. public high school seniors passed at least one advanced placement exam in 2007, showing they are better prepared for college than seniors were five years ago.[8]

Some 68 percent of high school students nationwide now go to college, and the percent of low-income students who say they want a four-year degree or higher has tripled, rising from 19 percent in 1980 to 66 percent in 2002.[9] This is a sound development, as from 1984 to 2005, those with some college education realized the strongest growth in family wealth (31 percent gain), and graduating from college contributed to a 10 percent increase in net worth.[10] In 2005, the average bachelor's degree holder earned $54,689; high school diploma holder, $29,488; and high school dropout, only $19,915.[11]

Accordingly, many large high schools serving low-income populations—schools organized for the last 30 years around *low* academic expectations—are busy now reorganizing around the opposite. Youngsters once seen as "at risk" are newly seen as "at promise." A reform leader maintains, "This is a transformational change. It's about the purpose of high school. It's about reinventing what high schools do."[12]

In short, even with the persistence of many hard-core social problems, many ongoing changes in our social mores, our government policies, and our educational realities have us substantially bolstering our future. America is experiencing moral advance even if the media have not caught up to it. This under-recognized story is one futurized schools can proudly share, and one youngster can profit greatly from learning, pondering, and in due course, helping along.

LOOKING ELSEWHERE

Likewise, a futurized curriculum would look overseas for progress that warrants overdue recognition. For example, over 135 million people emerged from poverty between 1999 and 2004, a stunning sign of progress. From 1950 to the present, globalization helped increase annual average income in the world, up from $2,100 to $7,000, thereby creating "the greatest mass exit from poverty in world history."[13]

Progress here owes much to growing control over fertility. The world's population is now growing at half of its pace in the 1960s, and so "world income per head has increased by more over the past five years than during any other period on record."[14] The worldwide baby boom of the 20th century, which threatened overpopulation and mass starvation, is subsiding. More children are getting schooling, escaping child labor, and enjoying improved life chances.

There is twice the number of fast-growing economies now than the world had from 1980 to 2000. In 2007, the developing countries produced over 52 percent of global growth, compared to 37 percent during the late 1990s. Their share of total world output has risen to 29 percent from 18 percent in 1995, and it may reach 56 percent by 2050. In 2008 the World Bank forecast their economies would grow 7.4 percent, compared to 2.2 percent in the old industrial nations.[15] More people have more access to more goods and services than ever before.

Arguably, "countries like Iran and China, which now seem so immune to the global democratic trend, stand a very good chance of becoming democratic in the next two or three decades."[16] In 2007, The Human Development Index, which combines adult literacy, education enrollment, GDP/capita, and life expectancy showed improvement for nearly all countries.[17] And there are far fewer wars raging now than in recent decades. The decline of violence is "the most important and underappreciated trend in the history of our species. . . ."[18] Countries that have not started a war in decades are in the majority. Humankind has never had it so good.

This is *not* to sugarcoat matters. Having traveled in twenty-six countries during the past thirty-six years, and having made demanding analyses of vexing trends a mainstay in my courses (the spreading income gap, the fear of terrorism that pinches our lives, the loss of millions of well-paying jobs, etc.) I know full well much needless cruelty, injustice, suffering, and terrorism persist.[19] Nearly 10 million children die each year because their families, communities, and nations are too poor to sustain them . . . and this happens on our watch.[20]

EDUCATIONAL CHALLENGES

To focus in on K–12 education in the nation's 124,000 public and private schools, nearly 13 million of America's 73 million children (17 percent) live below the artificially low poverty line (which has not risen in real terms in 40 years, and "probably understates the true depth of many children's misery"). Ironically, this adds up to substantially more youngsters than were poor 47 years ago—when the "War on Poverty" was declared—a "war" we have been losing ever since (37 million Americans, or 12 percent of all ages, still live below the line).[21]

Of no surprise was the recent reaction of a South Carolina state officer who unexpectedly dropped in to one of his state's typical rural public school: "I just couldn't really believe my eyes. It was the most deplorable building condition I've ever seen in my life. How the hell somebody could teach in an environment like that is really just beyond me."[22]

In the educational world I know best, a severe form of suffering, made all the more consequential and painful for being very private, involves the failure to graduate: the percentage of college students completing their degree work has been stagnant for over a generation.[23] Academically unprepared, emotionally disengaged, and vocationally aimless, far too many college dropouts take away only broken dreams and wounded self-esteem . . . a setback few college-bound high schoolers imagine as apart of his or her future.

Again, like you I know a lot about this . . . more anecdotes, facts, and linkages that bruise my soul, and vex me 24/7. I understand full well the aphorism, "pessimism of the intelligence, optimism of the will."[24] A futurized K–12 curriculum would pay age-appropriate attention to dark matters.

That curriculum, however, would accent actual and proposed reforms. It would not shy from their maddening contradictions and costly limitations, but would emphasize their intentional and also unplanned rewards. It would overshadow the mass media focus on harrowing spirit-wounding details (e.g., how many were murdered today? How did it happen? What was the killer like? The victim?). This enervating stuff ("death by a 1,000 cuts") feeds feelings of alienation and powerlessness in youngsters; it encourages cynicism and hopelessness about social change.

Our overarching goal would be to highlight efforts—here and abroad—to promote alternatives to misguided craziness and violence, and to invent ways to bolster collective benefits. Our students should gain confidence thereby in the ability of people worldwide to improve our shared future. Not coincidentally, in the process they should come to take pride in one of our greatest national strengths—we are the least fatalistic country in the world.[25]

OUTLINE

To help get us from here to there, that is, to help K–12 education make futuristics a preoccupation, I share eight chapters divided into three main sections. In Part I, we learn the meaning of futuristics, and take its full measure, especially where schooling is concerned (chapter 1). We also explore the why and wherefore of a school Futures Committee (chapter 2), and learn how an entire school curriculum might profit from greater-than-ever employ of futuristics (chapter 3).

In Part II we go into detail concerning a high school of the future, a training ground devoted to the preparation of tomorrow's professional forecasters. I discuss how the school might be named, what the school might resemble (grounds, buildings, classrooms, etc.), what its required courses might cover, how its implicit and co-curricula culture could compliment its mission, what its student government and its student clubs might tackle, and so on (chapters 4, 5, and 6).

And in Part III, we enjoy imaging what a biannual school Futures Fair might include, as this offers a unique opportunity both to show off and attract imitators (chapter 7). We move next in chapter 8 to ponder four high probability/high impact developments educators would best prepare for now (staff reeducation needs, human capital investment needs, the Artificial Intelligence Challenge, and the Climate Change Challenge). Finally, in the Epilogue I weigh the odds of soon making progress in this matter, and close by urging creation of a national organization to help advance K–12 gains from futuristics.

SUMMARY

Education remains the one public institution that "includes 90 percent of the next generation of adults . . . and has the explicit mission of educating for democratic citizenship."[26] Accordingly, much pivots on its creative employ or blasé underutilization of futuristics.

Fortunately, almost every K–12 professional I have ever met, here and abroad, seemed eager to improve schooling about tomorrow. Nations elsewhere are very active on this front: Australia (Sustainability Project), Canada ("Vision 2020"), England (FutureSight Project), Holland (Slash/21, etc.), and New Zealand ("Secondary Futures" Program) stand out. Linked to the "Schooling for Tomorrow" program of the Organization for Economic Co-Operation and Development (OECD), these projects have much to offer us, and, vice versa.[27]

Your readership has me now count you among the ranks of educators eager to get on with it. We have a bracing responsibility—you and I—to help keep education as future-focused as possible, and then some. If 90 percent of life is showing up, the other 10 percent is figuring out how to get there—and futuristics is a "map" of preference, a rewarding blend, like all maps, of "form, function, and fantasy."[28]

Much you will read about in this book you have probably thought about before, but may have wondered how to achieve it. The ideas for achievement ("map markers") I share hereafter work best if used in a custom-tailored way, as your school is its own unique world. Assessed creatively, frequently, and unsparingly, they can remain edgy rewarding aides, the kind we need to achieve the far-sighted educational system we dream of, "nimble, adaptive, and efficient."[29]

Working together, we can help futurize schooling and make history. Or we can allow K–12 schooling to drift, and become history. The risk of obsolescence is considerable. Our choice, as our students would say, is a no-brainer: *Time to futurize!*

HIGHLY RECOMMENDED READING

1) *The Top Trends That Will Reshape the World in the Next 20 Years,* by James Canton. New York: Plume, 2007. Explores the major changes now transforming our world; employs a cautious optimism regarding a surprising future.

2) *What Are You Optimistic About? Today's Leading Thinkers on Why Things Are Good and Getting Better,* edited by John Brockman. New York: Harper Perennial, 2007. Nearly two hundred especially thoughtful people share reflections about the sources of their hopes, as these are "born of expertise and hard, imaginative thinking" (vii).

NOTES

1. Amidon, Jane. *Radical landscapes: Reinventing Outdoor Spaces.* London: Thames & Hudson, 2001, 6.
2. Cohen, Roger. "Brazilian Lessons for 2008." *New York Times,* January 3, 2008, A–23.
3. Langley, Monica. "Michelle Obama Solidifies Her Role in the Election." *Wall Street Journal,* February 11, 2008, A1.
4. Carr, David. "News Isn't Wasted on the Young." *New York Times,* February 18, 2008, C1.
5. Bonin, Adam. "An Unfettered Internet Best Serves Democracy." *Philadelphia Inquirer,* February 21, 2008, A15. "John Edwards' campaign allowed ordinary Americans to prepare their own campaign ads, one of which on rural issues ended up airing in Oklahoma."
6. Wehner, Peter and Yuval Levin, "Crime, Drugs, Welfare—and Other Good News, *Commentary,* December 2007.
7. Brooks, Arthur C. "Happiness and Inequality." *Wall Street Journal,* October 22, 2007, A18.
8. McQuillen, William. "U.S. Students Showing Gains on Advanced Placements Tests." *Philadelphia Inquirer,* February 14, 2008, A7.
9. Rimer, Sara. "Urban Schools Aiming Higher than Diploma." *New York Times,* January 17, 2008, A24 (A1, A24).
10. Stafford, Frank, in Anon. "Rich and Richer, Poor and Poorer." *The Futurist,* November–December, 2007, 12.
11. Cetron, Marvin J. and Owen Davies. "Trends Shaping Tomorrow's World." *The Futurist,* March–April 2008, 43.
12. Dan Challenger, president of the Public Education Foundation (Chattanooga), as quoted in Rimer, Sara. "Urban Schools Aiming Higher than Diploma." *New York Times,* January 17, 2008, 24 (1, 24).

13. Easterly, William R. "Why Bill Gates Hates My Book." *Wall Street Journal*, February 7, 2008, A18.

14. Anon. "Grossly Distorted Picture." *The Economist*, March 15, 2008, 92. See also Walker, Martin, "Globalization 3.0" *Wilson Quarterly*, August 2007, 16 (16–24). Declines in dependency ratios "are responsible for about a third of the East Asian economic miracle of the postwar era; this is a part of the world that, in the course of 25 years, saw its dependency ratio decline 35 percent." Gladwell, Malcolm. "The Risk Pool." *The New Yorker*, August 28, 2006, 31 (30–35).

15. Hale, David. "Brave New Economy." *Wall Street Journal*. February 22, 2008, A14. See also Anon., "Don't Let Gloom Obscure Global Prosperity." *The Economist*, January 26, 2008, 23. The 2050 projection is from Jakab, Spencer. "Boomer Effect: Gloomy Forecasts." *Wall Street Journal*. March 28, 2007, B3.

16. Diamond, Larry, as quoted in DiGiovanni, Janine. "Democratic Vistas." *The New York Times Book Review*, January 20, 2008, 21. See also *The Spirit of Democracy*, by Prof. Diamond.

17. United Nations. *Human Development Report 2007/2008*. New York: Palgrave Macmillan, 2007, 6.

18. Pinker, Steven. "The Decline of Violence." In Brockman, John, ed., *What Are You Optimistic About? Today's Leading Thinkers on Why Things Are Good and Getting Better*. New York: Harper Perennial, 2007, 3 (3–5).

19. To cite just a very few relevant matters, I have worked on projects in prison-based parole rehabilitation, Job Corps system design, inner-school problems, and other such efforts. My wife Lynn and I have spent time in hardscrabble Rio *favellas* and in harrowing slums in Albuquerque, Beijing, Quito, and Vienna. We have lingered in museums in five concentration camps (Austria, Germany, Poland), in the Museum of Terror in Budapest and other nightmarish settings. In these and many related ways, we have tried to stay personally challenged by what some insist defies explanation, the better to help keep alive our faith in the redemptive possibilities of better social systems and life formulas.

20. Sachs, Jeffrey. "Common Wealth." *Time*, March 24, 2008, 38 (37–40).

21. Krugman, Paul. "Poverty is Poison." *New York Times*, February 18, 2008, A15. See also Vitullo-Martin, Julia, "Urban Decay." *Wall Street Journal*, March 14, 2008, A16: "To restore a city and its neighborhoods . . . fight crime successfully and everything else will start to fall into place. . . ."

22. Charles Way, former state commerce secretary, as quoted in a documentary, "Corridor of Shame," and cited in Herbert, Bob, "The Blight That Is Still With Us." *New York Times*, January 27, 2008, A21.

23. Brooks, David. "Fresh Start Conservatism." *New York Times*, February 15, 2008, A23.

24. Rolland, Rolland (French Nobel Prize–winning novelist, playwright, and intellectual). As cited in Fisher, David James. "A Statesman Without Borders. [Letter] *New York Times Magazine*, February 17, 2008, 10.

25. Anon., "Don't Let Gloom Obscure Global Prosperity," *The Economist*, op. cit.

26. Glickman, Carl. "If 'Change' is the Answer, What is the Question?" *Education Week*, March 19, 2008, 26.

27. See in this connection, OECD. *Think Scenarios, Rethink Education*. Paris: Organization for Economic Cooperation and Development, 2006.

28. Boutin, Paul. "A Sense of the Future." *Wall Street Journal*, January 26–27, 2008, W8.

29. Adapted from a thought of Professor Larry Summers, as cited in Chrystia Freeland. "Let the Bad Times Roll." *Financial Times*, February 2/3, 2008, 22.

32 Cautious Forecasts
March 2008

In the foreseeable future, K–12 educators are likely to be challenged by the varied impacts of at least these thirty-two very dynamic matters, all of which have connections—in varying degree—with one another. Pragmatic and creative preparations should be underway. While the future cannot be known, it need not blindside us.

THE NEXT BIG THINGS

1. Climate Change—Already underway; awesome in implications.
2. Energy Quandary—Can we achieve renewables in time? Rationing is possible. International innovation may help.
3. "Green" Technologies—Pressure builds to redo all as "green."
4. Cost of Living/Operations Rise—Driven by new buyers, new shortages. People and organizations face higher bills, as oil prices soar.
5. Water Shortages—The "oil" of the 21st century; water wars.
6. Nuclear Weapon Spread—Perhaps fifteen nations by 2020, up from as many as nine in 2008. Danger of terrorist access.

INFORMATION MATTERS

1. Informatics Gains—24/7 affordable broadband connectivity; open source user-generated software.
2. Mechatronics—Microprocessors embedded in almost everything.

3. "Intelligent Agent"—AI-based advocate of owner's well being; still very speculative, but a goal of many IT enthusiasts.

GLOBAL CHANGE

1. China, China, China!—Headline maker; troubled colossus. With India coming up fast behind, and Japan sharper than both.
2. Empire Fatigue—U.S. acceptance of multi-polar guidance of globe. More reliance on "soft power" and discreet negotiations.
3. Global Regulatory Gains—Solutions reach size of problems.
4. Fundamentalism—Ranks grow, as uncertainty grows. Violent?
5. Nation Fragmentation—Possible increase in split-offs from large nations; persistent agitation.
6. Polar Competition—Rivalry over resources under both poles, especially at the Artic.
7. Space Competition—China on Moon; joint Mars Mission.

HEALTH MATTERS

1. Biotechnology Gains—Awesome source of medical gains (nano).
2. Customized Medicine—From mass to narrow. Help extend life span.
3. Wellness Emphasis—Accent on proactive health care.
4. Eugenics—Quest for "Super Baby" engineering. The New Divide.
5. Pandemics—Ancient threat, exacerbated by increased travel.

MIND MATTERS

1. AI Gains—Biochips, Brain Research, "Smart" Robotics, etc.
2. Augmentation—Performance-enhancing chips and chemicals.
3. "Singularity"—A time when our advancing knowledge in biotech, AI, and nanotechnology merge into a single discipline, at which point, for better or worse, humans take charge of their own evolution.

SOCIAL MATTERS

1. "Gray" Power—Older Boomers coalesce in an AARP voting bloc. Lack of young workers undermines pension funding.
2. "Isms" Fade—Ageism, Racism, Sexism, etc., lose power.
3. Middle-class and Working-class Expansion—In emerging nations.

4. Middle-class and Working-class *Angst*—In developed nations.
5. Organizational Gains—Emphasis on "Tribe" membership, creativity, flexibility, retention of best employees, etc.

TECHNOLOGY MATTERS

1. Robot Ascendancy—Gains in "smarts," etc. Ever greater resemblance to humans, for better and worse. Key question is whether morality is possible in robots.
2. Space Weaponry—Renewed interest in "Star Wars" weaponry.
3. Nanotechnology—After climate change, THE Next Big Thing! May take decades to realize full potential, but likely to do so.

Prepared by Art Shostak, Emeritus Professor of Sociology, Drexel University, (shostaka@drexel.edu). Feedback earnestly welcomed.

Introduction:
The Time is Now!

"The future is not ominous, but a promise; it surrounds the present like a halo."

John Dewey

Drawing on my nearly half-century of involvement in K–12 education, and going beyond inspirational ideas earlier offered by other educational futurists, I highlight actions to help *futurize* K–12 schooling . . . that is, help us bring more of the art of futuristics into the art of education. I make a case for educational futuristics (a.k.a. "Anticipatory Learning"), and buttress it with examples of future-shaping changes proposed or under way, especially high probability/high impact developments likely to empower K–12 youngsters for the rest of their lives.

THE TIME IS NOW!

Given this outline of a task that might strike you as fairly overwhelming, I'd like to explain my cautious optimism. At the risk of preaching to the choir, as I anticipate your reading probably has you familiar with a good bit of what follows, I want to highlight three major reasons why I believe significant gains in K–12 futurizing can probably be made quite soon . . . and why this may be the best possible time to push for futurizing education. (Note: I say more about this in the Epilogue.)

First, "Generation Next" youngsters are not the children we once were; nor were their older siblings in Generation X or Generation Y. Instead, today's children have remarkable futuristic expectations of school. Second, many new teachers do also. And third, much that vexes educators (never-ending disputes involving charter schools, school choice, Columbine-like tragedies, doubts about the worth of expensive e-books, etc.) requires stronger than ever foresight on our part—a national strength best promoted by the futurizing of K–12 schooling.

1) GENERATION NEXT

When next possible, you might casually ask a youngster to share expectations about his or her future. In December 2007, I asked my nine-year-old grandson David and was intrigued by his thoughts.[1] After reflecting a moment, he wondered aloud what life might be like if global warming did not stop? What would take the place of animals that might disappear? He switched next to the challenge posed for his generation by the likely availability soon of pills that could make them smarter. He thought he would not volunteer to take any of them until he was certain users were not harmed in any way.

As for robots that got smarter and smarter, David looked forward to making close friends of some of them, as they would probably be easier to get along with than were some real people he had already met. He would welcome an opportunity to live for a while at a moon base station, though he would rather stay at a dome on the ocean floor since it would be closer to the Earth's surface, and there would be more people around to help him in an emergency.

David does not believe in the existence of extraterrestrial life, though he suspects our life-form began elsewhere, probably on Mars. He believes a baby born 50 years from now may have a life expectancy of about 140 years, thanks to really great improvements in health care, diet, and that sort of thing. The child will school only six hours a day in a school building (versus the nine hours David now spends there), and learn as much at home from really awesome tech tools.

David does not believe the future will have all the nations we have today; rather, he expects China and India to merge, and Argentina and Brazil to do the same. He is uncertain about America's ability to maintain its world leadership role, but not frightened by the prospect of having to share the role. While he expects his lifetime will include something resembling a world war fought by humongous *Star War* space technology (pieces of which he masterfully creates with Legos), he does not think it will involve nuclear weapons; David puts his hopes for avoiding that disaster in new American presidents.

On balance, then, my grandson's crystal ball musings earned my broad smile, as David was far more knowledgeable about future possibilities and perils than I could recall being at age nine. Or nineteen, for that matter.

Have-Much Youngsters

Explanations for the future-consciousness of American youngsters are not hard to come by. My grandson and his peers have been tutored by Saturday morning cartoons that often soar off to explore the future. They have grown up learning pro-Green "protect tomorrow!" lessons from "Barney," and from "Bill Nye the Science Guy." Some can mimic lines from futuristic movies like *A.I.* and *E.T.,* or from science fiction serials, from *Star Trek* reruns, and also from future-oriented series on cable TV (including material on The History Channel). Many explore future-oriented Web sites on the Internet.

Theirs has been a mind empowering "diet" from an $18 billion gaming market of Microsoft Xbox 360, Nintendo GameCube, Nintendo Wii, Sony PlayStation 2 or 3, and other electronic "edutainment" sensations (each complete with casual nonviolent cross-generational games that appeal to the more hip among their parents). Some still too young to ride a two-wheeler can already draw on their simplified computer. Items I grew up favoring, items without computer monitors, U.S.B. cables, and memory cards, "are seen by many children as obsolete."[2] Even the lowly Erector Set now comes with a little electronic brain (youngsters can assemble spy robots controlled by a home's WiFi network or via a Bluetooth connection).[3]

Preschoolers are learning computer skills from starter laptops that include educational games, e.g., ClickStart My First Computer, etc. A new generation of popular stuffed animals and dolls are now linked to Internet sites; for example, Webkinz (a plush toy with its own interactive Web site), Kookeys (a similar plush doll whose Web site stresses more educational activities).[4] Bib-wearing children "can cuddle and dress them one minute, and go online to social network the next."[5]

Many have spent untold hours glued to high-powered children's TV shows (*Futurama, Little Einstein,* etc.), most of which adroitly mix in sugar-coated educational stuff with their funny gooey stuff. Youngsters six and up can make movies with the Flix Max Video Camera (complete with 128 MB of onboard memory). Some better-off children even have cell phones, iPods, and other such colorful empowering things. In combination these items have "a way of making fourth grade sound like someplace you'd reach by space shuttle."[6]

(Robots for children, by the way, get better sooner all the time. A popular 2007 entry, the humanoid I-Sobot, contained seventeen motors with

which it moved its limbs, only three fewer than what you and I find necessary for most human movements. It responded to ten voice commands and
could speak about two hundred words or phrases. It required no assembly
or programming with a computer before a youngster could enjoy it. Its sale
price of $300 was a dramatic drop from the $1,000 asked by far weaker
predecessors.)[7]

Outside of their homes many of these children frequent modernized science museums designed "not to impart a body of static information, but to
stimulate discovery and scientific thinking by means of interactive installations."[8] Likewise, movies like *A.I.*, *E.T.*, and others offer exotic locales, involve easily digested learning, and challenge the imaginations far more
than did comparatively quaint and patronizing Disney (or inane "Three
Stooges") fare of yesteryear. And a robot called "Bender" on *Futurama* helps
youngsters accept the idea of such objects as human peers.

To lend some detail, consider this quick sketch from the mother of a 15-
year-old freshman at a California High School: "On a typical day after
school, you'll find Hannah in her bedroom, iPod charging on the desk,
headphones in her ears, cell phone in one hand, paperback book in the
other, television tuned to a *Gilmore Girls* rerun, and computer with display
divided among iTunes, YouTube, a *Pride and Prejudice* DVD, and, of course,
MySpace, which she constantly checks for messages from friends."[9] While
we adults scratch our heads, Hannah and her ilk rapidly move on, seldom,
if ever, even glancing at instruction manuals.

"At-Promise" Youngsters

This is not to overgeneralize. As dedicated teachers can testify, millions of
"have-less" youngsters contend with lives nowhere as privileged as those
pictured above (18 percent of all 73 million children, or 13 million, live below the federal poverty line).[10] Harrowing economic conditions, broken
families (especially absent fathers), and neighborhood anarchy handicap
these youngsters from the outset.

Youngsters who have drawn the short straw in life struggle to raise their
test scores above "basic" proficiency. They try and get by in schools where
simple building repairs can take months. Where dedicated teachers take
hundreds of dollars from their own salaries to plug vital gaps in school supplies. Where "teach to the test" pressures and outdated texts bruise learners
and teachers alike. Where ugly metal detectors and grim, burly building
guards are taken for granted.

While often behind grade, these youngsters, like all others, commonly
have considerable knowledge, potential, or talent. Many can and do take
advantage of the ongoing closing of the Digital Divide. Students in a third-
grade class in rural Oklahoma, for example, a class with a very high poverty

rate, start every morning interacting with computer-based educational programs delivered over a computerized "Smart" white board.[11] Similarly, high schoolers in low-income areas rely heavily on their cell phones, which they manage with high dexterity, as leery high school teachers can affirm (and as the acclaimed HBO show, *Wired*, made clear in its 2006–2007 season).

In low-income neighborhoods, America's best-selling game machine sells for less than its $130 list (the Nintendo DS), and among its 15 million-plus owners are many underprivileged students who qualify for school lunch assistance.[12] When low-income homes have computers, and many do, the machine they can afford makes the original Univac I, with its tiny memory of 12 kilobytes, "seem like a moron."[13]

Looking Ahead

In short, "our 21st-century students are media-saturated, tech-savvy, collaborative, and connected to a culture that has permanently altered the education experience."[14] Never before have so many youngsters—"have much" and "have less" types alike—had so many high tech communication devices with which to feed their natural curiosity about tomorrow. Most take an *interactive* way, rather than slough off as passive "listen-to-the-radio" or couch potato TV viewers.

Many, especially young cognoscenti, are first users of dazzling advances, such as their new ability in 2008 to use Sony's PlayStation Portable to make a free phone call to any other user of that machine anywhere in the world. Some may soon get a device to wear on their person that will combine phone, music and video player, PDA, camera, camcorder, electronic book, and so on. As hobbyists today have access to more processing power than MIT had in 1980, the dreams young people have of "wonder" high tech stuff tomorrow are not entirely wishful.[15]

Growing up immersed in a high tech environment, many youngsters expect K–12 education to adapt its curricula and pedagogies to new literacies. Little wonder that a close student of reading practices forecasts said, "today's kids are not going to want to pick up a big book and spend hours in a corner silently, passively reading. They're going to ditch the hardback and head over to Facebook."[16]

Many youngsters are quite good at abstract problem solving, and at the ability to adapt to new interfaces and find the information they need. At pattern recognition. At system analyzing with complex sorts of multiple variables. At system thinking, and at visual intelligence. They are the first generation to get beyond linear thinking. As geodesic thinkers they thrill to the possibilities in hypermedia use, and to life lived in a hyperlinked personal world.

Little wonder a writer who studies these youngsters believes "on all of these levels, kids are much brighter today than they were 20 or 30 years ago."[17] If and when Web 3.0 becomes operational, much of its open and flexible learning environment may be created by these youngsters themselves.

Tech-savvy youngsters expect *very* dynamic K–12 educational settings *as their due*. To judge cautiously from surveys collected in 2004 from 210,000 students in 50 states—they want educational settings that allow wireless access anywhere. Permit instant messaging all the time. And provide endless software upgrades.[18] As well, many of their taxpaying, school-board-electing parents expect much the same for their offspring. While the folks may still think "text" is a noun, even as their offspring recognize the word as a verb, the generations are as one in expecting razzle-dazzle change at school.

Given this orientation, we now have our first state (Michigan in 2007) that requires high school students to take at least one online course for graduation. We have our first school system (Charles County Public School District) to be wired end-to-end: "With a firm footing in the present and one eye on the future, [it] is well-positioned to take advantage of all the benefits educational technology has to offer."[19] And twenty-five states have now established statewide or state-led virtual schools.[20]

Likewise, youngsters at a typical path-setting school, Philadelphia's Science Leadership Academy, recently "studied atomic weights in biochemistry (itself a homegrown interdisciplinary course), did mole calculations in algebra, and created Dalton models (diagrams that illustrate molecular structures) in art. Learning [there] doesn't merely cross disciplines—it shatters outdated departmental divisions."[21]

2) APPLE FOR THE (NEW) TEACHER

Given the large number of teacher retirements expected in the next few years (as Baby Boomer staffers reach 65), new recruits will soon dominate the teaching scene—and many seem intent on increasing its modernization.

A middle-aged cohort, born in the mid-1960s (median age of 45), differs from their elders in having missed out on being adults during the culture wars of the 1960s. Many were essentially shielded as (underwritten) college and graduate students from economic setbacks and foreign policy reverses in the 1970s and 1980s. They have grown up in relatively privileged times, having "experienced low-inflation economic growth something like 95 percent of their adult lives—something true of no other generation in history."[22]

A younger bloc, still in their late '20s or early '30s, differs from their elders in that their life expectancies are much longer (a datum that has significance in choice-making). They have spent more time earning degrees, marry and have children later in life, attend church less often, are more tolerant of life styles and ethnic and religious diversity, and, at least in the 2008 primaries, voted at record levels.[23]

Taken together, many of both the middle-aged and younger types probably have a personal Web site, a MySpace page, a Facebook entry, and high regard for cell phone text messaging. At home in virtual worlds such as *Entropia Universe*, *Second Life*, and *There* (including the use of virtual classrooms at such Web sites), a third of all under thirty cannot remember their own phone numbers, and rely on their smart phones to do that for them.[24]

As teachers, many of the technophiles among the two age cohorts enjoy using Internet-based inter-active modes, including even after-hours Internet dialogues with their students. Some like exploring daunting subject matters in class, like the case for and against global warming, or the case for and against torture, along with other front-page aspects of our future. Many teach across disciplinary lines and scoff at the old-fashioned silo-like separation of subjects (regardless of what state licensing authorities prefer).

In short, those I call the New Faculty grew up with, and generally seem to appreciate the vast possibilities of our Electronic Age. Like Generation Next on the other side of the podium (actual or virtual), many New Faculty members champion a future-aware school culture that looks not only back and around, but also attentively forward. As a great many intend to stay on the job longer, and retire later than their predecessors, these teachers are serious about getting and keeping school settings futuristic.

Typical of the New Faculty is a 29-year-old primary school science teacher, Shakura Brown, who in 2008 chose to spend eight weeks teaching her courses from a base in Antarctica. The first African-American educator to do so, she used video conferencing and blogging to reach around the world. Dozens of other students learned via the Urban Science Corps, a NASA-affiliated nationwide after-school program Ms. Brown helped develop.[25]

3) FOR WHOM THE BELL TOLLS

Still another, and possibly the most significant reason to expect progress in K–12 futurizing is the growing recognition of our urgent need to bring along a new generation of aspiring futurists. That is, K–12 students who, years later as degreed adults, can help us better anticipate and respond to tomorrow's future.

Where K–12 education is concerned, recent "future shocks" include charter school controversies, school choice legislative battles, Columbine-like disasters, demands for Metal Detectors, a persistent Digital Divide, doubts about purchasing costly e-books, dustups over gay rights advocacy, and sharp differences of opinion about both bilingual schooling and main-streaming—to name just a few of many jolts to the system.

We ask, why didn't we see much of this coming? See it early enough to avoid being taken unawares, and have a better chance to dampen the cost and mount a sound response. Where is our foresight capability? Why can't we turn more high-quality anticipations to significant advantage? Why aren't we better users of futuristics?

As a society, we are not very sure about where we are going, though we seem to be going there rapidly. Many of us can still remember engineers wearing slide rules on their belts, secretaries operating out of typing pools, and movie-going requiring just that—going to a movie house. Today the once unimaginable rapidly becomes the unexceptionable—body part transplants from animals, fly-bys past Venus, a woman and a black male contesting their party's presidential nomination, and the Golden Arches selling "Big Macs" in Beijing, Moscow, Seoul, and Tokyo. Little wonder that Clarke's Law has wide acceptance: "Any sufficiently advanced technology is indistinguishable from magic."[26]

Kindergarten children in 2008 expect to graduate high school in 2021, by which time computer power may be millions of times greater than at present: "That which was impossible for our grandparents is now commonplace; that which seems impossible to us will be matter-of-fact for our children."[27] We need a citizenry with a higher Futures "I.Q.," and we need this yesterday. Even as we seem able to raise the test scores of certain youngsters, and improve metrics like attendance and on time completion, we need an improved capacity in K–12 schooling to anticipate much of what is heading our way, protect against the worst of it, and make the most of the rest.

We can no longer map the use of new technologies onto old curricula. The coprincipal of a suburban New Jersey high school concedes the classroom must compete with the flash of cyberspace: "We have to be interactive because they're accustomed to sitting in front of a screen, and they've got five windows up, and they're talking to three people at the same time."[28] Their example underlines the notion that the Internet is the "most radical transformation of private and public life in the history of mankind."[29]

SUMMARY

Prospects may be improving for futurizing K–12 schooling. A combination of Generation Next youngsters, New Faculty, and the impact of these dizzying times would seem to require it. Dynamic educational decision makers are likely to soon hold sway, and many seem to want K–12 schooling to be more forward-looking than ever. When asked in 1931 what he thought of Western civilization, Mohandas Gandhi answered, "I think it would be a good idea."[30] Likewise, a futurized school system would seem a very good idea.

HIGHLY RECOMMENDED READING

1) *Futuring: The Exploration of the Future*, by Edward Cornish. Bethesda, MD: World Future Society, 2004. A definitive overview of the history, state at present, and prospects of the field, by an insider who created the World Future Society.

2) *The Playful World: How Technology is Transforming Our Imagination*, by Mark Pesce. New York: Ballantine, 2000. Explores how a new kind of knowing and a new way of creating are transforming our culture: "Our children will know how to make sense of the playful world, an important lesson they will be happy to share with us, if we are willing" (272).

NOTES

1. Before it occurred to me to ask David his thoughts about tomorrow, I had been enjoying watching him play Mario Kart for DS Lite, a small $150 machine whose game then was a $35 Nintendo car racing game. Using its on-screen LCD keyboard functions with eight buttons and a control panel he could control a race car ("concert grands on fat tires") in any of five different modes, each rich with several levels of play. He was able to play alone or against as many as eleven others if they were all on the same WiFi setting (often true at parties and sleepovers). As he got better at it, the game tempts him to go further by offering ever-harder racing course and even other Mario games. (Silently I wondered, *What in school can match the magic of this game?*)

2. Richtel, Matt and Brad Stone. "For Toddlers, Toy of Choice is Tech Device." *New York Times*, November 29, 2007, A28.

3. Charney, Ben. "Technological Gadgets Smarten Up." *Wall Street Journal*, December 31, 2007, B3.

4. Richtel and Stone, op. cit. "Toy makers are worried that they may be losing their youngest, most devoted customers to the consumer electronics and video game companies." Additional evidence that today's digitally savvy K–12 enrollees have a distinct profile comes from the frantic ongoing search by the multibillion dollar theme park industry "to devise a new era of spectacular attractions rooted in technology." An executive admits "we [have been] trying to find out things we didn't even know to ask about." Sue Bryan, a Senior Show Producer at Pixar, as quoted in Barnes, Brooks, "Will Disney Keep Us Amused?" *New York Times*, February 10, 2008, BU8 (1, 8).

5. Richtel and Stone, *op. cit.*

6. La Gorce, Tammy. "Pop-Culture Exile: It's a Family Thing." *New York Times*, December 2, 2007, 8NJ.

7. McClaim, Dylan. "Not Exactly the Jetsons, but Getting Closer." *New York Times*, January 3, 2008, C6.

8. Gurewitsch, Allan. "Reinventing the Science Museum: A Cultural Conversation with Emlyn Koster." *Wall Street Journal*, November 28, 2007, D10.

9. McLester, Susan. "Technology Literacy and the MySpace Generation." *Technology & Learning*, March 2007, 17.

10. Viadero, Debra. "Poor Rural Children Attract Close Study." *Education Week*, February 6, 2008, 14 (1, 14).

11. Johnson, Sharon. "A Childhood in Poverty Informs Her Teaching." *USA Today*, January 14, 2008, 7d. The teacher is Valarie Lewis, a member of the 2007 All-USA Teacher Team.

12. Taub, Eric A. "With Wii and DS, Nintendo Has 2 Hit Game Devices." *New York Times*, December 31, 2007, C1.

13. Robinson, Frank M. *Science Fiction of the 20th Century: An Illustrated History*. Portland, Oregon: Collectors Press, 1999, 11.

14. Spence, Anne. "Closing the Science Gap by hand." *Education Week*, February 6, 2008, 25 (25, 27).

15. Hall, J. Storrs. *Beyond AI: Creating the Conscience of the Machine*. Amherst, NY: Prometheus Books, 2007, 253.

16. From Jeff Gomez, *Print is Dead: Books in Our Digital Age*, as cited in Liesl Schillinger. "Beyond the Cover, Who's to Know." *New York Times*, November 11, 2007, 14.

17. Johnson, Steven. As quoted in Anon., "Around the Corner." *Time*, March 20, 2006, 86 (84-89).

18. Corey, Murray. "Students See Tech as Necessity, Say Schools Fall Short." *eSchool News*, April 2004, 27.

19. Charles County Public Schools District (27,000 students), as recounted in Hoffman, Richard. "A Wireless World." *Technology & Learning*, March 2007, 30. It took several years to implement, and cost $1 million.

20. Armstrong, Sara. "Virtual Learning 2.0." *Technology and Learning*, November 2007, 26.

21. Smith, Fran. "My School. Meet MySpace." *Edutopia*, April/May 2007, 27. The school is one of four Philadelphia experimental high schools opened in 2006.

22. Barone, Michael. "The 16-Year Itch." *Wall Street Journal*, January 4, 2008, A11.

23. Riley, Naomi Schaefer. "A New Generation of the Young and the Restless." *Wall Street Journal*, January 18, 2008, W11. Draws heavily on a 2007, book, *After the Baby Boomers*, by Princeton sociologist Robert Wuthnow. Schaefer suggests, "thanks to Prof. Wuthnow, the boomers will know what the future holds."

24. Brooks, David. "The Outsourced Brain." *New York Times*, October 26, 2007, A25.

25. Rimer, Sara. "Harlem to Antartica for Science, and for Pupils." *New York Times*, March 28, 2008, A1, 20.

26. Swanwick, Michael. "The Edifying Odyssey of A.C. Clarke." *Philadelphia Inquirer*, March 23, 2008, H8.

27. Pesce, Mark. *The Playful World: How Technology is Transforming Our Imagination*. New York: Ballantine, 2000, 271. "Our children will come to apprehend a different reality than the one we inhabit. Because we have bestowed upon them eyes

and ears and hands we could only dream of, they will be granted a broader sense of self" (270).

28. Michael LaSusa, coprincipal at Chatman High School, Chatham, NJ, as quoted in Lee, Felicia R., "The Rough-and-Tumble Online Universe Traversed by Young Cybernauts." *New York Times*, January 22, 2008, B8 (1, 8) See also Prensky, Marc. "Programming: The New Literacy." *Edutopia*, February/March 2008, 48–52.

29. Siegel, Lee. *Against the Machine: Being Human in the Age of the Electronic Mob.* New York: Spiegel & Grau, 2008, 3.

30. Anon. "A Long Line of Stand-offs." *The Economist*, March 22, 2008, 94.

Great Expectations for the Future: Bridging Dickens to Dreams

By Alison J. George

Reports from the field are invaluable, as they lend authenticity and ballast. The report below of a successful exercise in adapting a course requirement to future concerns of teenagers can help show the way to many more such creative projects. The writer is an urban high school English teacher and a doctoral candidate with the Social Justice Program at the University of Massachusetts, Amherst, and she can be reached at alisongeorge@gmail.com.

JANUARY 30, 2008

Although I must have resisted aspects of own my high school education, my poor, highly transient, English language learning and ethnically diverse urban students enter the classroom much more disengaged than I remember being. That's not surprising as I attended a privileged, white suburban high school where our education was described as a stepping stone toward a "bright future." Teachers linked curriculum to college prerequisites, the guidance staff held frequent and well attended financial aid workshops, and all students were expected to apply to at least one university. As one of the few working-class students in the school, I received an exceptional amount of encouragement, guidance, and support, and went on to receive a scholarship to an elite private university. Even though my own parents had dropped out of community college, the high school's strong academic focus and abundant resources ensured I had everything necessary to succeed.

I became a teacher because I believed my experience shouldn't be unique; all students should have a high school education that truly prepares them for a "bright future." However, the pressures imposed by limited resources, state and federal content standards, and overwhelming testing mandates can make it challenging to offer as robust an experience as mine to my students. Frustrated by years of seemingly irrelevant and inaccessible standardized curriculum, many of my students enter my classroom balking at the list of "dead white men" required by our eleventh grade British literature course. (*"I hate reading." "This is boring." "Why do we have to read this?"*)

To make the course feel personally and academically important I developed a ten-week unit that uses Dickens' *Great Expectations* as a springboard for exploring the future aspirations of my students. I asked them to identify and research their professional and educational goals, meet with local adults they consider successful, write college application essays, and increase their sense of academic possibility.[1]

Given my students' relatively low reading levels (ranging from third to twelfth grade levels, with the majority reading two grades below level), and the length and complexity of the text, I opted to teach the 450-page *Great Expectations* as a ten-week unit. To help students develop independent work skills, allow for curricular differentiation, and accommodate a large number of students with limited out-of-school work time (due to work and/or parenting responsibilities), I used a reading-writing workshop model to frame the unit. Although this unit would be my first experience teaching, and my students' first experience taking, a reading-writing workshop, it was such a successful model that students requested to use reading-writing workshops for future novels.[2]

To breakup the monotony of a ten-week unit on a single text, and to facilitate students' acquisition of personally useful skills and information, each week I introduced a new topic related to students' developing "life expectations." For example, early in the unit, we spent several class periods discussing the concept of "success" and how it was interpreted differently in different social contexts (e.g., students' families, our school, the media). Students wrote essays exploring their personal definitions of success and identifying how they would become successful in their lives.

Subsequent lessons required students to interview people they considered "successful," and asked students to submit the names of family and community members that embodied success. Students suggested their siblings, parents, bosses, and other community members as examples of successful people; in a series of very well received lessons, I invited these people and other community members into the classroom to share their personal, educational, and professional journeys. In the first year I taught the unit, we had a social service worker, a professional singer, a baseball coach, a police officer, and two university faculty people address the class; students also conducted one-on-one interviews with local criminologists, lawyers, real estate agents, interpreters, child care workers, and even a zoologist.

In addition to infusing interesting (and often unexpected!) content into our class discussions, these guest speakers provided philosophically and culturally diverse models of "success" while affirming students' personal aspirations and dreams. Moreover, by involving students' families and other community members in class activities, these lessons increased the relevance and accessibility of a seemingly far-removed canonized text.

As students explored the ways Dickens' characters were affected by financial and social ambition, they reflected upon the values and skills they wanted to carry into adulthood. Although few of my students had family members who had attended college, many believed they would need some form of post-secondary education in order to meet their career goals. In an attempt to encourage these aspirations, as well as to increase their readiness for college, I incorporated a series of lessons focusing on selecting, applying to, and paying for college. In the first of these lessons, members of the guidance staff taught students how to use print and online college search engines; students then had two class periods to research, gather information about, and print the applications for two colleges they would like to attend.

Through this process, students learned about multiple colleges' prerequisites, costs, extracurricular offerings, and available majors. After completing their research and attending a financial aid workshop, students were charged with either a) writing an application essay appropriate for the college of their choice, or b) writing a resume and cover letter for the job of their choice. Although the resume and cover letter assignment would have required less work, one hundred percent of my students chose to write college application essays!

To help students begin their essays, I gathered "how to" articles from popular print and electronic sources. By incorporating advice written by "professionals," I was able to increase students' interest in and ability to translate a high school assignment into a college-level application essay; my reservation of a computer lab in which students could write and revise their essays (a hot commodity in my resource-starved school), further raised the bar of this assignment. After students had written, edited, and rewritten their essays, I compiled the essays into "college admissions packets" containing four anonymous student essays, admissions review team instructions, three deferral letters, and one acceptance letter.

In teams of four, students conducted mock college admission reviews during which they made specific recommendations to improve students' application essays. Although the feedback provided to students was rarely as specific as I had hoped, the process of reviewing other students' essays proved invaluable to students, own writing processes. Students' final drafts of their essays were easily their best pieces of writing, and all students filed their application essays with their guidance counselors for future submission.

Between completing the seemingly impossible task of reading and understanding *Great Expectations,* and taking steps toward meeting their own educational and professional goals, this unit left many students feeling ready to succeed in life after high school. In addition to proving useful, this was an enjoyable unit to teach, with students becoming increasingly excited about both the text and nonliterary assignments. Students' final evaluations of the unit included comments like "the most important thing I learned is about college, and where I would like to be in the future"; "I learned not to quit and to ask when I need help"; and "I learned how to balance a lot of work and not fall behind," with students' "favorite" lessons evenly split among literary, grammatical and college-readiness activities.[3]

In the words of my students: "I learned to read in depth and appreciate different types of literature. I also learned how to write a college essay, and not to quit when the work is too hard. This unit made me feel ready for college." "The guest speakers were interesting, and I learned it is important to start preparing for college early, because there is a lot to do that can't wait until the last minute." "In conclusion, I want the opportunity to strive for and have a great education. I don't only see [college] as a way to benefit from a vibrant community of people with a wide variety of backgrounds and experiences, but also as a way to contribute the customs I was raised with to build a stronger and more complete society around me."

Now, that's what I call success!

For more information about this unit, or for copies of selected unit materials and assignments, please e-mail the author at alisongeorge@gmail.com.

NOTES

1. I wish I could say the decision to teach what would become a creative and engaging unit on Dickens' *Great Expectations* was the result of my deep passion for Dickens; in reality, it was based on having sufficient copies of the text and access to other teachers' well-written unit materials for *Great Expectations* (see *Recommended Resources* below). One such unit, written by Mary Collins, proposes teaching *Great Expectations* as a thirty-lesson unit that integrates students' reading of the text with a mini-unit on their own life expectations, with an emphasis on how students might find and keep a job. Intrigued by the possibility of increasing the personal and cultural relevance of a canonized text, and deeply interested in fostering my students' current and future success, I adapted and supplemented Collins' unit to suit my students' needs.

2. I introduced the unit by distributing a fifteen-page unit outline to each student. Included in this packet were the unit objectives, a weekly reading schedule, a ten to fifteen word vocabulary assignment, ten to fifteen comprehension and analysis questions, an outline of all required assignments, and a weekly class schedule.

Most weeks, Mondays and Tuesdays emphasized group and silent reading, with me available to help students individually with upcoming assignments, reading comprehension, or other tasks. On Wednesdays, students turned in their vocabulary assignments, and we spent much of the period discussing vocabulary and grammar (e.g., Dickens' use of dialect as an indicator of social class) before students returned to their reading. Students' comprehension and analysis questions were due on Thursdays (with full credit awarded for "reasonable" answers, even if they weren't correct), and we spent the period closely analyzing content and themes from the week's reading. Fridays began with a fifteen-minute quiz on the week's reading and vocabulary content, followed by students' individual or group initiation of the next week's assignments. After the first two weeks, students rapidly adjusted to our schedule, and many students realized that if they worked diligently in class they could get most of their reading and vocabulary work done during class time, freeing up after-school time for other assignments. Moreover, the structure and schedule of this unit seemed to nourish students' developing organizational and time-management skills, and several students took the opportunity to "get ahead." (Why doing so made them feel like they were "getting away with something" I will never fully understand!)

3. Given the struggle to stick closely to mandated content while preparing students for the complex academic, personal, and professional demands of "real life," units that bridge canonized curriculum to personally and culturally relevant content offer real potential for promoting student success. By expanding a single text into a ten-week comprehensive unit, this unit enabled me to address multiple literary, grammatical, and compositional standards, while nourishing student engagement, academic confidence, and readiness to meet future success.

RECOMMENDED RESOURCES

Collins, M. (1999) *Great Expectations: A Unit Plan*, 2nd Ed. Berlin, MD: Teacher's Pet Publications, Inc.

Glencoe Literature Library. (n.d.) *Study Guide for Great Expectations*. New York: Glencoe McGraw-Hill.

I

"LIFT OFF!"

"To make the future is highly risky; it is less risky, however, than not to try to make it."

Peter F. Drucker

In the Preface I shared some biographical notes to give you an idea of where I am coming from. I rushed along to ask why bother to promote a greater-than-ever emphasis on the future in K–12 schooling? My answer placed particular emphasis on good news that seems under-reported in schooling, possibly to the detriment of children's expectations of tomorrow. I contend that educational futures can help youngsters appreciate a key precept from the Enlightenment: *We can and ought to improve what unborn generations inherit.*

I followed up in the Introduction by highlighting three reasons why I believe K–12 schooling is ripe for change; namely, youngsters coming along expect a future-oriented education, as do many younger teachers. And both cohorts seem to sense an imperative here: Either we change schooling, which is to say, rapidly and thoroughly futurize it, and thereby help make history, or we run the risk of our current version sadly becoming history.

OUTLINE

Now, in this opening part of the book, we get down to work. With all due modesty, and much is due, I share in chapter 1 some thoughts about *futuristics*, warts and all. We explore the implications of "a highly rational process of making reasoned extrapolations based on major trends that are now unfolding."[1] Strengths and limitations are reviewed, with attention specially paid to ways it can make a unique and valuable contribution to K–12 education.

In chapter 2 I urge you to form a Futures Committee in your school, an indispensable tool for promoting futures consciousness, craft, and confidence. I tackle such questions as who to invite on the committee? How can it become a "tribe"? What might it pursue? And so on. Over and over again a key point is made: One size does not fit all, and you must adapt my educational futures blueprint to your circumstances.

In chapter 3 I imagine an educational system designed as if the future mattered. I offer a sweeping plan for diplomatically and creatively expanding the part played by futuristics in the curriculum (explicit and implicit). I tackle such questions as what place does looking back have in a forward-looking pedagogy? What openings exist in standard courses for futures material? What should youngsters learn about futuristics per se?

Every chapter is followed by annotations for two highly recommended books, and many more are highlighted, along with articles, journals, and Web sites, in the Resources section at the back of the book. (Please send me your recommendations for later editions).

GAPS AND GUIDES

Before we can turn to chapter 1 attention is owed to some consequential matters of omissions and predilections. I omit five major topics you might reasonably expect to find here. And I allow three personal predilections to alter the book's tone and content (though, I would rather believe, not to unduly detract).

Disinclined, as I am, to plow a well-plowed field, I do not make a philosophical case for expanding futuristics in K–12 schooling. This is done exceedingly well in a 2005 book that inspired me to write this one: *Anticipate the World You Want: Learning for Alternative Futures*, by futurist Marsha Lynne Rhea. I especially like this closing thought: "We owe our ancestors deep gratitude for the knowledge they have given us. We owe our descendents the anticipatory learning that keeps the possibilities for their potential alive."[2]

I have chosen not to devote much time to how one actually does futuristics, touching on this at only two or three points, as this is the able focus of scores of fine books, with more appearing all the time. Outstanding on this shelf is *Thinking about the Future: Guidelines for Strategic Foresight*, edited in 2006 by Andy Hines and Peter Bishop. Drawing in part on ideas from many practicing futurists, they put our tools in a real-world context that helps underline their worth.[3]

I omit even a cursory review of the rich history and present state of futuristics, as this is quite involved, and covers multiple dimensions, all of which are quite well surveyed in *Futuring: The Exploration of the Future*, written in 2004 by Ed Cornish, the founder of the World Future Society. His closing sentence bears repeating: "Perhaps the best policy is to stop worrying whether the future will be as good as we hope or as bad as we sometimes fear, and just get on with the task of creating a future that we will try to ensure is good."[4]

I pass up the opportunity to share scenarios of highly likely and high impact futures, in part because this is beyond my ken, and also because I do not know where to start, as there are so many excellent exercises of this sort on my shelf. Exemplary in this regard is *The Extreme Future: The Top Trends That Will Reshape the World in the Next 20 Years*, by James Canton. He puts the challenge quite well: "The trends reported here are cast with hope, not alarm. We must strive to design the future we want."[5]

And finally, I slight, with regret, many ongoing overseas projects in educational futuristics. These are covered quite well, for example, in a 2006 essay collection, *Think Scenarios, Rethink Education*, published by the Paris-based Organization for Economic Co-Operation and Development.[6] In New Zealand, for example, an educational futures project drew on a concept from Aboriginal tradition that has respected noneducators invited to serve as "Guardians." As such, the outsiders brought a fresh perspective and helped create a safer place for dialogue. Likewise, a Glasgow 2000 project drew on art and literature to inject humanistic ideas into educational futures. These and other such field-tested ideas would seem to warrant adaptation.[7]

As for predilections that influence the book's tone and content, three merit mention: First, handicapped by "quantaphobia," I underemploy quantitative research. I regret this, as such material is at the edge of exciting new progress being made in forecasting, and I do not want you to be misled by my limitation. A juried academic publication of the World Future Society, *Futures Research Quarterly*, along with two others: *Foresight: The Journal of Futures Studies, Strategic Thinking, and Policy*, and *Futures: The Journal of Policy, Planning, and Futures Studies*, are all strong in this matter, and merit your consideration.

Second, I do not trust those who think they know the future. Some such forecasters exaggerate continuity, and maintain little of consequence ever really changes. I do not agree that time and change are an illusion, that "plus ça change, plus c'est la même chose." Instead, I am a surprise-focused futurist who expects almost daily to be awestruck by some new and possibly consequential development.

Likewise, I do not trust those whose thinking is clouded by a belief system for which there can be no testable evidence. I do not employ prophecies disguised as forecasts. I distrust ideas based on nonscientific thinking and on exotic exogenous events (such as the imminent Apocalypse, the imminent revolt of the masses, the imminent coming of the Messiah, etc.).[8] Instead, with the Enlightenment thinkers I believe the future is likely to prove more interesting that we can imagine, and I am persuaded we have considerable latitude to achieve deep and far-reaching change.[9] I believe that "without free will, societies tend toward nihilism and fatalism. And nihilistic, fatalistic societies cause all sorts of trouble."[10]

Finally, as I was raised to focus on the half-filled part of the proverbial "glass" I deemphasize—which is not the same as ignore—gloomy news of defeats and setbacks. My stripe of futuristics focuses on our ability to *make* a tomorrow worth experiencing, rather than merely sitting about and *anticipating* it. My approach is fundamentally optimistic and proactive. I agree with Senator Barak Obama in opting for "hope in the face of difficulty, hope in the face of uncertainty, the audacity of hope."[11] So, keeping all three predilections of mine in mind, *caveat*, good reader.

NOTES

1. McCain, Ted and Ian Jukes. *Windows on the Future: Education in the Age of Technology.* Thousand Oaks, CA: Corwin Press, 2001, 52. "Being able to [employ futuristics] is crucial to keeping the curriculum of the future relevant" (115).

2. Rhea, Marsha Lynne. *Anticipate the World You Want: Learning for Alternative Futures.* Lanham, MD: Scarecrow Education, 2005, 107.

3. Hines, Andy and Peter Bishop. *Thinking about the Future: Guidelines for Strategic Foresight.* Washington, DC: Social Technologies, 2006.

4. Cornish, Edward. *Futuring: The Exploration of the Future.* Bethesda, MD: World Future Society, 2004, 228.

5. Canton, James. *The Extreme Future: The Top Trends that Will Reshape the World in the Next 20 Years.* New York: Plume, 2007, x. See especially his discussion of four convergent technologies—nanotech, biotech, InfoTech, and cognotect (or neurotech) (153-182).

6. OECD. *Think Scenarios, Rethink Education.* Paris: Organization for Economic Co-Operation and Development, 2006. See also Hicks, David. *Lessons for the Future: The Missing Dimension in Education.* London: Routledge/Palmer, 2002, and UNESCO. *Toward Knowledge Societies.* New York: UNESCO, 2005.

7. Bentley, Tom. "Using Futures Thinking Strategically: Inward and Outward-facing Processes." In OECD, *Think Scenarios, Rethink Education.* Paris: OECD, 2006, 199 (196–200).

8. Nicholas Guyatt, author of the book, *Have a Nice Doomsday: Why Millions of Americans Are Looking Forward to the End of the World,* as quoted in Horn, Jordana. "Apocalypse Now?" *Wall Street Journal,* March 14, 2008, W11. Tens of millions of "End-State" religious fundamentalists and apocalyptic Christians "believe the Book of Revelation will literally be realized in the next few years . . . [and they] have an

incredibly specific vision of how the world ends; wars in the Middle East, the rise of the Antichrist, seven years of woe, and so on."

9. Helpful here is Orrell, David. *The Future of Everything: The Science of Prediction*, New York: Thunder's Mouth Press, 2007.

10. Last, Jonathan. "How the Dead Can Bind Communities." *Philadelphia Inquirer*, March 23, 2008, D5.

11. As quoted in Zakaria, Fareed. "What the World is Hearing," *Newsweek*, March 10, 2008, 45.

1

Futuristics:
Shaping Tomorrow

"The future offers more than we can foresee, but its nature will be determined largely by the way we think about it."

Thomas Hine, *Facing Tomorrow*, 1991, xiii

Recognition is growing that our weather isn't what it used to be, and increasingly isn't what we would prefer. This makes all the more vexing the fact that a prime suspect in the matter—the "Greenhouse Effect" (the sensitivity of Earth's temperature to changes in atmospheric CO_2)—was identified as long ago as 1896.[1] Likewise, experts began urging corrective responses over twenty-five years ago, though to little avail until very recently (and even then quite unevenly).

Why weren't early warnings heeded? Why do we find ourselves scurrying now to make up for lost time, and squabbling about what we should have done, should be doing, and might do next—all of this as in an irritable daze. Answers are many, and complex. But part of the explanation is surely our long-standing undervaluation of the art of forecasting, an art called *futuristics*. We cannot correct this dangerous attitude soon enough.

FUTURISTICS

To futurize is to upgrade any institution's orientation toward the future. Or, in the case of K–12 schooling, to gain more from futuristics (a.k.a. forecasting, foresight, futurics, future studies, and long-ranging forecasting) than previously sought or even thought possible. Futuristics can be defined as a "preoccupation with how we create the future every day, and on this basis, analyze the prospects for change—be it one day or a century from now."[2]

In the context of education, futuristics can be seen as "a framework for acquiring the knowledge and skills to understand future possibilities, and the ability to collaborate in creating a preferred future."[3] Like history, "it is a narrative-based medium: Futurists construct dramatic scenarios to portray how they think things will, or should, turn out."[4]

An ancient, creative, modest, and steadily improving art form, futuristics is as old as our species. Its roots can be traced to our inbred anxiety about the fragile uncertainty of our own lives (we can die in the next minute, though looking ahead might help us reduce the odds), and to questions we have about what tomorrow might bring (the better to make ready).

While the art form can be dressed up in flowery language that resembles New Age poetics, it is more soundly understood as offering unique insights into a timeless struggle over *power*——what many mandarins believe the past, the present, and the future are primarily about. Likewise, it should be understood to have two divisions: 1) A core that includes its history, methods, current applications, and potential advances and 2) its ability to advance any subject to which it is applied; for example, the future of art, of business, of culture, of death, of energy, of feelings, of Goodness, and so on.

Of relevance is an analogy of Sigmund Freud's. Psychoanalysis, he maintained, is "archaeology, the unearthing of meaning layered deep beneath an 'expanse of ruins.'" Futuristics can be likened instead to architecture, the building of meaning layered on top of a vast expanse of hopes and fears. In practice, like psychoanalysis, it is "closer to a detective story."[5]

Originally employed by astrologists, astronomers, seers, shamans, stargazers, and a wide assortment of other adventurous types, its early ranks also include many of the Fathers (and Mothers) of modern science. More than an intuitive skill, it has grown in recent decades into a coherent body of techniques and knowledge. Practitioners employ it "not as a guessing game, but as a way of glimpsing humanity's most realistic yet provocative possibilities, good or bad."[6] It has played a part in every culture over time and at every level of society.

Futurists wrestle with maddening contradictions, quirky contingencies, serendipitous discoveries, unanticipated encounters, and hard-to-expect outcomes. They appreciate the contingency, messiness, and even zaniness with which events unfold. They try and maintain an agile mind, one that values the contribution of play as well as that of logic, the contributions possible from flights of fancy along with those that only rigor can command. Little surprise, then, that along with sharp-edged mathematics and statistics, they employ subjective intuitions, random guesses, playful ideas, and fortuitous findings.[7] They understand deciphering clues means drawing on something more profound than the intellect alone.

To adapt a thought originally advanced about photography, while futuristics may appear an easy art, it is actually one of the hardest.[8] Concepts, insights, and techniques are forever being combined and recombined in systems greater than the sum of their parts. Practitioners understand they can never know their subject fully, and this enables them to "perpetually imagine sublimities beyond reason. On the margins of the known is the agile edge of existence."[9]

MODELS

On the margins of the known, futurists create helpful models of this "agile edge," this space we call "tomorrow." They use their models to help contain "stuff" (data, information, knowledge, wisdom), much as we use software folders. More significantly, the models can serve as illuminating portals, as rewarding ways to "see" further into the future. They help narrow an infinity of plausible futures into a manageable and meaningful few.

Three major models—classical, modernist, and recombinant—shed light on past and present thinking about tomorrow.[10] This approach can stand in for numerous others available to illustrate this methodology.

In the Classical model, popular in the U.S. before 1920, the future evolves inevitably, seamlessly, and risk-free out of the past. It is represented as a sign of steady evolution from savagery to civilization. A Classical future is understood as a "continuation and elaboration of the progress of the past——a future of ever bigger and better things made available largely through materialistic, quantitative, often imperialist expansion."[11]

Led by sober imperial missionaries of Empire, a Classical future promises "security," at least for the Overlords, as all sorts of animals will be hunted, coal will be dug, forests cut, minerals mined, oil pumped, seas fished, and so on, *ad infinitum*, much as if all is inexhaustible. In school, strict teaching and rigorous tests will dominate. Only that which can be measured will be supported. Admirers insist this future rewards by preserving the status quo. Critics condemn it for elitism, sexism, racism, and suicidal indifference to our need to curb growth and reduce exploitation of the planet. They believe this imbalanced future is stagnant and fatally unimaginative.

In sharp contrast, the Modernist model, especially popular in the U.S. between 1920 and 1964, offers a jarringly disruptive "Buck Rodgers" future. Its leaders, all of them earnest visionaries, expect a future that meets unprecedented needs and drives with scientific and technological breakthroughs, all of which will be free of unexpected and unwanted impacts. This model celebrates automation, efficiency, mass production, reduction, shortcuts, streamlining, and simplification. Modernists "look for wealth from the invisible——nitrogen from air, protein from microbes, energy from atoms."[12] Preferring the new to the old, their model disdains the Imperial excesses of the past.

Admirers expect this scenario to streamline consumption, production, and evolution itself. Critics, in turn, are leery of its extreme discontinuities, and prefer to hold onto the most rewarding aspects of the past. They doubt that science and technology can deliver, as modernists promise, certainly not as soon, as error free, and as affordable as held out. They condemn Modernism as "extreme, hubristic, and scary if taken straight——a fear reinforced by technological dystopias since the time of Mary Shelley."[13]

A third major scenario, the Recombinant model, has been in vogue since about 1964, though all three models ("Visions") overlap and blur in popularity. Less confident in the new than is Modernism, more eclectic and multicultural than is Classicism, its improvisational leaders intend to splice the Classical with the Modernist models, to blend the radicalness of the modern with the familiarity of the classics.

Admirers believe the Recombinant model is perhaps the most palatable and marketable of the three scenarios. It "may be the way many of us actually approach and experience the future: one foot forward, the other planted firmly in an imagined, decontextualized past."[14] Critics insist its transient and volatile character is more suited to a future of lightweight fads and fancies than to meeting heavyweight challenges like climate change, water and energy shortages, environmental degradation, and the world's widening income gap.

Whatever you make of the three models, of this effort to draw a reconnaissance map of possible futures, the methodological point should be clear: Model-building of this type can help us clarify our thinking. Sort out and assign to each model key aspects of the unfolding future. And recognize thereby consequential trends of value in identifying both preferred and preventable futures.

COUNTERFEITS

While we cannot "know" the future, at the same time we must question the "predictions" of those who brashly claim they do. Futuristics has nothing in common with colorful charlatans all too many in the public regrettably associate with it . . . card-reading fortunetellers, false prophets in supermarket tabloids, and clairvoyants and psychics in spooky storefronts.[15]

Nor does it have anything in common with supposed psychics who claim our fate can be revealed by their reading of our palm or our astrological horoscope. Or with professional readers of the iChing or tarot cards, paid interpreters of Nostradamus, or poetic diviners like cult favorite Edgar Cayce, all of them adherents of one or another stripe of determinism (e.g., apocalyptic "End of Creation" theories, etc.). Seemingly content to operate without a claimed basis in empirical or rational means, they have no doubts—unlike serious forecasters.

Likewise, futurists rue the part played by unscrupulous pollsters who manufacture "predictions" to help influence elections, and their partners in crime, amoral marketers who distort forecasts to sell things to the unwitting. These secular charlatans damage the regard the public might have for forecasting—and thereby seriously undermine public discourse about the future.

Quite apart are modern "prophets" of unquestioned integrity. In 2008, for example, Jim Wallis was getting attention for his forecast of a "Great Awakening"—an ongoing and soon-to-expand turning of church-going American people to social activism. Those in agreement hailed him as "a prophet in the popular sense—a guy who predicts what's going to happen—much as did his ancient predecessors. . . .").[16] Futurists are neutral regarding religiously-based arguments and faith-based forecasts, skeptical but not dismissive, and take them as matters for serious study.

Futurists themselves claim *no* predictive powers, as they understand the future is a zone of potentiality . . . undetermined, plural, and rife with possibilities, perils, and impossible-to-forecast surprises ("wild cards"). Surprises abound; for example, of the top eight political concerns in December 2007, four were not recognized as "comers" as recently as 2000 (the environment, fuel prices, immigration, and terrorism). About the sudden major troubles of Auction-Rate Securities in the winter of 2008, a shocked economist wrote—"Now, what wasn't ever supposed to happen has."[17]

Looking beyond our borders, no prominent forecaster expected India, with its economy of scarce skilled labor, to become a giant in skill-intensive IT and outsourcing, nor was the Philippines expected to gain command (72 percent) of the world market in electronic-integrated circuits.[18]

Forecasts remain contingent statements vulnerable to hard-to-anticipate erratic actions of often obscure others. To be sure, they gain strength from consistently reliable extrapolations we can make of inertial large system trends—demographic, economic, and social. Powerful accurate forecasting techniques enable accurate and widespread use of statistical extrapolations. But, our all-too-human wooliness still recommends humility and caution in the practice of our art.

APPLICATIONS

Futuristics does not reduce to an arcane matter only a few specialists can employ, and then only for deep-pocket global banks, firms, governments, or think tanks. Instead, it comes in a wide variety of responsible and accessible forms . . . many immediately applicable to schooling and school systems.

Today able users can be found in the employ of global corporations, every level of government here and abroad, international bodies (the EU, UN, World Bank, global NGOs, the Vatican, etc.), media conglomerates, think tanks, and the forward-looking like. Millions of investors, and especially their financial advisers, make 24/7 use of it. Serious investors "collectively anticipate changes in a company's earnings, so by the time they are announced, stocks often have already made their move."[19] As a discounting mechanism, the market tends to forecast at least six months ahead.

Regional and urban planners, along with the entire building industry (homes, industrial, etc.), rely on forecasts (demographics, economics, etc.), as do marketing specialists, who as trend watchers, endlessly test with sales successes or setbacks their ability to see ahead. Now, able to search ("mine") through continuously growing mountains of data, they improve their "read" of predictive patterns ("seismographs of change") regarding consumer buying preferences.

The entertainment industry has a wet finger in the air all the time, even as it attempts to also shape trends in a profitable direction. Politicians, in particular, endlessly read proverbial tea leaves (in the form of 24/7 polling), and promote popular mythology about ideal futures they, and they alone, can help secure. Pundits, in turn, employ futuristics to add intrigue to their stuff.

While nowhere as well recognized as warranted, nearly every school course students later remember closes with a session roughly entitled the future of X (the course subject matter). Futuristics, in short, is ubiquitous, even if seldom called by its proper name.

WHY FUTURISTICS?

Much of the art form's appeal involves helping us meet a deep-set need: We want to know what seems to be shaping events. And, what might we do about it? We want to grasp connections among events, assess developments, foresee opportunities for gains, and avoid losses. We want material that provokes us to think big thoughts, argue about ideas that matter, look at our lives and choices, help us understand why things are the way they are, and "imagine how they could be different."[20]

Futuristics can help us trace *pathways* that may link X to Y and then to Z; that is, link up seemingly unrelated, but possibly future-shaping matters ("connect the dots"). Where K–12 schooling is concerned I can imagine trying to trace a forecasting pathway among X (ever-better electronic-books),

Y (computers worn on the person), and Z (wireless broadband power "too cheap to meter"), as together these three could make a big difference soon in education.

We also want to clarify our *preferences* regarding future-shaping choices. Specifically, we might try to learn if local taxpayers are really willing to pay to modernize vocational education. Or if we are resolved to break large classes into far smaller ones. Or if we are really indifferent to the persistence of vast inequities in per-pupil funding outlays.

Always welcoming of good news, we want to imagine positive *possibilities*. In this connection I might try to learn if virtual reality technology is finally ready for large-scale educational use. Or if holographic technology (two-dimensional moving images that give the illusion of having three dimensions), which, until recently was a staple only of scientific museums, is now ready for classroom use. Or if cutting-edge psychopharmaceuticals for classroom use (other than Ritalin) are a possibility worth greater investment.

And we want—however hesitantly—to identify major *perils*, the better to have a chance to mitigate, if not escape them entirely ("... in thinking about the future, it is as important to be clear about what you don't want as about what you do").[21] In this connection I might try to learn whether expensive brain-augmenting biochips threaten to grievously distort childhood. Or if highly advanced robots, aided by dazzling software, increasingly threaten the livelihood of average Americans. Or if new classes of virulent viruses warrant extreme measures in school-based hygiene practices.

LIMITATIONS

Note my deliberate use above of the term—*try*—as futuristics, its many strengths notwithstanding, has long-standing limitations, only a few of which can reasonably be mentioned here.

Requisite data banks, for example, are often inadequate (rife with gaps, late in arriving, and weakened by proprietary exclusions). Models leave much to be desired; for example, "Until climatologists can model Earth as a single climate system—an achievement at best several years off—we are quite limited in our ability to forecast out decades or centuries."[22] We rely on organizations for data about themselves, and remain thereby vulnerable to their tendency to tell only a safe or flattering tale. Resulting "findings" are too weak to turn into statistically robust conclusions.

Alternative theories of change are often contradictory. And "wild cards" frequently upset reasonable expectations; for example, "9/11" left America profoundly altered, as did earlier the astonishing assassination of President Kennedy, our unexpected military setbacks in Lebanon and Somalia, the space shuttle Columbia tragedy, and so on.

Little wonder, accordingly, that our forecasts often miss the mark: For example, a major poll in 1998 that included many leading forecasters "didn't foresee the rise of a high-tech service sector in India. Nor did the experts anticipate how rapid, cheap communications across the Pacific would help China align its fast-growing factories with the appetites of U.S. consumers."[23]

Futuristics requires a fierce and unsparing humility, as it has *many* limitations (data gaps, inadequate theoretical models, biased partisanship, etc.). Practitioners know it is far from ready for prime time. They fully appreciate the limits of words in capturing important, though also slippery and elusive, aspects of tomorrow. They know self-interest shapes forecasts, both to defend the status quo or to disparage it: "To demystify forecasts we need to be more savvy about the rhetorical conventions, false dichotomies, inappropriate analogies, questionable assumptions, and dubious calculations that keep cropping up whenever the future is discussed."[24]

To hone in on the human element, unethical prognosticators can lose themselves in ideologies, and mask their sellout when forecasting. Power-holders make changes in response to a useful forecast, only to have mass media pundits scoff thereafter at a forecast that did not materialize. As if this was not enough, the speed of change can and does often overtake and trump the best of forecasts: "Ten years ago the average scientist, much less the average user, could not have predicted most cell phones today would contain cameras and color screens."[25]

Accordingly, the field is littered with the failed forecasts (flying cars, paperless office, teleportation, underwater cities, two-hundred-year life spans. etc.), many of which remain in the public's consciousness, and take a toll on the field's standing. As a wry critic puts it, "Human beings should have been cloned by now. Gasoline should be pumping at $5 a gallon. California, to the disappointment of many, has yet to collapse into the sea along its fault lines, metaphorically or otherwise."[26]

ENEMIES AT THE GATE

As if its honest shortcomings were not enough, futuristics is also bruised by unrelenting opposition. Many critics suffer from "status-quo bias," the belief that the way things are is the best way they can be.[27] Some archconservatives, for example, condemn it as irreverent, antitraditional, and unacceptably "modern."[28] They believe it stirs the asking of troublesome questions about traditional attitudes toward capitalism, culture, nationalism, religion, and sex—thereby opens the gates to barbarians within and without.

Critics of this persuasion prefer to "cope with an uncertain world through incremental and mostly unsuccessful innovation, not through extensive visions of the future."[29] Holding neo-phobic attitudes, they damn futuristics for reminding them change is indifferent to their fear of the New. The looking glass they seem to prefer is not a crystal ball, but a rearview mirror.

GUIDELINES

The better to help compensate for shortcomings, and vex their critics, earnest forecasters employ informal empowering "rules," three of which especially merit use by educators who would help futurize schooling. First, try to never use the words *will* and *will not* (e.g., the forecast that home-schooled children *will* out-perform others; language-immersion classes *will not* disappoint). We simply do not know enough to have a will/will not degree of confidence over unlimited time spans.

Second, do not use exclamation points, as do tabloid charlatans who hawk overblown "predictions." With rare exception forecasts are best regarded as cautious, tentative, and time-bound matters, available for correction at any time. They should rarely connote surety. In this connection, you might join those of us who boycott use of the word *prediction*, and use instead the word *forecast*. We cede the former term to pretenders, and claim the later term for humble practitioners.

Third, be leery of point forecasts—the suggestion this or that will occur, or not occur, by or in the year 20XX. Many such flamboyant "predictions" extend far beyond our forecasting prowess. They can create a false impression of (unwarranted) "certainty." They warrant skeptical regard, especially by impressionable young students. Assiduously avoided by the best forecasters, far too many point forecasts are often scams palmed off on the unsuspecting by the unscrupulous.

CONTRIBUTIONS

Provided the safeguards above are honored, K–12 schooling has much to gain from futuristics. Everyone—from a school bus driver or grounds keeper through to a teacher or Superintendent—can profit from learning how to anticipate more ably, prepare more effectively, fear less, and achieve more. A component of "existential intelligence," the ninth ability to be identified by Harvard psychologist Howard Gardner, futuristics facilitates pondering the meaning of life, and exploring both its possibilities and perils.[30]

To begin with, forecasters can help us explore our unexamined assumptions about tomorrow. Teachers, in particular, can profit from acknowledging their off-the-radar thoughts about possibilities and perils, for youngsters in their classes are good at picking up unintentional clues from them about such influential stuff.

Futurists identify the major paradigms with which we perceive the world and predict its behavior. Shifts in paradigms have, and continue to, trigger much of society's turbulence, especially as we cling far too long to outmoded ones ("Paradigm Paralysis, a terminal disease of certainty").[31] Paradigm pliancy would seem "the best strategy in turbulent times," as learning to identify the next dominant paradigm improves one's ability to anticipate the future[32]

Futurists try to find lessons in history, our own and that of all cultures, lessons that can take the form of repeating patterns or consequential cycles. For as Winston Churchill taught—"The farther back you can look, the farther forward you are likely to see."[33] Teachers can profit from getting beyond the sharing of dry dates and names in favor of sharing timely historic clues to the often unanticipated consequences of planned or accidental change.

Futurists try to draw on all valid forms of knowledge. They employ counter-intuitive notions, creativity, lateral thinking, gaming, intuition, playful thinking, simulations, statistical probability, and even the most intriguing of unorthodox ideas. In this way they set teachers a sound model of free-wheeling outreach across disciplinary lines. Picasso believed "art is not the application of a canon of beauty, but what the instinct and the brain can conceive beyond the canon."[34] Futuristics, an art form, is not the application of a canon of rules, but what the imagination and the brain can conceive beyond any canon.

Futurists employ a wide range of tools—only a few, like mathematical modeling, are beyond the ken of laypersons, but many more quite accessible to all. Trend forecasting, for example, is readily learned and taught, as is brainstorming, scenario writing, visioning, and other commonly employed methods. Scenario-writing, in particular, as a way of rehearsing the future, lends itself to K–12 education, since youngsters commonly enjoy questioning the inevitability of more of the same, a provocative starting point in this exercise.

Futurists try to assess major forecasts and generate ever-better ones based in part on exposed shortcomings. They regard constructive criticism from one another as a welcomed form of compliment, and set very high standards for awarding accolades. In this way they model for teachers a mature appreciation for assessment, transparency, and accountability. As youngsters need help recognizing and devaluing pseudo-futures silliness, especially horoscope nonsense, New Age mysticism, Nostradamus ambiguity, psychobabble, tabloid junk, etc. Futurists can help teachers teach the markers of third-rate stuff.

Above all, futurists try to highlight choices that might otherwise escape notice, the better to help people change their minds, and help develop a more informed citizenry. They bring to light options that current power-holders might prefer remain unnoticed. They call attention to overlooked choices, and also overlooked perils. Their goal is to enrich consideration, and thereby ratchet up the likelihood of a sound, or at a minimum, least-worse choice. In this way they remind teachers of their moral responsibility to help youngsters cultivate expectations of expansive, rather than constricting choices.

Little wonder this empowering art form thrives only in modern democracies: "The function of prediction is not . . . to aid social control, but to widen the spheres of moral choice. . . ."[35] It can best aid education in caring and democratic school settings where youngsters enjoy respect, age-appropriate rights, and meaningful responsibilities.[36]

SUMMARY

The future can be understood as a "spreading 'web' or 'tree' of alternative possibilities growing out of the present."[37] Still another appealing way of regarding it is as "that potentiality which makes us aware of the creative possibilities of the present."[38]

Futuristics, in turn, can be understood as "the systematic study, by basically rational or empirical means, of the possible alternative futures of human societies, and the special problems and opportunities relating to those futures."[39] Given its major goals—finding pathways, uncovering preferences, illuminating possibilities, and identifying perils—educators have a remarkable ally here for helping learners make more of their life possibilities.

Provided, that is, that we operationalize the art form in better ways than ever before. That you and I put it to work in as creative and sustained a way as possible. We may err at times, but it is far better that our errors be those of trying and failing than errors of omission.

HIGHLY RECOMMENDED READING

1) *Crucial Questions about the Future*, by Allen Tough. Lanham, MD: University Press of America, 1991. A leading futures educator asks nine fundamental, timeless questions like, Why do we act in ways that hurt our future? and How can we achieve a satisfactory future?

NOTES

1. Jenkins, Jr., Holman W. "The Science of Gore's Nobel." *Wall Street Journal*, December 5, 2007, A24. The scientist Evan Svante Arrhenius was awarded a Nobel

Prize in 1903, though for something else. However, some scientists think a stronger claim to the title of "first" to establish the carbon dioxide theory of climate change may belong to the 1938 work of Guy Stewart Callendar, or the 1959 work of Charles David Keeling. See Charlson, Robert J. "A Lone Voice in the Greenhouse." *Nature,* July 2007, 254.

2. Miller, Riel. "Future Studies, Scenarios, and the 'Possibility-Space' Approach." On OECD, ed. *Think Scenarios, Rethink Education.* Paris: Organization for Economic Co-Operation and Development, 2006, 95 (93–105).

3. I draw here on a definition not of futuristics per se, but of "anticipatory learning," as I believe it admirably captures what futuristics actually means for education. Rhea, Marsha Lynne. *Anticipate the World You Want: Learning for Alternative Futures.* Lanham, MD: Scarecrow Education, 2005, 2.

4. Belasco, Warren. *Meals to Come: A History of the Future of Food.* Berkeley, CA: University of California Press, 2006, x.

5. Stanley, Alessandria. "Four Days, a Therapist; Fifth Day, a Patient." *New York Times,* January 28, 2008, B1.

6. Boutin, Paul. "A Sense of the Future." *Wall Street Journal,* January 26–27, 2008, W8.

7. Belasco, *Meals to Come, op. cit.*

8. Lisette Model, a great modern photographer, as quoted in Plagens, Peter. "Is Photography Dead?" *Newsweek,* December 10, 2007, 96 (94, 96).

9. Wilson, Eric G. "In Praise of Melancholy." *The Chronicle Review,* January 18, 2008, B14 (12–14).

10. Belasco, *Meals to Come, op. cit.*

11. *Ibid.,* x. It was especially popular in the World's fairs of the late 19th and early 20th centuries.

12. *Ibid.,* xii

13. *Ibid.,* 214. "While many people were willing to jump ahead to a brighter tomorrow, they were not quite willing to reject the past."

14. *Ibid.,* xii. Belasco cites as examples new versions of the "smart" kitchen (a combination of high-tech gadgetry and artisanal ideals) and the recent enthusiasms for "functional" foods (which purport to engineer scientific nutrition into familiar forms).

15. For an account of an academic who takes phenomena like ESP and psychokinesis seriously, see Carlson, Scott. "The Truth is Out There." *The Chronicle Review,* January 11, 2008, B11–B13. It profiles Stephen E. Braude, past president of the Parapsychological Association.

16. Satullo, Chris. "Religious Right Gives Way to a New Prophet." *Philadelphia Inquirer,* February 19, 2008, A11.

17. Krugman, Paul. "A Crisis of Faith." *New York Times,* February 15, 2008, A23.

18. Easterly, William R. "Why Bill Gates Hates My Book." *Wall Street Journal,* February 7, 2008, A18.

19. deAenlle, Conrad. "How Long Will Profits Slump?" *New York Times,* January 5, 2008, C6.

20. Christensen, Linda. "Beyond Anthologies: Why Teacher Choice and Judgment Matter." *Rethinking Schools,* Winter 2007–8, 44 (42–47).

21. Hine, Thomas. *Facing Tomorrow: What the Future Has Been, What the Future Can Be*. New York: Knopf, 1991, 247

22. Anders, George. "Predictions of the Past." *Wall Street Journal*, January 28, 2008, B3.

23. Preston, Richard. "Will Forests Slow Global Warming—Or Speed It Up?" *WIRED*, February 2007, 114.

24. Hine, *op. cit.*, 264–5. "Especially suspicious are the transgressive, gee-whiz conceits of the feature pages . . . ."

25. J. Storrs Hall, PhD, *Beyond AI: Creating the Conscience of the Machine*. Amherst, New York: Prometheus Books, 2007, 248.

26. Boutin, Paul. "A Sense of the Future." *Wall Street Journal*, January 26–27, 2008, W8.

27. The concept is from Green, Ronald M. *Babies by Design: The Ethics of Genetic Choice*. New Haven, CT: Yale University Press, 2007, 23.

28. Hine, *op. cit.*, 247.

29. Krugman, Paul. "A Crisis of Faith." *New York Times*, February 15, 2008, A23.

30. Woodlief, Tony. "Intelligence Designer." *Wall Street Journal*, February 15, 2008, W11.

31. Barker, Joel A. *Discovering the Future: The Business of Paradigms*. St. Paul, MN: ILI Press, 1989 ed., 72

32. *Ibid.*, 74.

33. Anon. "Break Down These Walls." *The Economist*, March 22, 2008, 16.

34. Curator Note. Boca Raton Museum of Art. Attached to a Picasso sketch, "Nude Figures on the Beach."

35. Bell, Daniel, as quoted in Duncan, Otis Dudley. "On Forecasts." *The Public Interest*, Fall 1969, 107.

36. Rhea, Marsha Lynne. *Anticipate the World You Want: Learning for Alternative Futures*. Lanham, MD: Scarecrow Education, 2005, 2.

37. Kauffman, Jr., Draper L. *Teaching the Future: A Guide to Future-Oriented Education*. Palm Springs, CA: ETC, 1976, 296.

38. Bussey, Marcus, on his web site, www.futuresevocative.com.

39. Kauffman, *op. cit.*, iii.

Future Problem Solving Program International

It is with great pleasure that I include here several examples of some outstanding educational work available from one of the world's leading organizations of its type—the Future Problem Solving Program International (FPSPI). Created in 1974 by creativity pioneer Dr. E. Paul Torrance, FPSPI stimulates critical and creative thinking skills and encourages students here and abroad to improve their vision for the future.

We begin with the topics in the current FPSPI program, their brief descriptions and the questions raised illustrating FPSPI's reputation for timeliness and variety of challenges. In the Scenario Writing component, students select one of the five Future Problem Solving topics and then work for several months developing a 1,500 word scenario. These are evaluated on the following areas: Futuristic Thinking, Creative Thinking, Character Development, Style, Purpose, Audience (recognition of intended audience), and Mechanical/Structure. The top three students in each affiliate program may be submitted for the international writing competition.

For the 2006–2007 school year, Australia, Canada, Hong Kong, Korea, Malaysia, New Zealand, and Singapore participated, as well as forty-one states in the U.S., while Russia, Japan, and Great Britain were piloting the program. Approximately 250,000 students participate in FPS annually, and, in 2006–2007, the program had 6,000 booklet teams (made up of four students each, plus alternates) throughout the affiliate programs. There were also 200 Community Problem Solving projects, 400 individual booklet writers, 190 scenario writers, and many students involved with FPS within the curriculum who choose not to compete.

"Scenario writing provides an opportunity for gifted writers to create for an audience. Authentic assessment is provided by between three to six evaluators so that these young writers receive supportive criticism and means to improve in multiple areas" (Marianne Solomon, Executive Director, FPSPI; personal e-mail correspondence, March 14, 2008).

Next are two expanded descriptions of specific challenges within problem solving topics (Climate Change/Climate Threat, and Caring for Our Elders), each with a story and characters to illustrate some of the issues entailed. The scenario that follows ("Back to the Old Dayes") was written in response to the Caring for Our Elders challenge by a student participating in the 2006-07 program. We conclude with a final example of prize-winning student work which, in combination with the other pieces, should whet your appetite to have your school and students join this time-proven, mind-expanding, learning adventure (www.fpspi.org).

2007–08 FUTURE PROBLEM SOLVING PROGRAM INTERNATIONAL

PP#1	Body Enhancement
PP#2	Simulation Technology
QP	Neurotechnology
Final/Bowl	Debt in Developing Countries
IC	Child Labor

Please note that some affiliate programs change the topic order in their affiliate.

Body Enhancement

Cosmetic surgery, brain implants, computerized prosthetics, tattooing, and body piercing are all forms of body enhancement. In some cultures, tattooing and excessive body piercing are seen as antiestablishment, while in others, indigenous peoples are reverting to these ancient rituals as a statement of their cultural belonging and pride. Plastic surgery has evolved from assisting badly burned or maimed soldiers to those today suffering from body dimorphic disorder due to imagined needs to change his or her appearance. New technology now enables paraplegics to control prosthetic devices using only their thoughts and forecasters foresee nanorobotics boosting other mental abilities. Where will the concept of body enhancement end? How far will people go not only to correct deformities or disabilities but to enhance their otherwise normal, healthy bodies to superhuman or "super-perfect" proportions?

Simulation Technology

As computer technology improves, photos can be "corrected" to show perfection. Video of any individual can be altered to show whatever the programmer chooses. This could be a wonderful opportunity for actors to vacation while movies that include them are made. It might also allow someone who is overweight to see what they might look like as a thin person or for parents to see what their new baby will look like as a child or an adult. Images can be manipulated to show almost anything. What implications could this have in court evidence? Could it impact employment? What other amazing things could be accomplished with this technology?

Neurotechnology

Neurotechnology is technology that makes it possible to manipulate the brain. Already one young patient has had a chip embedded in his brain, which allows him to control a computer using his thoughts. Instruments and techniques used in developing neurotechnology include brain imaging systems (MRI, PET, EEG), biochips (DNA microarrays, protein chips, RNA chips), genetic engineering techniques, cellular implantation, and electronic stimulation. Neurotechnology offers hope to sufferers of brain disorders and spinal cord injuries to lead a normal life again. It also has the potential to enhance brain functions in normal people. What are the ethical implications of neurotechnology? Should it only be used for recovery from illness and injury or is the use of it for augmentation also a possibility?

Debt in Developing Countries

For many years, the world's poorest countries have been forced to take out loans in order to afford essential goods and services for their people, such as national security, health care, public safety, and education. In the short-term, deficit spending can create jobs and fulfill basic needs. But it also leads to higher interest rates that stifle economies, and imposes obligations on future generations to repay the debt. Many activists and world leaders now argue that the debts of third world countries, which are largely owed to wealthier foreign governments and multinational corporations, amount to a substantial obstacle to sustainable development, security, and stability in those countries. Pleas to forgive the debt of poor nations have evoked much sympathy in recent years, but opinions remain divided over how best to remedy the situation.

Child Labor

Child labor is a pervasive problem throughout the world, especially in developing countries. Africa and Asia together account for over 90 percent of total child employment. Children often work because of poverty, particularly in areas where the capacity to enforce minimum age requirements for schooling and work is lacking. Children are major contributors to family income in developing countries. Traditional cultural and social factors increase child labor. Child laborers are often subjected to extreme exploitation leading to deprived lifestyles. There is no international agreement defining child labor, making it hard to isolate cases of abuse, let alone abolish them.

Climate Change/Climate Threat
Junior/Middle/Senior Division Future Scene
Future Problem Solving Program International
Practice Problem #1 2005–2006

"Mother, look over there!" Ivan pointed to a small group of Arctic seals on a nearby ice float. He spoke into his media watch, "July 12, 2025: 3:37 p.m.—four adult seals, two seal pups." Then he clicked on the global positioning system to record the exact location of the seals. "I hope I see polar bears this trip," he exclaimed.

Ivan and his mother stood on the deck of *Seadragon 4* as it slowly navigated through the famous Northwest Passage. (The passage runs below Iceland and Greenland, north of Canada and Alaska). Ivan's family owns a fleet of ice-breaking tugboats with reinforced hulls and sophisticated navigation devices. These tugboats, the Russian *Seadragons*, are hired by international shipping companies to lead massive vessels through the passage safely. The international world of commerce is thrilled that the passage is finally open on a regular basis; and since Ivan's mother is considered one of the best navigators in the Arctic, her business is flourishing.

Ivan's mother nodded at the seal sighting. "I'm glad to see the seals, Ivan. I see fewer animals each year. Unfortunately, I see less ice each year too."

Ivan was puzzled. "But, isn't that a good thing? I mean, less ice means even more ships will want to travel through the Passage."

"Yes, it's good for my business," his mother responded. "But, what you're seeing is only part of a much bigger picture. For example, you can't see that the permafrost is also thawing—that's land that used to stay frozen year-round. Inuit villages in the area rely on the permafrost ground to prevent erosion from the ocean storms. Several villages have already had to relocate. So, what's good for us isn't necessarily good for everyone else." Ivan's mother hooked her pocket computer onto Ivan's belt and turned on his audio receiver. "Listen to the report I'm working on, Ivan. I need to get back to work."

Ivan listened intently to his mother's research. She had analyzed statistics from the International Science Foundation which is continually monitoring the region's marine ecosystem. Although the entire world is expected to be ten degrees warmer in 2100, these scientists report that no place is warming up faster than the Arctic. In fact, the Arctic temperature is increasing twice as fast as anywhere else on earth. The Foundation scientists predict an ice-free Arctic Ocean every summer by 2050. Not only does the increasing temperature melt ice and permafrost, it also creates extreme changes in the area's weather. Violent thunderstorms, once rare in the area, now appear regularly during the summer—a major concern for both the inhabitants and the shipping companies.

The Foundation reports that in addition to the oceans rising from the thaw, the oxygen level of the water is also rising. Microbiologists report the shifting of ocean plants and crustaceans into deeper water making them out of reach for walruses and seals. New marine predators are now able to feed in the Arctic area, competing with the indigenous species that require frigid weather.

However, scientists don't necessarily agree on what causes the thaw. Most say that it is the result of increasing carbon dioxide, methane and other harmful gases—human interference. A few scientists disagree. They claim that the thawing cycle is natural—due in part to continual warming and cooling of ocean currents or changes in the sun's intensity.

Ivan spotted a polar bear in the distance. As he logged it into his media watch, he sighed. He had hoped to see a lot more wildlife on this trip, but his eyes confirmed his mother's report. He was only seeing the "tip of the iceberg."

Like Ivan, scientists agree the continuing Arctic thaw is a climate change that has far-reaching implications. Use the FPS six-step problem-solving model to identify challenges, select an underlying problem and produce solution ideas relating to one of the major challenges of the Arctic thaw.

Caring for Our Elders
Middle/Senior Division Future Scene
Future Problem Solving Program International
2006–07 Affiliate Bowl

Human Molecular Genetics Online Journal Article Abstract: I Sing the Body Technological Bunkyo-ku Tokyo, Japan, 2035 January The Hostel for the Elder Biosphere located in Tokyo, Japan, is the prototype for elderly care of the future. The cost of elderly care hit an all-time high last year. Due to technical advances in medical care, the elderly now outnumber the workforce. Medical advancements have been a major factor in prolonging lives with age-related disabilities, creating escalating expenses in the quadrillions. Doctors have learned how to lengthen life, but not how to reduce the debilitating, costly effects of aging.

To solve problems created by prolonged life and the drain on the world-wide economy, medical associations from Japan, Europe, the Americas, Australia, Asia, and Russia formed the Center for the Global Geriatric Genome (CGGG). Doctors gather DNA information from the elderly on gene variants known as "snips" to perform personalized automated real-time monitoring of body systems. With nanostructures called dendrimers, genetic engineers can repair or re-engineer genes that underlie disease and disability. This new technology will reduce the cost of elderly care by using molecular assemblers to build new organs and body systems to replace aging ones. Contributions from governments and the public have poured in as the greatest minds in gerontology and medical engineering join with the CGGG.

2035 December
Tokyo, Japan

"Will she even know who I am?" Keiko's eyes met her mother's as she unhooked the carabiner that latched her into the airwave transporter and stepped down onto the Temachi Substation platform.

"Of course she will, Keiko. Akiko Obaachan hasn't changed. She's just . . . well . . . protected from all the things that could harm her. Don't worry. Grandmother will know who you are. At least we can actually visit her instead of having to use the WIpod. Families who live faraway aren't so lucky. I know our visit will boost her spirits."

The family of three latched in their 'biners and accelerated toward the next stop, the Hostel for the Elder Biosphere. The building front appeared massive and solid. Keiko realized it was a digitally-mastered facade; Tokyo had no room for large expansive hospitals, but the façade made her feel protected and calm. The biosphere's motto was etched into the granite-like entranceway, "Re-engineer: Regain, Remember, Remain." She repeated the words to herself as her family glided along the path. Stone structures morphed into the halls of a biomedical unit.

Keiko's grandmother, one of one thousand patients, was part of the CGGG's first experimental study. To be considered, each participant must be sixty-five years or older, reside in one of the countries working with the CGGG, and be willing to sign legal guardianship over to the CGGG during the six-month to one year period of residential care as their body systems are re-engineered—little to ask for a chance at a healthy, prolonged life.

The family disembarked at Section 93. Father keyed in the code to enter Grandmother's room, but instead of opening, the door transformed into a screen. Akiko Obachaan's geriatrician, a biomedical engineer and architect of body systems, appeared on the screen and greeted them. "Re-building Tanaka Akiko's immune system and repairing and replacing aged body systems will take six months or longer. As her treatment continues, so does the risk of disrupting the process and contamination. Her doctors have determined that physical visits could be detrimental during this period. Quarantine is necessary, but feel free to use the WIpod for weekly updates and contact.

"She is making remarkable progress. The engineering approach coupled with nanotechnology may be the missing link in reducing effects of the aging process. This action-oriented method uses dendrimers, three-dimensional man-made molecules containing sticky spaces for chemicals. Acting as vehicles, they target and deliver diagnostic and therapeutic products to re-engineer genes—the ideal building block for biotechnology to redesign aging humans.

"You will be able to see Tanaka Akiko today but not meet with her. She may be slightly disoriented and unresponsive, but her medical successes may provide treatments for millions of elderly in the future." The geriatrician's image faded away on the screen. Keiko was lost in the facts and statistics. She just wanted to be close to her grandmother. As the geriatrician's image faded, the atoms in the wall in front of Keiko morphed into transparent glass revealing her grandmother in bed. Keiko waved to her. Akiko Obaachan appeared weak and dazed as she tried to raise her arm.

This new form of treatment for the elderly is still in the beginning stages. Its success could change the future of mankind. As outside observers, your FPS team is asked to identify challenges of CGGG's medical advancements for the elderly, produce solution ideas, and develop an action plan.

Terchan Newman of Martin Luther King Middle School in Texas wrote this scenario in response to the 2006-2007 FPSPI topic Caring for Our Elders. "Back to the Old Dayes" took 2nd place in the Texas Future Problem Solving Program Middle Division, International Scenario Writing Competition.

Back to the Old Dayes

As Earl sat in his La-Z-Boy recliner listening to the golden oldies on his radio, he thought of his family that he had left behind. He cringed, for his flashback was most unkind. In the home of Christy, his great-granddaughter, things had not worked out for him. He had complained about the tasteless food she prepared on her sterile Cook Master 3000, about her husband's super project-a-screen television, about her daughter's holo-babies which cried all night more loudly than any real baby ever could, and about her son's roof-rocking Super Jam-a-lator Music Ball. It had been too much noise, too much movement, too much, too much of everything, twenty-four hours a day, seven days a week.

"Turn that crap off, Andy!" he had yelled. "You'll go deaf listening to that junk!

Sometimes Earl had wondered if the boy had already lost his sense of hearing because he never responded to anything his great-great-grandfather said to him.

Oh, he had thought his life was so miserable. He had wanted to leave, but the Seniordences that had been built for elderly citizens during the last fifty years were so high-tech, so perfectly prepared to care for their every physical need, so coldly impersonal. Android robots picked them up if they fell, medicated them when they were ill, bathed them, and combed their hair; they even brushed their teeth, trimmed the hair from their ears, and clipped their toenails. The elderly unable to care for themselves and who had no family members were sent to one of the Seniordences whether they wanted to go or not. Only those with family willing to take them in and provide total care were allowed a choice in the matter. Earl had family willing to take him in. Christy. She loved him; he adored her. They just didn't seem to live in the same world.

Earl had wanted to go back to the world he knew; his great-granddaughter, had reluctantly let him go.

Earl looked around the room, his place in time. The familiar pictures and fixtures brought him no comfort now. "Be careful what you wish for, boy; you just might get it," he murmured, recalling the long-ago words his own grandfather used to say to him. "Oh, Pops, I should have listened," he sighed and closed his tired eyes.

There in his memory lingered Christy, like a ray of golden sunlight. "Oh, dear girl," he addressed the glowing image, "what an old fool I was!"

"He's so unhappy here," Christy said to her husband Larry one Saturday morning while surfing the Universalnet on her touchfree PC Pod. "He really wants to leave, but none of the Seniordences please him. What are we to do, Larry?"

"There is that Old Dayes space community near Mars that I told you about last month. Remember?"

"I remember, but you said we would not be allowed to visit him."

"No, we would not be allowed to visit. According to their ad, visits from family tend to upset their clients. Tell you what, why not talk it over with Papa Earl? Let him decide, Chris."

"I'm afraid he'll decide to go."

"He has that right, honey."

Her husband was right, of course. Although he shared her firm belief that families should stay together regardless of the sacrifices involved, he knew that at this point it was not their decision to make. The thought that her wanting to keep Papa Earl with them might be a selfish violation of the older man's rights saddened her deeply. "He needs us," she said, biting her bottom lip in a futile attempt to control its uncontrollable trembling.

"Talk it over with him, honey." Larry leaned over and kissed the top of her head. "You know I'm with you all the way."

At dinner that night, Earl complained about the high-tech house, the holograms, talking walls, cleaning robots, and magic doors without knobs.

"Now when I was a boy on the farm," he launched into one of his back-in-the-day reminisces, "a man opened the door for a lady, and walls did not talk! Why, if I ran into a wall, my head swelled like Elmer Fudd's." As a memory of Elmer chasing Bugs Bunny crossed his mind, a soft smile crossed his face.

"Who's Elmer Fudd?" Christy laughed, seeing the old man's smile.

"Oh, just a cartoon character from way back before your time," he chuckled. "That was back when cartoons made us laugh." So much had changed. Too much. With that thought his smile faded. "When can we leave for the Old Dayes?"

Christy was stunned. "You said you would think about it, Papa Earl."

"I'm done thinking."

There was nothing more Christy could say.

As Earl, Christy, and Larry toured the Old Dayes community, Earl pointed excitedly to a man dialing a telephone and exclaimed, "Look at that!" He was overjoyed to learn that each residential community in the Neighborhoods of the Decades was built to reflect a specific decade. Sections 1950 and 1960 had a collection of Elvis Presley's music. They even had farms! Earl's grin stretched from ear to ear, and his face shone like a full moon. "When can I move in?" he eagerly asked Ms. Nancy Anderson, their guide.

Ms. Anderson laughed, "Not so fast. We do have a week-long orientation for you and your family. If you decide to stay with us, we have a six month trial period."

When they made it to the Victorian-styled front office, Christy stared at the doorknob, a peculiar look on her face. "Must all the doors be opened manually?"

"You bet!" said Earl. "That's the way it's supposed to be."

"No, it isn't!" Christy disagreed. "Larry and I have never touched a door in our entire lives! Why, it's . . . it's inconvenient, to say the least, and . . . and unsanitary!"

Earl looked around. "Here they have created a world like the one I knew; here is where I want to spend my remaining years."

At the end of the week of orientation, Earl said his good-byes to Larry and Christy. He had found the life he wanted among other seniors like him who wanted to return to a simpler place in time. He refused to allow Christy's final argument to dampen his joy.

"Papa Earl," she had said, "it's a make-believe world, a long way from your real home with us. We must keep moving forward, Papa Earl. That's the way life is. We can't go back to the old days no matter how badly we want to or how hard we try. They are selling you a dream." As Larry had led her away, she had turned to Ms. Anderson and choked out, "Remember our agreement."

Earl had looked one last time into Christy's tear-filled eyes, those bright, honest eyes so much like those of his beloved late wife Elizabeth.

Now Earl sat in his lonely La-Z-Boy recliner listening to his lonely golden oldies on his lonely radio. Modern science had extended the life span of so many elderly ones, and modern inventions had created well-equipped homes for them. Although he had good neighbors, they could not take the place of the family he had rejected, the family that had so lovingly taken him into their hearts and their home. His initial joy of being in the Old Dayes had evaporated months ago as he gradually came to realize that the entire setup was nothing more than a fancy Seniordence designed especially for fools like him who thought they could live in the past. It was an antiques warehouse for antiques like him, he thought sadly. "I'm stuck," he said aloud, well aware that the six-month trial period had passed months ago, making him a permanent resident.

A soft knock at the door interrupted his thoughts. He rose slowly from his chair, and shuffled across the room to open the door. He stared into those eyes he had thought never to see again. "Christy!" he choked out and gripped the doorknob to steady himself.

Christy looked into her great-grandfather's moist eyes. "Well, we were in the neighborhood."

Earl looked behind Christy where Larry stood with their two smiling children. His family.

"We thought you might need a ride home, Papa Earl," Andy said, and they all laughed. They laughed later as they waved farewell to a smiling Ms. Anderson who had honored her agreement with Christy to double the six-month trial period; they laughed as they left the Old Dayes behind them to board their earth-bound flight; and they howled with delight when Papa Earl fed a crying holobaby, tapped his foot to the beat of Andy's roof-rocking music and asked, "Who needs a doorknob?"

Written by Paul Nelson, homeschooled, Iowa Future Problem Solving Program, this scenario was a 1st place winner in the Senior Division of the International Scenario Writing Competition. Topic: Cultural Prejudice.

Different

"Heads up, scrub!"

Nate looked just in time to see the yellow glideball smash into his face. He fell to the ground, followed by his pile of holobooks. His thick black glasses tumbled across the floor.

Howls of laughter echoed through the glassy corridors of Neo-New York High School. Nate's face flushed with shame as he faltered after his glasses. His myopic eyes struggled to focus on the hazy world around him.

"Never mind a glideball . . . with those things on his face, he should be seeing Lunar City!" taunted an obnoxious voice. Nate froze. Nearsighted or not, he recognized the husky silhouette standing over him: the school jock, Trevor.

"Hey Nate! You ready to get those eyes replaced and join the rest of us in the twenty-first century?"

Nate stood up, shakily. "Can I have my glasses back, Trevor?"

The blurry, muscular blob snorted. "Whatever, scrub."

Nate felt his glasses being roughly shoved back onto his face. He straightened the bulky plastic frames, relaxing slightly as the world came back into focus. Trevor gave Nate another scornful laugh and walked away.

Trevor's nickname of "The Cyborg" was well-earned. Bioplasm implants of all sorts covered the boy's body. From the bulging biceps underneath his shirt to the neural uplink imbedded in his skull, the blue glow of artificiality emanated from every anatomical region.

Nate remembered the day bioplasm had arrived. His first-grade teacher had squirted a blob of the blue gel into each student's hand, exuberantly explaining the wonder of it all: how the byproducts of genetically-modified algae could, with the application of highly sophisticated treatments, be transformed into synthetic analogues of biological tissue. Bioplasm could create muscles that were more dense, brains that were more compact, and bones that were far stronger than their human parallels.

As Nate gathered his books ashamedly, he looked around at his fellow students. Nearly all of them had replaced body parts with bioplasm "augments," as the kids had termed the devices. The school population reflected perfectly a culture consumed with gaining and keeping every edge. But Nate Weirz, his parents, and six hundred thousand other citizens of the world were exceptions to this overarching trend. They formed a unique fragment of modern society, a subculture that kept their bodies unaltered. And as he picked his last book off the floor, Nate had no idea why.

Nate took a cautious step off the school's hovertram, nervously looking down the street toward Trevor's house. Seeing no one, Nate plodded toward his own residence. He opened the door and was greeted by the affectionate buzz of the household computer system.

"Welcome home, son!" Doctor Weirz stepped out of his study, smiling warmly. Nate gave a desultory "Hi," threw himself down on the couch and flipped on the telepanel. His father, a gray-haired, studious man in his mid-forties, raised an eyebrow. "Trouble in school again?"

Nate remembered that very little escaped the eyes of his physician parent. "Yeah."

His father grunted, staring at the screen with his son. "You feel like talking about it?"

Nate shut off the panel and shrugged. "Not really."

A pause. "Your mother's not back from Cerberus yet; she said she'll be a few more days." More silence. "I hear there's a refill tanker docking tonight; you wanna see it?"

The bioplasm in human augments needed to be replaced every six weeks. Huge *Leviathan*-class supertankers shipped the product from off-shore farms to major population areas on a regular basis. The gigantic ocean-going vessels were always a sight to see. Normally, Nate would have jumped at the chance to glimpse another of the engineering marvels.

"Not really," he repeated. "I've got a ton of homework."

His father looked surprised, but nodded. "Good boy. I have a holo-conference in an hour; I'll try to have dinner ready after that. See you then." He started walking back toward his office.

"Dad?"

The doctor turned around. "Yes, son?"

Nate took a deep breath. "Why do we choose to be different?"

His father let the office door slide shut. He walked over to the sofa and sat down next to his son. He was silent for a moment, considering each thought with care.

"Is this about what's been happening in school?" he asked finally. Nate nodded.

His father smiled. "Does it bother you that we're different?"

Nate knit his brows. "Yeah, Dad, it does. Why do we want to stand out from everyone else?"

His father stood up and walked to the window. "Look out there, son. What do you see?"

The lights from the distant metropolis glimmered on the horizon. "I see the city," said Nate.

"No," his father said, staring off into the distance. "You see the Earth. You see temperate grasslands, scorching deserts, frozen wastelands, and dripping rainforests. You see a variety of habitats unlike any other world this galaxy has shown us. And yet human beings manage to inhabit each and every corner of this globe. How?"

He turned toward his son. "Variety. For thousands of years, humans have survived because they adapted their ways of living to the environments in which they found themselves."

"But things have changed, Nate. These . . . these 'augmentations' we've devised for ourselves . . . they don't make us unique or equip us for changing circumstances. At one point in time, man could be supremely independent; he could live off the land, surviving by the sweat of his brow. Now, son," his father chuckled sadly, "he can't even go six weeks without a refill of bioplasm."

Nate felt his father's hand on his shoulder. "You know I don't hate technology. And you know your mother and I want to give you every opportunity for the future. But we also want you to develop the body with which you were born. We want you to learn how to be independent—how to adapt. That is why we choose to be different."

Nate sat, thinking over his father's words. He knew his parent was right ... but the ramifications were so hard to accept ...

Exhausted from the stress of the day, he slumped over and fell asleep.

Nate awoke with a start, throwing the remote control off his chest with a startled yelp. The device fell to the ground, inadvertently forcing the telepanel on. Nate breathed heavily for a few moments, slowly gathering his shattered thoughts. Suddenly, he focused on the telepanel. The newswoman had an unusually anxious tone in her voice.

"All signs point to a malformed protein that contaminated the latest shipment. Casualties continue to mount as the investigation continues. Police and firefighters have struggled to maintain order as their own implants break down; civil services have been heavily equipped with bioplasm augments since the Standardization Act of 2037 . . ."

Nate noticed the woman's bioplasm arm hanging awkwardly at her side. The device's typical blue glow had been replaced with a sickly, pallid green. Something was wrong.

Nate's father burst from his office, running toward the front door. "Nate!" he said, noticing his son. "There's been an accident . . . the bioplasm shipment was tainted. People are dying all over the city . . . I'm heading to the clinic to see what I can do. Don't leave the house, son; you'll be safe here!"

"Wait, Dad!" Nate yelled, sprinting after his father. "What about Mom?"

But his father was gone. Nate listened as the doctor's vehicle roared out of the garage. A moment of indecision, and Nate sprang for his own jacket. He was not going to cower in a corner until the crisis was over.

Smoke rose over the Weirz's neighborhood, its dark tendrils obscuring the moon. Distant cries for help mingled with the stench of burning diesel as Nate stumbled down the front steps. He ran into the middle of the street, stopping to look at the hovercar that had smashed into the lamppost outside his house. Its driver-side door hung open.

"Help . . . me . . ."

Nate whirled around. Scant yards away from the wrecked car lay its former driver. The injured adolescent lay disabled on the sidewalk, every one of his augmentations inert. The teen's eyes—one tinged green with the pallor of infected bioplasm—stared pleadingly at Nate. Nate gasped. It was "The Cyborg": Trevor.

A maelstrom of emotions arose within Nate's heart. The pity he had felt for helpless mankind was nearly overwhelmed when he glimpsed his paralyzed oppressor. The repressed rage of a decade finally welled to the surface in a tidal wave of fury, flushing Nate's cheeks and quickening his pulse. The bully's ignorance, his refusal to accept Nate's uniqueness, fiercely compelled Nate to leave the boy where he lay.

Trevor's dimming eyes saw a hand reach down into view. He looked upward into the face of Nate, whose eyes were smiling behind his thick glasses. "Come on," said Nate. "Let's get you to a hospital."

Nate's anger withered as he heaved the boy off the ground. He had never been more thankful to be different.

2

Futures Committee: Showing the Way

"No matter how much you study the future, it will always surprise you. But you needn't be dumbfounded."

Kenneth Boulding[1]

We can start now to imagine a customized multiyear campaign to help futurize much you and I value in the educational mission. The operative word here is *customize*, as I have no intention of insulting you with prescriptive "wisdom." In this, and almost everything else, one size does not fit all. Many years of learning from your counterparts have caused me to appreciate your insider ability to tweak to advantage the ideas for change of others like myself. We both know you can make more of them than I can imagine.

For openers, you, or, if necessary, a recruit much like you, must embrace taking a leadership role . . . one that is heartfelt and empowering. Onlookers have to sense both your deep commitment to the endeavor, and also your buoyant (if privately sober) expectation of more successes than setbacks. Futurizing begins with an inspired leader: "It starts at the top so that the courage to invent can be felt and supported throughout an [organization] . . ."[2]

As a widely respected, experienced, and insightful person, it will help if you also have a good sense of humor, a patient way with people, and more than a little charisma. A natural salesman, you should stand out as a creative thinker and an energetic doer. You will be expected to diplomatically share credit for all campaign gains. And, if necessary, to take the heat for errors, guide a creative midcourse recovery, and, above all, help the futurizing campaign stay the course.

It would help if, at the outset, you can agree to stay committed (as one of the inner circle, if not the leader) for at least three years, so as to ensure accountability and follow-up. This includes grooming your possible successors, as one measure of an astute leader is the presence of able replacements in the wings. (Known as "lead users," they are not just early supporters, but also leaders capable of figuring out things you have not thought of).

Given the specialized nature of futuristics, it helps if you are a self-proclaimed futurist, a person who finds tomorrow's possibilities and perils a compelling interest, though this identity can develop rapidly from this point on. (*Relax*: It is a comparatively easy identification to assume—no certification, no secret initiation or handshake, no degree requirement—just a commitment to think beyond the obvious about future-shaping events and choices).

You would do well to become a member of the nation's only formal organization of futurists, the 15,000-member World Future Society (www.wfs.org), the largest category of whose members are—like you—in K–12 careers. You can make good use of its publications—*The Futurist, Futures Survey, Futures Review*—all of which also belong in your school's library. Especially valuable is the education section of the WFS Web site, where like-minded teachers trade real-time advice, and so on.

If there is a local chapter of the WFS nearby (a directory is on its Web site), you might become a regular attendee. In addition, you should try to join over one thousand forecasters from around the world at the three-day annual Global Assembly of the WFS. Starting at 8 a.m. and running through 10 p.m., a track of school-related sessions regularly highlights ongoing projects of relevance to your futurizing campaign. (The 2008 Assembly includes sessions entitled "2021 Vision for Elementary and Middle Schools in a Global Society," "Some Suggested Priorities for Futuristics in the Classroom," and "Teaching Futures and Future Education.")

You will also find it useful to subscribe to free Internet-based discussion lists that regularly help futurists stay up with the latest ideas about tomorrow (see Resources at the book's close). Likewise, magazines such as MIT's *Technology Review, Scientific American*, and various "Green" publications belong on your "must scan" reading list. Responsibility for covering such resources in search of relevant articles should be shared with colleagues, as their number otherwise overwhelms.

CREATING A COMMITTEE

As a futurizing campaign is beyond the capacity of any one of us, you will need to recruit a band of kindred souls, a sparkling cadre, so to speak, of enthusiastic first-responders. Together you can create your school's first *Futures Committee*, an overdue development of lasting significance (though, to be frank, this remains for your group to prove, as it is not self-evident). In addition to yourself as initiator, this committee will be key to the success—or failure—of the entire campaign.

This point cannot be exaggerated: Unless and until a Futures Committee becomes a dynamic, respected, and effective change agent, your futurizing campaign will remain in danger of reducing merely to good intentions, blah-blah, and faint accomplishments. At the top of a list of critical things to accomplish is the formidable task of creating, maintaining, and steadily improving the committee. Having myself led a comparable group for over 30 years—the Philadelphia Chapter of the WFS (the oldest in the Society)— I know from experience how vital it is to nurture a committee in ways both obvious and out of sight.

You may groan—*Not another committee!*—so leery are you and I of their propensity to waste time, misdirect effort, and finally produce only marginal gains. This one, however, can and should do much better: Drawing, for example, on the ability of members to often meet virtually, rather than in real space, and to employ other 21st century high-tech cutting-edge tools (such as Blackberry instant-messaging aids), a school's Futures Committee should show peers and the entire school district superior ways to employ this time-honored organizational form.

With this as backdrop, we can now consider twelve guidelines likely to help you keep your sanity, buoy your spirits, protect your personal relations, minimize mistakes, and maximize gains—provided, that is, you tweak all twelve and make these guidelines your own.

1) Welcome All

In your school—indeed, in school districts—among all district staffers, there are almost always a few good men and women. Once they learn of the opportunity to help futurize schooling, they are likely to join you. To get the word out, and ask for more volunteers, you could use the Internet, and a new Futures Committee Web site created pro bono by Web-savvy cyber-wizards/netizens among your first recruits.

Diversity is critical to the committee's success. Political savvy recommends including as many types as possible, lest the committee be perceived as a "private club." This goes beyond race, gender, and sexual preference to also include recruitment from all age blocs, time-in blocs (those new to the school; those long there), subject blocs (the arts, the humanities, the sciences, etc.), home locale blocs (urban, suburban, rural), life style blocs (singles, parents, near-retirement), and especially, political persuasion (conservatives, liberals, libertarians, radicals, and so on).

Since most interest groups tend to be homogeneous, fostering diversity means breaking with convention and, if the political scene permits, inviting into membership a representative of the elected local school board. This person, presumably a volunteer aligned with the cause of futurizing your school, can prove an invaluable link to power-holders, a buffer against unwarranted criticism, and a sound spokesperson for those neighbors whose role includes helping to keep things "real."

Diversity has more going for it than merely moral exhortations. New research draws here on formal mathematical models used by forecasters (particularly those concerned with anticipating financial markets or voting patterns). It finds that diverse groups outdo homogeneous ones at problem-solving. The former get stuck less often as their varied members draw on more and different ways of seeing a problem, and thus, have richer ways of forecasting. Researchers suggest the more diversity, the fewer the errors in a group's forecasting: Diversity "makes everything we do more powerful."[3]

Attracting diverse types is not easy, and holding them in membership is harder yet. It will require extraordinary tact, self-conscious forbearance, and the capacity to nip in the bud misunderstandings and seeming slights that if not arrested, can magnify and overwhelm all. This not withstanding, the effort must be made, as the committee's educational focus—*tomorrow*—is far too important to have onlookers think it a "captive" of only the Greens. Or the whites. Or the males. Or the humanities. Or the newcomers, the Do-Gooders, and so on. It should belong to everyone—as does our future.

2) Students as Members?

In the best of circumstances, this should be a no-brainer: Of course, students should be welcomed as full-fledged junior colleagues, with the privileges and responsibilities of all others. In this way they can learn at first hand the rewards of intellectual curiosity, cultivated intuition, and commitment to Vision.

Apart from their roles on the committee, these student volunteers may in due course help "futurize" student-led school organizations, e.g., encourage the Drama Club to stage "R.U.R," a classic play about robotics, or get the French Club to sponsor a forum about early French utopians whose influence is still felt in futuristics (Saint-Simon, Rousseau, etc.). A model student UN might tackle issues raised by World Government advocates and detractors.

Of course, at the outset, your Futures Committee may not be ready to welcome young people as equal members. At the very least some student representative should be invited to attend as observers, or as "voice, but no vote" members. Once such students have demonstrated the distinctive and valuable contribution they can make—as their perspective often eludes that of their elders—they should be offered membership.

To fly the flag of future-concern is to shun ageism (and all other restrictive "isms") as soon and as thoroughly as possible. It is also to recognize that "the grand challenge for schools is to empower students to contribute actively to a preferred future." (Rhea, 2005, 107)

3) Power Sharing

As the committee's leader, you must generously share power and responsibilities. Recruits must recognize the committee as a genuinely collaborative effort, rather than a one-man band. It must model a new way of getting things done—a 21st century collegial way—and not undermine itself by clinging to the tools of yesteryear's organizational models (authoritarianism, identity politics, Machiavellian wiles, etc.). Members should feel useful, valued, and affirmed.

A sound, indeed, indispensable initial activity for a Futures Committee involves a technique known as scanning. Every committee member identifies information resources they ordinarily enjoy learning from (such as magazines, radio and TV shows, Web sites, etc.). Once duplications are known, each can volunteer to monitor specific sources using a retrievable format placed on the Internet by the committee. This will enable the committee to keep up with trends, fads, and other manifestations of significant change. Everyone can profit thereafter from the easy availability of shared information not otherwise available.

Creating many subcommittees is also a sound way of assuring power-sharing and boosting efficiency and effectiveness—provided innovative use is made of information technology to manage the multiple activities. Automatic checkup e-mails could usefully go to subcommittee heads, and they in turn could monitor progress of colleagues using similar Internet techniques. The committee's Web site could publicly track progress, red-flag hindrances, and in 101 other creative ways, attest to both the organization's wide range of interests and its democratic ethos.

4) Virtual Planning Process

Much of the committee's planning process can be accomplished in a virtual mode online rather than by relying solely on face-to-face contact. As this is likely to take some members far from their comfort zone, they may ask—*Why not stick with familiar methods?* To which other members might diplomatically remind all that a futurizing campaign should demonstrate a decided preference for innovation, as a distinction of a futurizing process. A judicious mix of Old and New would seem the wise course.

5) Mapping the Field

To assure sound planning, it is advisable to initially conduct a school-wide survey of what is already underway, lest your new Futures Committee embarrass itself by appearing to reinvent the wheel or charge through an open door. One or more farsighted teachers may have ongoing curriculum units that explore this or that aspect of tomorrow, and it is politic to know this ASAP, not the least reason being your ability to sincerely extend the committee's keen and smiling admiration for such pioneering efforts.

A particularly good tool for conducting agenda-setting research is a technique known as appreciative inquiry, a new and overdue mode of research that accents the positive. It helps users reframe realities in a positive way, in this case, enabling you to ask everyone how they imagine attention to the future might improve K–12 schooling in general, and your school in particular. Emphasis is put on no-holds-barred imagination, and on conjuring up attractive images of the future, rather than on staid analysis. The survey data should highlight energizing opportunities to grow (glass half filled), rather than (demoralizing) problems to solve (glass half empty).

6) Capturing a Vision

Buttressed by the findings from an appreciative inquiry survey, and from ensuing creative and pragmatic discussions, the committee should draft a dynamic three-year Web-based master plan for your futurizing campaign and post it on the committee's Web site. It should be reviewed at half-year intervals. Bold and inspiring, your vision statement should be guided by the notion that "nothing important was ever begun in a prudential frame of mind."[4]

As vision-capturing exercises have been a mainstay of educational change in recent decades, this process should start with a thoroughgoing review of the literature. The mission statements, vision statements, and other like documents of comparable schools (here and abroad) should be scrutinized. Sound ideas (and language) should be adapted to the special circumstances of your school. Intent on not reinventing the wheel, your committee should borrow with attribution, and improve on the best others offer. Above all, your vision statement should bolster morale (on and off your Committee), clarify goals, and point the way.

7) Prepare to Defend

In alliance with relevant departments your Futures Committee should help protest unwarranted cuts in resources, as in right-brain subjects (the arts, the humanities, the social sciences, etc.) that do not lend themselves to the testing mania now in sway. The committee could mobilize the growing body of research demonstrating the distinctive ability of these so-called "soft" subjects to promote exactly the strengths needed in our future—strengths like imagination, ingenuity, social concern, and the vital like.

Sometimes overlooked in this connection is the need to protect (if not even expand) the time available for recess. Here is where youngsters can make major gains as "junior" futurists, though adults seldom understand this: Play can help give children hope for a better tomorrow. Imaginative play uniquely helps create persons "who believe in possibilities—an optimist, a creative thinker, a person who has a sense of power and control."[5] A close student of play explains "What is adaptive about play may be not only the skills that are a part of it, but also the willful belief in acting out one's own capacity for the future."[6]

Likewise, in alliance with departments in your school under direct attack, your Futures Committee should also prepare to protect academic integrity, a vital bulwark of futurizing. If weakened, a school's curriculum can be reduced overnight to joke status, the sorry stuff of a cable news freak show. No seriously wounded curriculum is likely to have a place for your futurizing campaign.

There is growing pressure, for example, in some "Red" States to teach "alternative theories" alongside of Darwinian ideas about evolution. Those eager to trump scientific education with their personal religious beliefs want biology teachers, in effect, to have to end class with, "And it's all so amazing, a lot of people think you-know-who designed it!"[7] Your Futures Committee could help colleagues fight back, as such anti-scientific notions undermine what is meant by scientific theory and method, which are both vital in the study of tomorrow.

Likewise, your Futures Committee should prepare to protect students from the emotional stresses that invisibly build in high-pressure settings; pressures to overachieve that can result in a frenzied student culture and burned out teachers. Fierce rivalries are common among student subcultures—and in the worst of circumstances, school-related suicides or even school-place homicides. Your committee can help your school push back against inordinate pressures for superachievement, pressures many sage educators think incompatible with a preferred future for us all.[8]

8) Prepare to Provide

Again, in alliance with relevant departments your Futures Committee might look outside school walls to engage a wide-range of constituencies. Its members include parents of your students, school alumni, retirees, officeholders, influence-shapers (clergy, journalists, etc.), local employers, and other adults curious about various aspects of the future (many such citizens, not incidentally, vote for school board members and vote on school bond proposals).

In due course, a series of engaging evening programs could address some of the vital information needs of adults. For example, a forum could explain such Web sites as *Divide the Ride*, a new carpooling Web site designed to help busy parents by drawing up shared calendars based on their availability and the school schedule of their children (dividetheride.com), Another free Web site, Cappex (cappex.com) offers a "matchmaking" service that pairs high-school students with colleges looking for specific types of candidates. Three other Web sites provide free comparisons among K–12 schools, including demographics, test results, teacher-to-student ratios, and percentages of students eating free and reduced-price lunches (Education.com, GreatSchools.net, SchoolMatters.com).

Another type of forum could address surreptitious viewing by curious youngsters of wildly popular Web sites for the Mad magazine set; e.g., Ebaumsworld, which typically shows har-har videos of skateboard wipe-outs, but also offers such dark stuff as bodies ravaged by crack cocaine. Or LiveLeak, which features videos of extreme real-life violence, including executions, murders, and torture. Some parents fear their children are being harmed by the stuff on gross-out sites. Does it warp a child's morality, and thereby his or her future, and what does its availability suggest about our future as a viewing public?[9]

A related forum run by your Futures Committee could address common fears that children might become laptop-addicted Internet zombies or video-game-addicted isolates. Panelists could urge attention to defensive aids like the Entertainment Software Rating Board website. The point might also be made that at a certain point that immersion in the cyberworld—especially by youngsters still gingerly making and maintaining real-world personal contacts—can have more merit than fault (it allows experimentation, risk-taking, etc.). Whatever the topic, these forums should provide fresh information, fair-mindedness (which is not the same as neutrality), and ethical rigor.

9) Prepare to Recommend

Your Committee could provide thoughtful advice. For example, schools increasingly confront the question of what to do about lighting? The 2007 Energy Bill has written *fini* to the plain vanilla incandescent light bulb in four billion U.S. sockets: By 2012 it will no longer be for sale, having long since failed to measure up (it costs 30 percent more energy than acceptable).[10] Mandated energy-saving replacements at $3 a spiral light bulb—six times the price of their outlawed predecessor—are expected to last four times as long (10,000-hour life), use less energy, and save power.[11]

While a school's net lighting costs over time may reflect savings, the initial acquisition cost may be considerable. As well, critics point out the new "Green" bulbs contain mercury, which they warn can build up in dumps when millions get discarded years from now. After possibly first hearing from area libertarians and conservatives who, on principle, resent this sort of future-making federal legislation, and also hearing from those focused on the mercury hazard, your school Futures Committee might favor a well-publicized pro-Green switchover, or carefully explain its well-buttressed opposition to this move.

Apropos teaching as such, your Futures Committee might recommend a free open source online course-management system called Moodle. With its password-protected access, it addresses the anxiety of parents who oppose having teachers direct their children to a site on MySpace for classroom resources and homework assignments. Moodle, and many counterparts (the Sakai project, etc.) use a user-friendly modular design that allows teachers to start with a few basic tools, and add others later, without knowing or understanding HTML or other computer languages.[12]

10) Above the Fray

Note that recommendations are *not* the same thing as forecasts. It is best to avoid having your Futures Committee offer forecasts. As explained in chapter 1, this should be left to professional forecasters. It would be a costly mistake for the committee to get closely identified with one or another of the warring camps where forecasts are concerned . . . to be thought, for example, a "captive" of the Greens or Globalizers, or of their opponents. Far more desirable is a reputation as a fair-minded forum for all responsible points of view.

This point cannot be made strongly enough, as certain members of your Futures Committee are likely to take a passionate stance in favor of the Committee issuing strong forecasts; that is, strong political statements papered over as "forecasts." There is NO one future to hail through forecasts, only a myriad of possibilities to endlessly anticipate, assess, and respond to in a proactive way. It would be a grievous mistake for a school Futures Committee to get sucked into partisanship where academic neutrality is called for.

In a related way, it is best to constrain those Committee members whose enthusiasm for the campaign might have them wanting to shout its merits from the rooftop. This would be a costly mistake, as it could force opponents into high gear. Your goal is not attention, and an ensuing confrontation: it is the inclusion of many futuristic components inside the framework of the state's basic curriculum, achieved quietly and possibly under the radar.

A low-profile exercise brought along on "cat's paws" is always advisable. Young learners should gain from age-appropriate exposure to the art of forecasting (short-term, long-term, value-neutral, evaluative) and creativity exercises, discovery learning, scenario writing, trend analysis, and other straightforward aspects of futuristics almost all youngsters find fascinating.

In a deliberately cautious way your school and its Futures Committee should avoid provoking others stirred by any trumpeted use of futuristics. Not the least reason is that the subject is associated nowadays with environmentalism which has been targeted by anti-Green activists. (Typical is the charge by a former U.S. Senator that "too many global-warming zealots appear to worship the creation instead of the Creator, and view man and his actions as only suspect disrupters of nature."[13]

These earnest citizens insist global warming is not a seismic shift taking place, but only what used to be called summertime. They oppose "Green" changes, especially those that upset the status quo in schooling, as overbearing, misguided, and inordinately expensive . . . changes they trace in part to airy forecasts from elitist practitioners of fault-ridden pseudoscience. Pro-Green citizens, in turn, charge their opposites with ignoring the factual evidence and turning their faces from, instead of facing the looming future.

Accordingly, inside your school your futurizing campaign is likely to raise hackles. At the very least, there will be thoughtful doubters, colleagues who warrant respect and a diplomatic response. Certainly, any campaign to purposefully shape the future will have earnest opponents who must be artfully countered, and hopefully neutralized, or possibly even won over in time. Make no mistake: a futurizing campaign seldom escapes opposition, since it challenges privilege, shibboleths, turf, and the status quo.

All of this notwithstanding, once your school's many futurizing projects have proven of significant value, your committee can then skillfully bring your campaign out of the shadows. If your circumstances do not require this sort of defensiveness, all the better. While remaining alert and agile, your Futures Committee can begin an upfront campaign on many different fronts, recognizing from the outset that each front has its own prospects, and its own unique set of stakeholders.

11) Prepare to "Teach"

Over the long haul your committee should make itself available as a very cordial, diplomatic, and yet also effective mentor to colleagues. The goal of earning newly enthusiastic collaborators, and of winning community buy-in, is a vital one.

Given the neglect of futuristics in typical teachers' college curricula and in BA/BS teacher preparation programs, it is unlikely that many colleagues will immediately feel ready to take on a role in the futurizing effort. It is not easy to grasp the present as the past of the future. All sorts of excuses can be expected ("My plate is full," "I don't know enough," "It just sounds weird," "Yes, but," etc.).

Mentoring, offered in a very cordial way, should help these adults rapidly reach a sound level of knowledge and related confidence. This last attribute is vital, as teaching future-related ideas can lead to unsettling questions from curious young learners: At such times it helps to remember that "learning comes in the cracks when we are open and willing to deal with the uncomfortable conversations, the unpredictable question, and the spontaneous outburst."[14]

Mentoring should ease attainment of "transparency of meaning and lucidity of thinking—qualities good educators hope to inculcate in children."[15] Students, by the way, profit from observing teachers learning anew, especially when the adults are doing this in front of them. They provide fine models of how to deal with change.

Typical of nitty-gritty matters that mentoring could help with is establishing policies governing the use of laptops in class. After consultation with student members of your Futures Committee it might be agreed that all teachers would ask their students to confine use to lecture note taking and/or real-time research that bears on the matter directly under discussion. Students could be put on their honor to curb irrelevant uses, even as they put their cell phones on silence when entering class.

12) Outreach

Please remember: whatever way you introduce your school to its new Futures Committee—whether by announcements, displays, events, projects, and so forth, or a combination of them—your material should be temperate in tone. Any projects you refer to should be capable of being accomplished swiftly and with clear rewards for youngsters.

First impressions are vital, and you want to make one that draws smiles and expressions of positive interest from youngsters and adults alike (including visiting parents and school board members). Some committee members are likely to urge bolder, more ambitious efforts than seem advisable. Sounder views should trump such zeal, and discreet equivalents of "speed bumps" are advisable.

Once matters seem under control, your Futures Committee might take a leaf from the example of American Legacy magazine and outfit an eighteen-wheeler tractor-trailer with interactive displays (its 2008 exhibit, which visited 11 cities, helped schoolchildren and adults learn about black history, play games, view photo exhibits, and trace their ancestry online.)[16] Your exhibit—perhaps a converted school bus—could highlight both selected aspects of the future, and appealing methods of teaching futuristics. It could visit area schools on a "Johnny Appleseed"-like tour, and help spread word of our futurizing campaign far and wide.

Finally, your Futures Committee might encourage the administration to offer cost-effective distance learning and online interactive courses on Future topics. For example, the Florida Virtual High School, which is the largest such venture in the United States, invites Tallahassee legislatures—those who hold the purse strings—to experience any of their online courses first hand, in order to help win their critical support at budget allocation time.

SUMMARY

Without an inspired volunteer, hopefully YOU—or possibly a cadre that operates, for all intents and purposes, as a single entity—the futurizing process cannot get beyond wishful thinking: All too often we "tend to devote years to studying what to change and little if any time to actually making change."[17] A close-knit group, your Futures Committee should enjoy a sense of mission, mutual regard, and an energizing "can do!" spirit.[18]

The route thereafter should prove manageable and rewarding, albeit requiring agility, creativity, and diplomacy. Done well, the process should create a long-lasting "community of practice," an empowering form of social learning that nurtures ideas, innovations, and solutions.[19]

HIGHLY RECOMMENDED READING

1) Future-Focused Leadership: *Preparing Schools, Students, and Communities for Tomorrow's Realities*, by Gary Marx. Washington, DCL ASCD, 2006. Outstanding combination of theory and applied material. Includes sixteen trends that will profoundly affect education, eight ways to scan your environment, a four-step management process. And sixteen activities that make up an effective future-focused communications system. 2) *Anticipate the World You Want: Learning for Alternative Futures*, by Marsha Lynne Rhea (Lanham, MD: Scarecrow Education, 2005). Outstanding introduction to future thinking and methodologies as applied to a learning environment. Predicated on the notion that "the grand challenge for schools is to empower students to contribute actively to a preferred future."

NOTES

1. Cited on p.119 in Barker, Joel A., Discovering the Future: The Business of Paradigms. St. Paul, MN: ILI Press, 1989 ed.

2. Gobe, Marc. *Brandjam: Humanizing Brands through Emotional Design.* Allworth Press, 2007, 306.

3. Dreifus, Claudia. "In Professor's Model, Diversity = Productivity." *New York Times*, January 8, 2008, F2. The research was by Prof. Scott E. Page of the University of Michigan and economist Lu Hong of Chicago's Loyola University.

4. David Brooks. "In Iraq, America's Shakeout Moment." *New York Times*, May 18, 2004, A23.

5. Henig, Robin Marantz. "Taking Play Seriously." *New York Times Magazine*, February 17, 2008,. 75 (38–45, 60, 75).

6. Brian Sutton-Smith, as quoted in *ibid.*

7. Thomas, Mike. "Don't Monkey with Science in Our Schools." *Orlando Sentinel*, January 13, 2008, B1.

8. While I was finishing this book, a scheduled high school talk by a Nobel laureate climate researcher was cancelled after some conservative townspeople objected to what they mistakenly thought would be a one-sided advocacy of Green reforms. The speaker told a reporter, "Our generation caused the problem [global warming], and I want to talk to high schools because they are the generation that will solve the problem." Robbins, Jim. "Climate Talk's Cancellation Splits a Town." *New York Times*, January 17, 2008, A19.

9. Heffernan, Virginia. "Cabinets of Wonder." *New York Times Magazine*, February 17, 2008, 25 (25, 26).

10. Kranhold, Kathryn. "His Bright Idea: Dominate Energy-Saving Light Bulbs." *Wall Street Journal*, December 27, 2007, B1, B2. As new fluorescent bulbs will contain mercury, burnt out bulbs will require costly recycling.

11. Carney, Brian M. "Bye Bye, Light Bulb." *Wall Street Journal*, January 2, 2008, A10.

12. Trotter, Andrew. "Market for K–12 Course? Management Systems Expand." *Education Week*, February 27, 2008, 10.

13. Santorum, Rick. "McCain Must Change Views on Social Issues." *Philadelphia Inquirer*, March 13, 2008, A15. Mr. Santorum was the Republican Senator from Pennsylvania, 2000–2006.

14. Tolentono, Heidi. "Race: Some Teachable—and Uncomfortable—Moments." *Rethinking Schools*, Fall 2007, 50 (46–50).

15. Kozol, Jonathan. "Beware the Jargon Factory." *Rethinking Schools*, Fall 2007, (38–41).

16. Clark, Vernon. "Heritage, History on Wheels." *Philadelphia Inquirer*, February 21, 2008, B10.

17. Wood, George H. *A Time to Learn.* New York: Plume, 1999, 175.

18. Logan, Dave, et al. *Tribal Leadership: Leveraging Natural Groups to Build a Thriving Organization.* New York: Collins, 2008.

19. Davenport, Thomas H., et al. "Putting Ideas to Work." *Wall Street Journal*, March 10, 2008, R11.

Schooling in 2015:
Beckoning Possibilities

Below is a vision of mine that carries a critique of our current K–12 scene within it, but appropriately accents the positive: I like to believe it beckons us on.

By 2015 more extraordinary and desirable changes could occur in K–12 schooling than many previous decades. If parents insist local school boards and the state do the right thing, the schooling of our children, whether public or private, could be much better, and far different than anything you and I can recall, thereby unsettling as well as thrilling us.

Consider the radical changes in education made possible by fast-coming advances in computer applications. To educate is to first communicate, and the gadgets coming our way are remarkably powerful communication aids. Electronic books as portable libraries, computers as cell phone-aided "wearables," information agents as allies, and virtual reality labs as "way out" simulations, offer much, especially as they achieve affordability, simplicity, and versatility. Whether or not we will take full advantage of their potential, however, remains uncertain.

By 2015 many teachers and youngsters could be savvy users of remarkable computer-aided electronic books. They should enable a child to carry around an entire bookshelf programmed into one lightweight attractive volume (and easily reprogrammed as the teacher and/or the child wishes). Each can have a built-in dictionary, a thesaurus, word-search capability, excellent screen resolution, wireless connectivity, and long battery life. Each will enable a child to rewrite the story itself, as by putting him or her into the tale. An embedded voice chip can help tutor the child eager to learn how to read better, and could provide immediate self-scoring quizzes with which to assure a youngster he or she is really "getting it."

By 2015 many teachers and youngsters could also be savvy users of very powerful wireless computers carried on their person. Known as "wearables," they may take the form of a cell phone worn on the wrist. Users will speak to, and be spoken to by wearables whose small size belies their very great significance.

Imagine your child able to learn almost anything he or she is curious about, whenever they want, wherever they might be, and in such a way as to bolster the youngster's self-esteem, natural curiosity, and love of learning. Imagine your child able to do this alone or with others. In small doses or for hours on end. In the company of brothers or sisters, or in immediate touch with youngsters from around the world. Imagine all of this in sync with the values of your family, and free of hazards otherwise posed by unfriendly cyberspace material. Neat, yes?! And, thanks to wearables already previewed in 1999, highly likely to characterize schooling in 2015.

When a large, heavy, and awkward computer is no longer left behind on the desk, or lugged about as a six-pound bulky laptop, but is instead a very convenient small wireless aid, school children will be empowered as never before. Any question of information posed by a teacher can be whispered by a child into his or her wearable. An information broker hovering nearby in cyberspace will be eager to sell information from vast data banks for a trivial sum. The broker will "sell" the youngster a good answer in nano- or picoseconds. This sort of regurgitation of facts, an outmoded form of miseducation, should give way to far more creative mind-stretching challenges.

Housed in a child's wearable is likely to be a 21st century version of Merlin, Puff the Magic Dragon, Jiminy Cricket, Tinker Bell, Aristotle, and many of the other magical "ah ha!" aides of which a child might dream. Known technically as an Intelligent Agent, it amounts to artificial intelligence software programmed to do its creator's bidding.

A child would essentially "train" his or her Agent by patiently answering its endless stream of ever-more-refined questions (e.g., what are your favorite toys? Why? Least favorite? Why?). In this way the Agent will get to "know" the youngster (whose well-being would be at the heart of the software's "existence"). Much like a Furby, the 1998 Christmas gift sensation, the child's Intelligent Agent would get "smarter" with use, grow on (and with) one, and occasionally surprise and delight its young caretaker.

Any question that might occur to a child could be asked of its Intelligent Agent, which, in turn, would rapidly research the matter in cyberspace, using search engines vastly improved over those crude upstarts familiar in 2008 (Yahoo, AltaVista, etc.). In school, one's Agent would stand by ready to provide whatever information its young "creator" might need.

As if this wasn't enough, a child might "train" his or her Agent to provide counsel, solace, support, advice, or just plain friendly chitchat, much as every child occasionally wants. At home, the Agent could offer a shoulder to cry or lean on, provide a wise head with which to argue, and in 1,001 other ways, be a nonjudgmental, unflappable, and thoroughly reliable pal.

As if electronic books, computers as "wearables," and Intelligent Agents were not enough, K–12 schooling in 2015 could also employ the most exotic learning tool of all, virtual reality aids to education. As long ago as the mid-1990s especially adventurous school districts created VR labs in which youngsters could don goggles, take a joystick in hand, and "magically" transport themselves via VR computer simulations inside of molecules, algebraic formulas, or oceans they wanted to study. These "wrap-around environments" enabled children, as telepresences, to "drop in" on VR recreations of the signing of the Constitution, Dr. King's seminal address at the 1963 Civil Rights March, or the impeachment of President Andrew Johnson or President William Jefferson Clinton.

A dramatic complement to the 4,000-year-old conventional classroom system, virtual reality programs enable youngsters to feel like they were "there," interact with other participants, and explore what it would mean to modify the (artificial) world itself. VR breaks down the traditional and costly distinction among work, play, and education. It offers the possibility of a class choosing to "meet" in a simulation of Antarctic, Brazil, Croatia, Denmark, or Ghana. It allows participants to explore the enormity of our solar system by "moving" around in it, or get inside the microworld of bacteria. Best of all, VR essentially dissolves the wall of the schoolhouse and offers educational access to the universe.

Naturally, to host such ed tech advances, K–12 classrooms should house phone lines, cutting-edge modems, and/or infrared equipment designed to help a youngster move with his or her wearable (and Intelligent Agent) effortlessly from room to room. Teachers could rely on timely material drawn immediately from the Web, and made available on the screen of every child's wearable. Learners will be able to input ideas into everyone else's wearable, thereby elevating educational dialogue ("interactivity") to a new plane. Ideas should crackle around high tech-aided classrooms now finally as vital and as engaging as is playtime in the schoolyard.

Lest the impression be left that ed tech alone is all that could and should improve by 2015, it is critical to also note the urgent need between now and then to reduce the size of classes, employ more new findings about learning, raise the pay of the staff, emphasize the arts, upgrade standards—and spend the vast amounts necessary to "walk the talk."

By 2015 no subject is likely to prove as central as the arts, for they stand out in their ability to celebrate our human distinctiveness. Youngsters are likely to inherit a world where "smart" equipment, exemplified by the Intelligent Agents in their wearables, take the place of humans in doing rote, repetitive, programmable tasks (those that require precision and are hugely intolerant of error). The jobs left to human job seekers will require creativity, ingenuity, inventiveness, resourcefulness, and even zaniness, fantasy, and fun. The arts uniquely help youngsters nurture their natural gifts in these domains, and learn to accommodate the messy, imprecise ways of their fellows. Playfulness will prosper as never before in K–12 schooling.

Which is not the same thing as saying content loses. Standards will be more critical than ever: In order to graduate from high school in 2015 all teens (not just college-bound youngsters) could be required to pass no-nonsense statewide exams in American history, English, global studies, math, and science (as in New York State since 1999). All may be required to try out career options via co-op stints, and also satisfy a community service requirement. As well, high school graduates could come with a "money-back" guarantee—if he or she cannot do the job, they can be "returned" by a supportive employer for additional free remedial schooling (as in Los Angeles since 1997).

Similarly, before new teachers can be hired, they could have to pass several difficult tests and get a license from a thirty-five-state consortium begun in 2003. Special attention should be paid to their "usability" craft, their ability to make sound and creative use of high tech educational tools. Accountability could be crisply measured, merit pay could be a significant portion of total compensation, and teacher's unions could be in the forefront of the entire reform effort, as so often in the past.

By this time you have undoubtedly noticed the use over and again of the word "could." There are no guarantees in any of this. Many previous waves of technological innovation have disappointed. Classroom use of TV in the 1980s was supposed to make the difference, as was computer-assisted instruction in the 1990s, but both appear mixed blessings. Similarly, recently only one child in four was being offered any arts education (music, arts, theater) at least once a week in school.

Nothing, not ed tech gains, staff aids, curriculum changes, and/or boosts in standards are sure things. The only sure thing is that achieving any these digital-based reforms by 2015 will require many hard-to-raise tax dollars.

Why, then, are they still good bets? Because the other way guarantees local and national disaster. Governors know jobs and new businesses early in the 21st century will go only to states with a top-notch entry-level work force. They understand how fierce is competition among the states for educational bragging rights ("the best schools in the East"). Either we invest substantially in K–12 possibilities, or we will fall farther behind forty-nine other state competitors, watch our best graduates increasingly pack up for better jobs elsewhere, and wanly rue our short-sighted mistake.

Similarly, between now and 2015 we have to close the educational gap between Information Have-More and Information Have-Less neighbors. The contest in the world is not between the top fifth of every nation, but between the four-fifths of every nation's work force. Unless and until the vast number of Americans get out of the Have-Less category none of us will have the security and well-being we want for all. Not until every child has the advantages characteristic today only of affluent school districts and high profile private schools will our position in global economic competition be secure.

If we elect to short-change our offspring, and nickel-and-dime our educational efforts, not even our Intelligent Agents in 2015 can keep us from social and economic disaster. But in a bold new world of ubiquitous computing, with the help of such Agents, of versatile electronic books, computers as "wearables," exotic virtual reality labs, and other mind-boggling educational aids, we may yet achieve an educational system as delightful and rewarding as our children (and their caring teachers) have always deserved.

3

Futuristic Schooling: Moving Parts

"This time, like all times, is a very good one if we but know what to do with it."

Ralph Waldo Emerson

To help bring futuristics into the K–12 curriculum is to first fully appreciate its unique nature (as touched on in the Introduction). After recently earning a Master's Degree in the subject, a friend e-mailed me this reflection:

Futuristics is a mixture of art and science, of the quantitative and qualitative, right and left brain, with a dash of heart and soul. It must not be pigeonholed into a pre-existing category of study . . . [It] studies the big picture. The most valuable part of my future studies education was learning to see and seek connections everywhere. This has given me a perspective on the world I'm not sure I could have learned elsewhere.[1]

This "big picture" perspective can be promoted through seven different educational formats:

1) It can influence curriculum and all other school activities—as explained at length hereafter in this chapter and in chapter 4.
2) Or be featured in an open enrollment elective course.
3) Or in an Honors elective.
4) Or in a course open only to "gifted" students.
5) Or in an after-school non-credit elective or club.
6) Or as a Career Academy embedded in a high school.

7) Or as the focus of a magnet high school, where teenagers might study long-range forecasting in depth, and weight it as a career (see chapter 4).

Each of these approaches warrants a book discussion of its own, and I hope someone soon undertakes to treat them in this way. In this book I have chosen to deal only with options #1 and #7, though I would like to believe my ideas have some value to the other five options as well.

In the best of situations, all seven options would coexist in every school system. Each would have comparable and ample funding and support. The resulting synergy would be a sparkling boon to each. More likely, however, is piece-meal progress throughout the nation's fourteen thousand school districts, with new components added only after predecessors have proven their worth . . . and then only thanks to the patience, persistence, and commitment of school Futures Committees (including, of course, yours).

To achieve success with any of the seven options is to improve a school system's ability to answer the question: What are the fundamentals of a futurized education? What is it that any of America's school systems should be able to boast if they are to ready youngsters for our dizzying times? What is it that America's three million teachers should come to smile appreciatively about when the term *futuristics* is mentioned?

FUNDAMENTALS

Thanks to a school Futures Committee, youngsters in schools that are better attuned to the future should be able to:

learn how to identify future-shaping lessons from the past;
uncover their own hidden assumptions about the future;
draw insights from the arts into the future;
find futuristic ideas everywhere;
explore progress in shaping the future being made in America and overseas;
look into tomorrow's job market;
understand more about globalization; and
learn to look to one another for ideas about the future.

Each of these abilities is discussed below, with emphasis placed on their application in the pre-high school years. Later, in chapter 4, "High Schools of the Future," I switch attention to a total educational design for the upper grades, as research has revealed a critical divide between the learning abilities of preteens and teenagers. *Everything* below *is* applicable to the entire K–12 world, though my material in chapter 4 goes far beyond.

1. Looking Back

In keeping with an emphasis on the "big picture," and on learning to see and seek connections everywhere, a curriculum sensitive to the future should study the past. Youngsters should learn how to delve into history *and* also reach into the future. For to forecast without having studied the past, as some anonymous sage once advised, is to sow with cut flowers.

Seeking clues to the unfolding of events, attention should go to histories commonly overlooked, such as that of women, and of the working class. Little told stories of vanquished peoples here and elsewhere should be explored for future-relevant lessons (cycles, tipping points, etc.) as well as for their intrinsic majesty——the anguish, art, folklore, heroics, insights, and so forth, of many such sagas . . . often astonishing in their contemporaneity.[2]

2. Digging Into

An effort should be made to help youngsters (and teachers, administrators, board members, etc.) acknowledge their previously unexamined assumptions about tomorrow, as these mental maps significantly shape the decisions we make on our way into the future.

For example, do we believe we can meet the challenges posed by accelerated climate change? By large disparities in life chances? By persistent *isms* (ageism, racism, sexism, etc.)? By pandemics of devastating toll? By extreme water shortages? By acts of terrorism? By the threat of nuclear war? And if not, why not? From a less harrowing angle, what do peers and teachers assume about bright possibilities? How much help can we expect to soon get from alternative fuels? From artificial intelligence? Biotechnology? Cloning? Nanotechnology? Space ventures, and other widely-anticipated breakthroughs?

Only as we acknowledge our less-than-obvious beliefs and biases, and dare to reconsider them, can we begin to reduce their restrictive effect on our creativity and vision. Indeed, there is reason to suspect that clarifying and validating our long-term assumptions may be *the* single most important thing any of us can do in coming to grips with the future.[3]

3. Taking In

The *arts*—broadly defined as both a participatory and an observer activity—are a remarkable portal into the future. They make possible new ways of seeing things with new eyes. As writer Daniel Pink explains,

"Left-brain thinking—rule-based, linear, SAT-style thinking—used to be enough. Now, right-brain thinking—artistry, empathy, narrative, and synthesis—is the big differentiator."[4]

In art courses, for example, youngsters could be invited to experiment with digital art, which can take many forms; for instance, children can generate images of paintings, drawings, or comic or film characters they like—and be tickled by predictable or randomly-generated changes that appear in the art. Or they can explore virtual reality projects that use data gloves and headsets to send them soaring into immersive, navigable, and sophisticated 3-D artificial worlds.

Youngsters could draw aliens, or futuristic cars, or moon base life, or post-global warming cities. They could have classroom (or virtual) chats with artists who do sci-fi magazine covers, ads with future themes, and the like. Field trips to area museums could focus on paintings, such as those by Hieronymus Bosch, or etchings by William Blake, that depict the future as envisioned centuries ago. Likewise, sites like the Space Museum on the Smithsonian Mall are treasure troves of futuristic art, albeit primarily of a technophile variety.

The school *drama* department, in turn, could stage future-connected works like William Saroyan's play, *The Time of Our Lives*, and also provocative dramas like Karel Capek's classic play about the first robots, *R.U.R.* Youngsters could be encouraged to write short one-act comedies or dramas set years, decades, or even centuries ahead, and aspiring student filmmakers could be encouraged to make computer-animated shorts about intriguing aspects of life tomorrow.

In and outside of a *film course*, students and staff could discuss such films as *AI, Alien, Blade Runner, Brazil, Children of Men, Close Encounters of the Third Kind, Colossus: The Forbin Project; Cloverfield, Fahrenheit 451, Forbidden Planet, Futureworld, Gattaca, Independence Day, Martian Child, Metropolis, Outland, Planet of the Apes, Star Wars, Solaris, The Postman, The Sum of Our Fears, Things to Come, THX 1138, Waterworld, Westworld, 12 Monkeys, 2001, 2010,* and scores of others, the better to extract insights into both the unfolding, and the imagined future.

A course in the *media* could discuss TV episodes of *The Simpsons* comedy show that had a robot fall for Marge, with much ensuing silliness, and yet also wry insight into our relations with artificial intelligence. Or, explore episodes of *Babylon 5, Star Trek,* or *The X-Files*. Similarly, ideas could be analyzed from *Jericho*, a futuristic TV series that "examines the role of American communities after a nuclear disaster."[5]

Particular attention could go to insights from the TV reality show—*Kid Nation*. Fans maintain it sheds valuable light on a key future-shaping question—Will youngsters left to their own devices create a democratic idyll or a savage anarchy? Critics, however, maintain, "the children, urged to build a better town (read 'world') than their forefathers, were manipulated into the copycat media culture."[6]

Music classrooms could use computer-based piano labs, and midi-interfaces and software that can create and edit music manuscripts in minutes, a task that used to take days. Youngsters could enjoy "composing" by adding and subtracting with snippets of prerecorded music available from a classroom computer. Likewise, attention could go to Educational Math Music (a smart cooptation of the braggadocios and confrontational spirit of gangsta hip hop, whose real value "is in its entrepreneurial, speak-your-mind, and hold-your-own spirit").[7]

Left-brain thinking is enormously useful with its rule-based, linear style strengths, but it is no longer enough, given deep-reaching changes in the mental world around us. Right-brain development by young learners is now of the utmost importance. Artistry, creativity, empathy, narrative, playfulness, resiliency, resourcefulness, risk-taking, and synthesis are assuming unprecedented importance: "Over the next twenty years we will endow ourselves with creative abilities beyond any we have ever known . . . the creative [play and media] world of children has become manipulable, programmable, and mutable . . . where our children are already going, we look to follow."[8]

(Full Disclosure: Over three decades of sharing ideas in schools with K–12 educators has left me persuaded that the arts are THE most vital part of a futurized curriculum, and I am zealous in their support.

The arts are valuable for aiding cross-cultural understanding, and giving experience in teamwork. They stand out in their capacity to aid imagination, ingenuity, and inventiveness, to say nothing of empathy, fantasy, and zaniness—all traits that set us apart from our inanimate rivals aided by artificial intelligence (AI). As such, the arts may help preserve a niche for us in a future world where decisions may increasingly be made by AI machines.

Today's neglect of the arts in K–12 education and the persistent denial of adequate financial and curriculum support is a mistake of the first rank, one we cannot rectify soon enough if we are to help keep awake a sense of wonder in the world.)

4. Draw Futuristics In

The language, and better still, the ideas and methods of futuristics can be employed lightly throughout a blended elementary school curriculum, one that integrates futuristics with everything else, and no one course or special emphasis is required. (This approach contrasts dramatically with a high school of the future, as explained in chapter 4).

Much futuristic material can be incorporated into conventional courses. For example, and arranged hereafter alphabetically, a course in *American*

Government could tackle changes that might be made in the U.S. Constitution and Bill of Rights. Many of our problems of governance can be traced to the events that seem to have gotten beyond the reach of the iconic documents (matters of privacy invasion, use of torture, etc.). Teenagers could weigh revisions and updates, as in possibly replacing the Electoral College with direct voting for the president, and limiting campaigns to six months before the election.[9]

A course in *Geography*—after first attending to test-preparation responsibilities—could wrestle with the adequacy of an existing town plan. After students have experienced many guided walks around town, and have studied the present master plan and interviewed its makers, they could design a PowerPoint presentation of their own ideas as prospective dwellers, and share it with the authorities. (A model project in 2007 led a teacher to conclude that his students had begun to "realize their place in the future, and understand they can be the principle architects of that future in their own community."[10])

A course in *history*—after first attending to test-preparation responsibilities—could note the tools used over time to "divine" the future—tools like astrology, legends, magic, mysticism, shamanism, theology, wizardry, and so forth. Attention should be paid to their limitations, and also their strengths (as in quieting anxiety, unifying a group, etc.).

A *language course*—after first attending to test-preparation responsibilities—could have students study the language via the exciting use of videoconference technology. American youngsters could sit in on a French language class being conducted somewhere in France. As well, the futures literature could be slipped into in the language under study. For example, the seminal 1972 work by Alvin Toffler, *Future Shock*, exists in French, and many other languages. Guest futurists could also be invited to address the class in a language other than English.[11]

(Full Disclosure: I believe a study of a second language should be mandatory, as do most Americans, and in the best of worlds it would begin in prekindergarten and be reinforced throughout—much as is true overseas, where youngsters have commonly command of more than one tongue).

A *literature* course—after first attending to test-preparation responsibilities—could enjoy paying attention to science fiction. By questioning society's basic rules and speculating about how other worlds might work, this literary genre raises fresh and provocative questions. With its distinct ability to illuminate alternative lives, it is a mainstay of arcade games, videogames, "hip" Web sites, and anime movies and manga comics—all of which are teenage favorites. Science fiction in these popular formats—purposefully and robustly studied in class—could become a powerful "edutainment" tool.

Mathematics instruction—after first attending to test-preparation responsibilities—could draw on teleconference technology. Students in two widely separate "worlds" (by ethnicity, gender, geography, race, or social class) could gather their own answers to such questions as how many expect there is human-like life elsewhere in the universe, or expect to vacation off-planet or experience the end to war in their lifetime? Each class would tally its answers, create an electronic spreadsheet, select a graph to represent the information, and then compare all of this with the other class. Both could then exchange insights into what mathematical thinking can reveal in the data.

Likewise, spreadsheets could be used to explore a contemporary puzzle. Students could compare the costs of operating four types of cars (conventional, diesel, hybrid, hydrogen), including the costs of extraction and transportation of fuel. To top off this project they could calculate the costs of a school converting its buses and cars to any of the four types, and later share their findings with your school's Futures Committee (which might leverage them to everyone's advantage).

Another present-day issue a mathematics course might tackle involves endangered species. A class could begin by identifying animals and plants in the immediate area that urgently need protection. It could then compare the costs of alternative modes of protection, and use statistical formulas to forecast likely numerical changes in the population of the animals and plants. As with the car findings above, the results could be shared with local media, much to the interest of the school's members and neighbors alike.[12]

Physical education courses could explore extraordinary changes underway here at Formula One "Grand Prix" speed. Long part of the socio-cultural fabric of civilization, sport is caught up now with escalating technological interventions that draws on artificial intelligence, bio-genomic and molecular engineering, imminent digital media platforms, and interactive materials. Students could study controversies about computer-aided prostheses, chemicals that add bulk, and other exotic future-shaping sport options society is struggling to come to terms with.

A course in *physics*—after first attending to test-preparation responsibilities—could draw on the popular video game Halo 3, a first-person self-organizing shooter game that allows players to link up with others around the world. To the delight of many teenagers, they learn through trial-and-error experience, and organize their own "education." A physics teacher could use Halo "as a microworld, setting up measurements to see how the physics behaves, if it is realistic, and so on."[13]

A course in *political sciences*—after first attending to test-preparation responsibilities—could wrestle with what is arguably the greatest threat to our future—nuclear terrorism ("the ultimate preventable catastrophe").[14] Students could weigh calls for negotiations toward global abolition of nuclear weapons against counter-calls for maintaining our nuclear superiority.

A *science course*—after first attending to test-preparation responsibilities—could explore far-reaching neuroethical questions recast in age-appropriate ways: For example, "should functional magnetic resonance imaging (MRI) be developed to detect lies while questioning crime suspects? Or job applicants? Or blind dates? Is it ethical for healthy people to use drugs to enhance cognition or improve their moods? How might the government regulate such drug use?"[15]

A course in *social change*—after first attending to test-preparation responsibilities—could explore how financial incentives can make a BIG difference! Specifically, the X Prize Foundation announced in 1995 a multimillion dollar competition that drew twenty-four teams, had them spend over $100 million on R&D, and in 2004 resulted in one of them successfully sending a manned rocket craft into suborbital space. In 2006, the Foundation announced a $10 million prize for the first team to sequence 100 human genomes in ten days at a cost of less than $1 million. (Four teams were busy in 2008 pursuing this goal). In 2007, it announced a contest for the first one hundred MPG production car. And, in 2008 it created a $30 million prize that will go to the first private group to land a robotic rover on the moon and send images and other data back to earth. Supporters claim this colorful method can light a fire under future-shaping innovators everywhere.[16]

A *social studies* course—after first attending to test-preparation responsibilities—could explore the extraordinary psychological and sociological lessons possible through engagement with educational simulations like the Sims series—Sim City, the breakthrough game (1989), followed by SimEarth (1990), SimAnt, SimLife (1992), SimFarm, and SimWorld, all together the best-selling computer game franchise of all time.[17] Simulations formerly confined to graduate school use, such as "Stranded on the Moon," have been adapted for use in elementary schools.[18]

5. Explore Progress

As first mentioned briefly in the Preface, a major goal in futurizing education is to help students choose to appreciate progress we make in shaping a finer future. Taking care not to gloss over persistent problems and unwelcome setbacks, this emphasis highlights our ability to make a desirable difference.

Youngsters should learn America is tackling overdue social repairs. Abortion rates are down. Drug use is down. Divorce rates are down. In some areas, "like crime and welfare, the progress has the dimensions of a sea change. . . . We have learned progress can happen faster than many people thought possible."[19] Little wonder that, in terms of happiness, our level is above that of most of our European allies, and is little different regardless of social class (the same is true regarding optimism about the future.)[20]

6. Tomorrow's Job Market

Onlookers, especially parents of your students, are likely to think sound job forecasts are *the* most valuable contribution a futurizing campaign can make. They do not want their offspring preparing for yesterday's jobs, and graduating into a disconnect between what they have to offer and what employers are "buying."

Accordingly, your Futures Committee should attempt to help teachers do job forecasting so well that graduates for years after will give it credit for help of lasting value. Fortunately, considerable resources exist to bolster your effort, ranging from sound, if prosaic, job forecasts from the federal Department of Labor, through to colorful, if more speculative, forecasts from futurists of every stripe.

A hallway display—large and prominent—could be dedicated to this topic. Charts could highlight both immediate local and also national labor market forecasts (this year, five years out, ten years out). Updated every quarter or sooner, the data could be merged with feedback from alumni, and articles from current newspapers, magazines, Web sites, and so on.

Particular attention could go to future-related jobs already with us, for example, aquaculturists, cloning technicians, cyber crime technicians, eugenics counselors, feng shui professionals, hydrogen fuel technicians, and the like. As well, many blue-collar jobs (now retitled "Green Collar") are expected in environmental areas. For example, between 2009 and 2014 in the desert southwest massive construction is scheduled to begin on large commercial solar projects.[21] The Apollo Project is a leading joint effort by labor unions and environmentalists to win large-scale job-generating projects, a goal with widespread support.

All the more intriguing is a "far out" job forecast list that suggests by 2015 we are likely to have biofuture therapists, cancer cure enablers, and organ cloners. By 2020, global headhunters, and nano-bio entrepreneurs. By 2030, antiterrorism technicians, climate change forecasters, hydrogen marketing managers, poets, solar fuel developers, and space market planners.[22]

Should your Futures Committee publicize the list above, as well it might, it should simultaneously reassure all that alongside of these seemingly esoteric jobs there are likely to be many more we know and value today—positions for attorneys, bakers, builders, clerks, drivers, entertainers, salespeople, and teachers—though the number of people in them may steadily drop as "smart" robots replacing them.

To help the student body make sense of all this, interactive forums—actual and virtual—might be held with speakers from local companies invited to explain current and anticipated realities of the labor market. Speakers could be encouraged to share—warts and all—what will be involved tomorrow in specific positions of greatest interest to youngsters: job content, rewards, limitations, and so on.

7. Look Elsewhere

Globalization, arguably the most significant development in modern history, sets your Futures Committee the challenge of helping youngsters adopt a global perspective, and assume a sense of global citizenship. They need to appreciate their unprecedented global connectivity, and get enthusiastic about making a rewarding place for themselves in our new "Flat World."[23]

Progress overseas especially warrants classroom attention, as it is often overshadowed by the media's enervating emphasis on dark news. K–12 students should learn that more people today than ever live above their nation's poverty line, and the number of poor people in the world is falling very fast. Birth rates in developing nations are beginning to match those of the industrialized world, and infant mortality is at its lowest level in history. The middle class in poor countries "is the fastest-growing segment of the world's population . . . and will almost double in poor countries [by 2020]."[24]

More democracies and near-democracies exist now than ever before in human history—and more develop annually. Human violence is in steady decline, and "as bad as it is in Darfur, relatively few people in the world today are likely to die at the hands of others. This trend will almost certainly continue . . . it just won't seem like that when you watch the news."[25] Millions can now "afford to have dreams as well as possessions, and to think about the years to come with some confidence rather than dread."[26]

8. Look Homeward

Finally, look to insiders for fresh curriculum and project ideas. In addition to having student members on your Futures Committee, you could conduct biannual surveys via the Internet to get student ideas about ways to bolster your futurizing campaign. Feedback, warts and all, should be widely shared and made part of the committee's Web site.

Every component of the school should be encouraged to "listen": The school library, for example, although a chockablock wonderland of familiar resources (books, comics, CDs, DVDs, journals, magazines, and VHS films), might lend new models of e-books to student product "testers," and take quite seriously feedback from these prospective users. (Some such e-books are "the size of the bill they bring the bill in at the end of a meal, and can hold thousands of novels, thanks to a [plug-in] flash-memory add-in card.")[27]

A growing national movement "is putting students' voices—and their work—front and center in the push to raise expectations and results in schools . . ." and your Futures Committee would do well to be counted among its prime supporters. The leader of a successful effort to upgrade the "Green" quotient of a middle school notes—"Asking a group of 8- to 11-year olds how they would like their school to look and feel is a first step to engaging and empowering them as a community."[28]

Likewise, many teachers in the trenches are busy showing the way. Some have profited from use of TeacherTube, a free video-sharing site for educators and students. Teachers share their own instructional videos around the world. Many draw as well on SchoolTube, which mainly hosts videos produced in class by students aided by their teachers. Both sites vet videos to assure they are appropriate for K–12 use, though they steer clear of judging accuracy or quality.[29]

Bright ideas and field-proven techniques can be had from a cadre of K–12 educators who annually showcase new learning strategies and tools at the WFS Meeting. These pioneering school leaders continue to make headway adding futuristics to formal curricula they already influence. The WFS Web site has a section for educators, and related ideas are available from www.rethinkingschools.org (and more such aids are noted in the Resources section at the book's close).

Empowering magazines like *Edutopia*, *Rethinking Schools*, and *The School Administrator* are very rich sources, as are scores of Web sites (see the Resources section in this book). Each member of your Futures Committee could volunteer to thoroughly cover one such source on behalf of all, and distill its content to share fresh program ideas to aid your futurizing campaign.

EXAMPLES

Lest you think we are still back at the starting line, it seems wise to close this chapter with some examples of very different ongoing advances, one or two with a reassuring familiarity, others of the brow-arching novel type.

In 2007, for example, the Pennsylvania Middle School Association ran an old-fashioned essay contest, but one with a fresh angle: Youngsters in Grades 5 through 9 were challenged to answer the question, "Where do I see myself in 10 years?" The best essay writers got age-appropriate prizes, and their school received $1,000.[30]

Similarly, in 2008 the Urban Revision Project sponsored a nationwide poster contest for high school and middle school students. Youngsters were invited to create art in answer to such questions as: What will your community look like in the year 2050? What will people be doing, driving, wearing? Where will their water, energy and food come from? Participants were urged to "design the future, and win an outdoor adventure trip."[31]

New essay and poster contests could have students tomorrow answering such questions as:

"Would you want to be a homesteader in space?"
"Would you want an electronic brain implant?"
"Should we allow enhanced athletes?"
"What difference might it make if we discover life elsewhere in the universe?"
"What do you hope for most from the future? And how do you intend to help secure it?"
"What do you especially fear the future might contain, and how might we prevent it?"[32]

Here, as in every other like situation, some of the best questions are likely to come from youngsters themselves.

Going beyond these essay/poster standbys, a K–12 futurizing process can tweak seemingly resolute physical assets. For example, in 2007 New York City unveiled an ambitious plan to renew 290 largely decrepit school playgrounds by 2010. They will be converted into attractive, usable public spaces open to the general public as well as to school children after school hours, during weekends, and when school is not in session. Nearby residents and schoolchildren will help design these future-shaping renovations. New York's initiative, the largest such transformation in the country, resulted in sixty-nine playground overhauls in its first year, and is expected to eventually cost more than $100 million in public and private money.[33]

As well, a K–12 futurizing process can involve root-and-branch changes in an educational culture. Prominent here are complex efforts under consideration, or even underway to "Green" an entire school system. Proponents envision an ecological/environmental showcase that "teaches" by its very existence. Initial gains can be as modest as giving up the use in the cafeteria of throwaway Styrofoam trays (they do not decompose). Or as far-reaching as covering a school roof with solar panels, and/or adding a hydroponics station, or novel innovations to the school grounds.

The futurizing process encompasses the entire country. On January 31, 2008, an organization called Focus the Nation sponsored "Choose Your Future," the biggest teach-in in history. More than ten thousand volunteers created learning events at over 1,200 schools, faith and civic organizations, and businesses. After studying the costs and benefits of alternative Green policies, along with the winners and losers, attendees chose Top Five Policy Solutions to address climate change. Promoters saw the event as "an opportunity to debate the steps the U.S. government will need to take in the next couple of years if we are indeed, going to choose the future, and hold global warming to the low end" (www.focusthenation.org).

The process can also cross oceans: FIRST (For Inspiration and Recognition of Science and Technology), is an international competition run every year since 1989. It has teams of youngsters design and build a remote-controlled robot that competes in athletic-type matches. Its accessible, innovative programs build not only science and technology skills and interests, but also self-confidence, leadership, and life skills. (www.usfirst.org).

Future Problem Solving International, as noted earlier in this book, has sought to help students ages 9 to 19 develop their vision of the future. It involves over 250,000 students annually in the United States and several other countries. Its 2008 focus is on Body Enhancement, Child Labor, Debt in Developing Countries, Neurotechnology, and Simulation Technology. Youngsters, for example, after learning that neurotechnology makes it possible to manipulate the brain, will be asked if it should be used only for recovery from illness and injury, or also be available for augmentation (www.fpspi.org).

At its colorful Web site, an organization called WebQuests features over 1,500 activities sorted by subject and grade level, requires a youngster to draw most or all of the information sought from the Internet, thereby promoting creativity and high-order thinking. Typical is a Martian Haiku Quest, a 15-minute internet-based lesson that asks learners to team up, do the research about the history of the planet, write a haiku about Mars and its relationship to earth, and present it to the class (www.webquest.sdsu.edu).

As such projects seem widespread, diverse, and rewarding, their prospects in recent years seem to have been ratcheted up not a notch, but a logarithmic leap.

SUMMARY

The melancholy reality is that futuristics, a neglected stepchild, is not getting the attention and use in schools our times requires. An educational status quo that neglects it costs America far too much, especially given the extraordinary challenges we now wrestle with—the age wave, biotech options, energy shortfall, and so on. From now on futurism should be everyone's "second profession."[34]

Schools, especially those already strong in their cutting-edge combination of bricks-and-clicks (physical site and Internet distance learning courses), can and should raise the Futures I.Q. of students and teachers alike. There is much from futuristics that should permeate the core curriculum. Field-proven ideas and tools already exist to bolster a futures curriculum. This is an achievement waiting for you and me to help make it happen. We are called to share the art of horizon scanning, in all of its empowering aspects, with young learners eager to get on with it.

RECOMMENDED READING

1) *To Want to Learn: Insights and Provocations for Engaged Learning*, by Jackson Kytle. New York: PalgraveMacmillan, 2004. A wide-ranging exploration of what education might resemble as an act of creativity and hope. "If you believe that schools should create students who can dream, experience joy, and use their imagination in the interest of creating a better world, this is the book to read." Henry A. Giroux (Book Jacket) 2) *Foundations of Futures Studies: Human Science for a New Era*, by Wendell Bell. New Brunswick, NJ: Transaction, 1997. Volumes 1 and 2. Seminal exploration of the complex interplay between the values and visions of the future: Tackles "the toughest question that futurists, politicians, and ordinary people can ask: 'What is a good future?'" Theodore J. Gordon (Book jacket)

NOTES

1. Krukin, Jeff, a graduate of a Masters Degree program in Futuristics (University of Houston, Clear Lake City). E-mail to the author.
2. Particular attention should go to overlooked aspects of American history, such as the little-known contribution of colonial era black activists in shaping the future of our nation. Newman, Richard. "A Founding father with a Vision of Equality." *Philadelphia Inquirer*, February 14, 2008, A23. Major figures here include Richard Allen, James Forten, Prince Hall, Absalom Jones, Phyllis Wheatley, William Hamilton, and Peter Williams, etc.
3. Typical of great free Internet resources is the daily Listserv, *The Munirah Chronicle*, which tells of the day's black historical events, facts, and bio notes. Comparable daily exercises in historical recall exist for other races, ethnicities, etc.
4. Pink, Daniel. "Tom Friedman on Education in the 'Flat World.'" *The School Administrator*, February 2008, 12 (12–16, 18).
5. Storm, Jonathan. "'Jericho' Comes Tumbling Back to Faithful Fans." *Philadelphia Inquirer*, February 12, 2008, D1. See also Stelter, Brian. "A TV Show Hopes to Cover a Lot of Ground in Postapocalyptic Kansas." *New York Times*, February 12, 2008, E7.
6. Goodman, Ellen. "Kid Nation: Creating Little Capitalists." *Rethinking Schools*, Winter 2007–8 33 (32–33).
7. Strambler, Michael. "Debate through a Hip-Hop Lens." *Philadelphia Inquirer*, December 31, 2007, A9.

8. Mark Pesce. *The Playful World: How Technology is Transforming Our Imagination.* New York: Ballantine Books, 2000, 12. See also Daniel Pink in "Tom Friedman on Education in the 'Flat World.'" *The School Administrator,* February 2008, 12 (12–18).

9. Coates, Joseph F. *A Bill of Rights for the 21st-Century America.* Washington, DC: The Kanawha Institute for the Study of the Future, 2007. See also Sabato, Larry. *A More Perfect Constitution: 23 Proposals to Revitalize Our Constitution and Make America a Fairer Country.* New York: Walker & Company, 2008.

10. Mitchell, Ted. "Students as Town Planners." *Green Teacher,* Fall 2007, 31 (29–31).

11. High schoolers can draw on authors with the prowess of H. G. Wells, Jules Verne, Aldous Huxley, George Orwell, and, more recently, Margaret Atwater, Octavia Butler, William Gibson, Walter Mosley, Bruce Sterling, Neil Stephensen, and other luminaries. As well, there are extraordinary films available for analysis, the names of which many teenagers can easily rattle off.

12. I draw extensively here on a model article: Tuttle, Harry Grover, "Making Math Work." *Technology & Learning,* March 2007, 32.

13. Kurt D. Squire, as quoted in Ash, Katie. "The Halo 3 Question." *Digital Directions,* Winter 2008, 9.

14. Allison, Graham. *Nuclear Terrorism: The Ultimate Preventable Catastrophe.* New York: Times Book, 2004, 204.

15. From the course description for PSY 418: Neuroethnics, taught by Professor Charles G. Gross. In the *Princeton Alumni Weekly,* February 13, 2008, 7.

16. Mossman, Kaspar. "X Prize Foundation." *Scientific American,* January 2008, 43. See also Peter H. Diamandis, as quoted in Stone, Brad. "A Google Competition, with a Robotic Moon Landing as a Goal." *New York Times,* February 22, 2008, C3.

17. Copeland, Michael V. "Game of the Year." *FORTUNE,* February 18, 2008, 28 (27–30).

18. Prensky, Marc. "Simulation Nation." *Edutopia,* March 2007 38 (34–39).

19. Wehner, Peter and Yuval Levin, "Crime. Drugs, Welfare—and Other Good News, *Commentary,* December 2007 (www.commentarymagazine.com).

20. Brooks, Arthur C. "Happiness and Inequality." *Wall Street Journal,* October 22, 2007, A18.

21. Smith, Rebecca. "Wind, Solar Power Gain Users." *Wall Street Journal,* January 18, 2008.

22. Canton, James. *The Extreme Future.* New York: Penguin Books, 2006,109.

23. Thomas Friedman's 2005 book, now in two updated revisions, is possibly the best-known, and most read futures book among today's K–12 educators: *The World is Flat: A Brief History of the Twenty-First Century.* New York: Farrar, Straus, & Giroux, 2005.

24. Naim, Moises. "The Growing Pains of the Middle Class." *Foreign Policy,* February, 2008; as reprinted in *Philadelphia Inquirer,* February 18, 2008, A15.

25. Diamond, Larry, as quoted in DiGiovanni, Janine. "Democratic Vistas." *The New York Times Book Review,* January 20, 2008, 21. See also *The Spirit of Democracy,* by Prof. Diamond.

26. Anon."Don't Let Gloom Obscure Global Prosperity." *The Economist,* January 26, 2008, 23.

27. Gomes, Lee. "The Year in Technology: Pirates, Flash Memory and Hobbies—Oh, My!" *Wall Street Journal*, January 2, 2008, B1.

28. Morrow, Rowenna, "Images of a Sustainable Primary School." In Mack, Timothy C., ed. *Hopes and Visions for the 21st Century*. Bethesda, MD: World Future Society, 2007, 321 (#01-323).

29. De Avila, Joseph. "Teachers Tap Video-Sharing in the Classroom." *Wall Street Journal*, March 26, 2008, D1.

30. Len Ference, Executive Director, PMSA (Lference@mbgsd.org).

31. www.urbanrevision.com. The organization has much to offer educators, and its Web site is well worth a visit.

32. Adapted from Platt, Charles. *When You Can Live Twice as Long, What Will You Do?* New York: William Morrow, 1989.

33. Anon. "NYC School Playgrounds as Public Spaces." *New York Times*, July 8, 2007. Unpaged.

34. Cleveland, Harlan, As quoted in editorial, "Futurism is Not Dead," www.wfs.org/futurism.html.

Design a City: An Individual Renewable Energy/Resource Recycling Project

By Katherine Spalding and Kelly Smith

The "Design a City" project below is the culminating activity in a seventh grade Resources Unit. Students were asked to design a city integrating four of the renewable energy technologies they had been learning about with at least one form of resource recycling. They also had to do a model or drawing along with an essay describing their city and its climate/location, the ways that they integrated energy use and resource recycling, and why their plan made their city a better place.

In just the first year of the project the authors (teachers Spalding and Smith) got "some very thoughtful and creative cities, and it seemed to help the students understand the idea of integrating environmentally friendly technologies into current and future lifestyles."

DESIGN A CITY!

This portion of the project is to be done individually, utilizing the information you found during your poster project gallery walk.

Your job is to design a city that is powered by renewable energy sources, and includes recycling of materials.

Your city must include at least four of the six types of renewable energy that we have researched, and use recycling in at least one way.

You should clearly label the different energy sources, and what they power.

Your city should include things like houses, businesses, a school, people, etc.

You may do this as a poster, drawing, or model. It should include *color*!

You should include an explanation about each source of power you chose, relating it to your city. (For example, if you have geothermal energy in your city, explain what it specifically does within your city, as well as include a general description of it.)

Because it affects your energy sources, you should also include a brief description of the location of your city and the weather patterns. (For example, you would not be able to use geothermal energy just anywhere; you would need to be in specific parts of the country/world to use it.)

You should also include a description of how your city uses recycling. What material(s) do you recycle, what do you make with the recycled materials and how do you close the loop?

Your explanation should be seven paragraphs: an introduction that describes your city and its location and weather patterns, four paragraphs describing how you use renewable energy (one for each source), one paragraph on how you use recycling, and one conclusion about why your city is a better place because of the way you use these technologies.

Katherine Spalding and Kelly Smith, 7th Grade Science, Mechanicsburg Middle School, Mechanicsburg, PA.

II

"JEWEL IN THE CROWN"

"Thinking is more interesting than knowing, but less interesting than looking."

Goethe

In Part II, we explore the exciting possibility that a school somewhere in America might soon become world's first high school whose entire curriculum focuses on tomorrow, and, thereby deliberately helps teenagers assess whether or not they might go on in Higher Education to become professional forecasters (chapter 4). Innovative courses required in the school—many of which other schools might eventually adopt—get their own discussion (chapter 5). So rich is the learning possible in this unique high school the chapter that follows is devoted to its non-credit-giving aspects, its tacit and co-curricular components (especially a host of student clubs) (chapter 6).

In chapter 4 I offer advice concrete and actionable. We tackle such questions as how to name the school (no easy matter!), how to select students (including those less well-prepared than desirable), how to assure classrooms and facilities are futuristic, and what sort of classroom technologies warrant use. I bring along as touchstones-of-sort two more of my grandchildren—Benjamin and Elena—as pleasant thoughts of their matriculation at the school (and possibly also that of my third grandchild—David—whom you met in the Introduction) help me better imagine what they would welcome.

In chapter 5 we explore eighteen required courses, divided into three clusters. The first builds a solid foundation for everything that follows, as its ten courses, listed in a recommended order of matriculation, include "the usual suspects": History, Methods, Science Fiction, Film, Slighted Futures, Assessment Processes, Claims, Community Service, Disputes, and Limitations. The second cluster addresses matters of personal development, and its two courses are entitled Social Competences, and Love and Human Sexuality. The closing section ventures into the art of forecasting per se: its six courses are called Collapses, Crisis Anticipation, Cross-Cultural Patterns, Reforms, Possibilities, and Utopian Ideas/Projects.

Taken all in all, Part II offers a blueprint for a long-overdue addition to the American (and world) educational scene—a network of high schools likely to help assure the nation an urgently needed supply of the most able and creative futurists possible. When our nation is blindsided by something we could and should have seen coming (a slowly developing economic recession, a sub-prime mortgage crisis, a natural disaster that was "an accident waiting to happen"), I think part of the blame can be traced to the absence in America of high schools to help bring along aspiring futurists . . . an educational gap we *must* soon close.

4

High Schools of the Future: "Boot Camp"

"The only thing we have to fear is when, as a species, we don't believe in the future anymore."

Yves Behar, *Brandjam*, 2007, vii

Somewhere in America there is a school system destined to become famous here and everywhere else. I would like to think you are on its staff. An innovative school superintendent, the school's creative principal, and dynamic teachers on the school's Futures Committee (see chapter 2), will soon jointly announce their development of the first high school in the world to make teaching futuristic skills its central concern.

This is an announcement to which attention will be paid, here and overseas. Every level of government, major global corporations, planning organizations, think tanks, far-sighted NGOs, and others will applaud. Sophisticated onlookers know they stand to benefit from the school's long overdue development. They know full well anything and everything that promotes the availability of educated forecasters is in their best interest, for they all make big bets on the future.

In the best of all possible worlds, our nation's K–12 school system would employ futuristics in 101 creative ways. Even as we campaign to achieve this, we can also promote development coast-to-coast of magnet high schools devoted to futuristics. While these allied causes go better together, and near-simultaneous achievement of both offers unique synergistic gains, they can—if necessary—be pursued independently.

High schools of the future would resemble those already specializing in the performing arts, the sciences, international affairs, the health sciences, and so on—but as schools that take tomorrow seriously to heart, they would promote the creative study of probable, possible, preferable, and preventable futures. In further distinction from other schools, they would differ in ten ways:

 1. Selection (choosing a student body and staff)
 2. Naming (choosing an empowering name)
 3. Planning the Premises (designing a "future-feel" space)
 4. On the Grounds (experiencing a "future-feel" space)
 5. Classroom Technology (equipment and strategy)
 6. Basic Curriculum (teaching the subject's foundation)
 7. Implicit Curriculum (bolstering the foundation)
 8. Co-curriculum (non-credit aids to learning)
 9. Career Focus (guides to employment as futurists)
 10. Student Forecasts (seniors look beyond)

The first five are discussed in this chapter, the Basic Curriculum in the next chapter, and remaining four topics in chapter 6.

While I will continue below as your main guide, after some opening matters are addressed (Naming, Selection), I will also introduce in the narrative Benjamin and Elena, two more of my three grandchildren (you met a third child, David, in the Introduction). I enjoy imagining their (prospective) experiences in their "high school of the future" . . . and I especially like thinking that one or more of the three may yet choose to become a professional forecaster.

1) SELECTION

In the best of circumstances, teenagers who seek admission will have already gotten a fine introduction to futuristics on which to build. Possession of this "tool kit," signaled by the reputation of the youngster's previous school, and also vetted by some friendly probes during an admissions interview, should serve as a screening "gate." Everyone should know such candidates are given preference over all others.

If, however, in this imperfect world, especially promising candidates are not prepared, they should expect to complete remedial work as part of their conditional admission. As discussed in chapter 3, they would learn to:

 • identify future-shaping lessons from the past
 • Uncover their own hidden assumptions about the future
 • Draw insights about the future from the arts
 • Appreciate the place of futuristics in every subject

- Recognize progress in shaping the future being made at home and abroad
- Understand the dynamics of future job creation
- Understand globalization and
- Draw on ideas from one another, and from concerned adults (teachers and their parents, relatives, neighbors, etc.).

As this material is substantial, mastery of it could require attending a special catch-up program on Saturdays throughout the first year.

Likewise, in choosing staff, a selection committee should look for a defining personality trait of the 21st century—*a sense of confidence in our ability to thrive in chaotic times.* Candidates should also evidence at least a passing familiarity with futuristics, and an eagerness to learn more about it. As teachers, they should prefer the role of coach on the side to yesteryear's "Sage on a Stage." And they should appear knowledgeable about frontiers in their own discipline, the better to highlight these future-shaping matters in class.

A special effort should be made to secure as diversified a student body and staff as possible. Naturally, all the standard criteria should be employed: diversity by ethnicity, gender, race, place of residence, social class, and so on, but also diversity by aptitude (athletic, artistic, scientific, spiritual, etc.) and by orientation (commercial, communications, governance, humanities, politics, sciences, technology, etc.). The wider the diversity, the more zestful the mix . . . and thereby, the better the prospects for creativity, fun, and "deep" learning.

2) NAMING PROCESS

As this school flies a banner that reads "Futuristics," is organized around the subject, and hosts a student body and staff that enjoy immersion in it—it should boast a related and significant name. People should smile for years to come at its mention, as they link it to positive aspects of futuristics (creativity, conscience, contribution, craft, etc.). A school's Futures Committee cannot pay this branding matter enough attention.

In the school's first year, an upbeat major contest could be formulated and happily promoted to everyone (school people, their families, neighbors, etc.). While no hasty decision need be made, it is a fitting accomplishment with which to crown a school's premier year.[1]

Consideration could go to highly-regarded historic figures in futuristics—luminaries like Sir Thomas More, Leonardo DaVinci, Edward Bellamy, Jules Verne, H. G. Wells, Aldous Huxley, and George Orwell. More recently deceased figures worth attention include Arthur C. Clarke, Teilhard de Chardin, Peter Drucker, Buckminster Fuller, John Kenneth

Galbraith, Charles Handy, Ivan Illich, Herman Kahn, Marshal McLuhan, and Carl Sagan.

Living heroes and heroines also merit review; for instance, Norman Borlaug, 93, is hailed for being the father of the "Green Revolution," a future-shaping use of agricultural science to reduce world hunger. While gains varied widely (far more successful in Asia than in Africa), he is credited with saving a billion lives, more than anyone else in history.[2]

Care, of course, must be taken to avoid using a name associated strongly with political leanings (such as Ayn Rand, on the right, or Michael Harrington, on the left), as this would bias perception of the school. Likewise, names of controversial "pop culture" types, such as Edgar Cayce or Madam Blavatsky; or biblical prophets, like Isaiah; or controversial legendary or historic figures like Cassandra or Nostradamus, should be regarded as off-limits from the outset.

Students are likely to urge use of hip names like Kirk, Picard, Bones, Worf, or Spock of "Star Trek" fame. Or Boba Fett, Chewbacca, Han Solo, Luke Skywalker, Princess Leia, C-3PO or R2-D2 of "Star Wars" fame—or perhaps John Carter of Mars, or Michael Valentine Smith. All of these are cute ideas, but best side-lined for use instead by a student Futures Club.

If all else fails, a school could resort to an impersonal, though relevant name, such as Apollo, Challenger, Delphi, Discovery, Forethought, Future Look, Future Vision, Great Expectations, New Hope, New Horizons, New Tomorrow, New Vision, Possibilities, Vision, or Vision Tomorrow.

Once the matter is settled (albeit no choice will please everyone), the high school could arrange a well-publicized naming ceremony. Attendees could enjoy a tour of the school, and be invited to talk informally with teachers and students about the new venture. If done well, a naming event in the first school year can serve much like a successful NASA "liftoff," a memorable event of lasting value.

In the second year a new contest could help identify a school motto, perhaps a variation on one of these appealing corporate mottos; for example:

Adding Tomorrows Every Day; Advance; Answers for Life; Believe You Can; Hope Lives Here; Ideas for Life; Imagination at Work; Inspired by the Past; Knowledge, Skill, Duty; Let's Get It Done; Life's a Journey; Making Every Day a Better Day; Moving Forward; Not Your Typical Bank; Proud to Be Different; Smart Move; The Power to Know; The Pursuit of Perfection; Thinking Ahead; Your World Delivered[3]

Or, inspired by the iconic Labor Union motto—"Bread and Roses!" Or by a line from the popular contemporary musical "Les Miserables," "One more day!" Or, a thought adapted from another tongue; e.g., *Si no somos parte de la solución entonces, somos parte del problema.*

In the third year, another contest could help choose a school mascot—though certainly not a Crystal Ball or the Oracle at Delphi, as both images erroneously link forecasting to fatalism and mysticism. More useful candidates might include the International Space Station, the Moon Landing, the "Starship Enterprise," and other such iconic images (but not the murderous "Hal" from the *2001* film), along with appealing fictional characters like Data, Merlin, or Obi-Wan Kenobi.

3) PLANNING THE PREMISES

In the best of all possible worlds, school systems would have the funds to build their high schools of the future from the ground up—fresh, experimental, and path-setting. Unfortunately, few, if any, have the necessary funds. If backers nevertheless press for expensive new construction, opponents are likely to highlight the financial losses likely to hurt existing schools and programs . . . a very poor trade with which to launch a futures educational venture.

A wiser course of action might have backers avoid any suggestion of new construction in favor of urging instead the renewal of an existing facility, especially one standing where critics would not have expected it (as in an inner city neighborhood, or a poor rural area, rather than in a privileged enclave, whether urban or suburban).

Before a window is repaired or a wall repainted, a subcommittee of the Futures Committee should have studied ideas proposed in a virtual building mockup of the high school.[4] Student views, in particular, should play a very large role in the decision-making.[5] The final plans should promote a space at once airy, light, safe, and distinctly modern looking. Its architecture and setting should help raise ambition and morale, as both offer clues to preferable futures.

4) ON THE GROUNDS

Early in the 2020s the first thing my grandson Benjamin and granddaughter Elena might notice as they bicycle toward school is a tall wind turbine busy generating electricity for use in the building.[6] At its base signage could explain its cost, its rewards, and when, with savings from reduced consumption of commercially produced electricity, the school expects to make back its investment in a wind system. The names of area venders could also be noted.

Creative outdoor art signed by the maker—a teacher or a student—would enliven the setting. In the place of yesteryear's ornamental lawn (a source of much pollution from chemical pesticides, fertilizers, etc.) the school grounds would house only native plants in different colors and shapes that promote biodiversity. Many vegetable gardens, each supported by a different class eager to assume environmental stewardship, would have value. Fruit trees, chosen with knowledge of the climate, would reward the cafeteria almost daily. Teachers could enjoy leading Benjamin and Elena on educational fieldtrips without leaving the grounds.

A Buckminster Fuller geodesic dome might serve as a portable classroom or a large greenhouse. Administrative offices would have glass walls so students can look in and staffers look out. An expansive open-space floor plan would boast many live plants. Rooftops might be covered with sod and plants to help moderate inside temperatures. And a small fleet of official school cars, many, or even all of them advanced hybrids, or electronic cars, or high-tech diesels, would be parked outside. Adjacent are enclosed bicycle racks where almost everyone—staff and students alike—leave their wheels with those of Benjamin and Elena.

Anyone stepping inside would know they are in a *very* imaginative place. Building floors would be terrazzo made with recycled glass. The lobby might contain a giant replica of our planet, with the ceiling indicating distances to the sun and fellow planets. A video system could circle the space making available streaming electronic news of the moment. Dynamic electronic display cases could feature colorful accounts of current and proposed future-shaping educational projects either at the school or around the world—"best practices" and upgrades of note.[7] And a geothermal heating and cooling system would assure comfort.

Hallways would sparkle with student art on futures subjects, along with artwork from the covers of science-fiction magazines and from brilliant future-oriented illustrators (such as Florida's Jacque Fresco and Roxanne Meadows, etc.). Photos—perhaps taken by students themselves—could highlight newly constructed buildings around the school (even at a day's car ride). Those chosen would probably be quite creative, as architects have long since broken through to a future whose buildings are "whimsical, sensual, and possessed of a substantial wow factor."[8]

Classrooms well lit by natural light might have the architecture, furniture, coloration, and "feel" of a Mars or Moon base (Benjamin's). Or an ocean-floor domed colony. Or an interstellar "Star Ship" (Elena's). Or any other such simulation, provided it stretches the imagination, intrigues the mind, and augments one's education, even while held to code, and affordable. As schools should be places students *want to be*, these "Gee Whiz!" settings have much to recommend them.[9]

Green-oriented students like Benjamin and Elena might help monitor the daily environment through specially installed measuring devices. They could raise edible fish (tilapia, etc.) in on-site tanks in the school basement.

A campus greenhouse could feature cutting-edge experiments with plants that might prove new food sources. Rain water runoff and soiled water from the lunchroom kitchen (or even the toilets) could be recycled and made ready again for use by groundskeepers and building cleaners. Bathrooms could offer use of a composting toilet, one that was odorless, required no chemicals, water or plumbing; and produced a safe non-offensive compost called humus.

5) CLASSROOM TECHNOLOGY

Students and teachers who co-design their classrooms are likely to have set out to nurture a culture of curiosity; that is, "environments driven by inquisitiveness and imaginative thinking about the future."[10] Accordingly, an effort would be made to employ cutting-edge learning aids, and even serve as beta test sites for technologies still not ready for the market. Serving much like first responders, budding futurists could test, adapt, and critique technologies worth much wider adoption, or, rejection across K–12 schooling.

Clicker technology is a good example of interactive approaches. Much to Benjamin's delight, it sets students against one another in a good-natured competition. They respond to the teacher's quiz by pressing the right key on a hand-held clicker. An animated plasma screen at the room's front displays each student's responses in real time, using unique personal symbols assigned by the system; e.g., spaceships, Segways, ATVs, and so on. This permits everyone to compare their own performance anonymously.

Teachers appreciate the easy ability to transfer students' data wirelessly to their learning management systems. They can quickly see what is, and is not, getting across, and to which learner, especially those who do not actively participate in classroom discussions.

The device helps bring Benjamin's classroom alive, encourages class participation, and enables students to study their own displayed answers in real time. When used in high schools of the future, the system could be recoded to promote collaborative learning by small groups, rather than individual cutthroat competition as at present.[11]

Brand new gadgets could be tested to a fare-thee-well better to help wavering administrators reach sound technology adoption decisions. Typical is the expected offering late in 2008 of an advanced pen-computer that uses microdot reading technology to enable Elena to draw a calculator on a piece of paper, for example, and use it to perform everything from additions to square roots by tapping on it. She and other "testers" can help your Futures Committee determine whether to recommend purchase of the gadget, or urge changes in it.[12]

Likewise, aspiring futurists might appropriately be among the first to test a $300 headset that lets users control simple actions, as within computer games, by using their thoughts. To Benjamin's fascination, the device measures electrical activity in his brain, and works with software to let him record a particular pattern he associates with a command used in the game (such as *move right*, or *lift that object*). To execute the command, a helmet wearer need only think the thought. Student futurists could weigh what, if any, educational gains are possible.[13]

Naturally, much use is made of computer-based gaming and simulations. The very popular Sims series, and Civilization IV, Rise of Nations, and so on, serve handsomely as both teachers and motivators, as they offer problems of considerable complexity and sophistication. Players must learn different skills to survive, better yet advance. The best of the simulations stand out in their ability to help players understand system interactions and take prudent risks in pursuit of objectives, make ethical and moral decisions, work in teams, and employ scientific deduction—all critical matters in doing futuristics.

Attention could also go to Internet-based massively multiplayer operations (M.M.O.). For example, a 2007 offering, Tabula Rosa, a science-fiction game complete with ethical parables and problems, especially appeals to Elena. Its creator sought to "present the player with dilemmas akin to the global war on terror: How far are you prepared to go to do what you think is right? To defeat the enemy, are you prepared to poison a river your peaceful allies depend on? Or to destroy large swaths of your allies' forest home? Are your allies expendable in the sense that you're fighting over there so that you don't have to fight over here?"[14]

School workshops (computer repair, graphic arts, robotics, space technology, etc.) would explore the use of experimental materials, as from nanotechnology and biotechnology, along with more familiar standards (metals, woods, etc.). Indeed, flashy gadgetry and materials, even of the cutting-edge variety, would not be the mainstay. Students and teachers understand they are trumped by creativity and the ability to have fun: "A skilled teacher equipped with cheap, hands-on tools like Legos, ping-pong balls, and hair-dryer-powered hot air balloons can work magic in inspiring future scientists."[15]

SUMMARY

The high school of the future "concentrates on creating the conditions under which all interact with one another in mutually supportive ways."[16] Two of its many novel components stand out: Its career focus helps teenagers consider becoming professional long-range forecasters—an offer with no precedent in K–12 education here or abroad. And, its requirement of student forecasts has graduating seniors leave behind a cache of intriguing material succeeding classes can mine for years to come.

Distinctive, and also quite demanding (as made clear in the chapter that follows), the nation's high schools of the future should quickly prove a national asset of great worth. Over their lifetime their graduates (hopefully including some or all of my grandchildren) will enjoy the cachet of a diploma from the world's first public "boot camp" for new futurists.

HIGHLY RECOMMENDED READING

1) *Leading Beyond the Walls*, edited by Frances Hesselbein, et al. San Francisco: Jossey-Bass, 1999. Twenty-three original essays on how we might take ourselves and our organizations "beyond the walls to new levels of performance and positive changes in the lives of people" (2). 2) *The Sport Business Future*, by Aaron Smith and Hans Westerbeek. New York: Palgrave Macmillan, 2004. A sweeping, bold, and imaginative exploration of far more than the future of the sport business; rather, it sheds valuable light on the human experience of life and sport decades ahead—a topic of keen interest to many teenagers.

NOTES

1. Consideration could be given to honoring a relevant area resident, preferably alive and well (even if long since retired). A highly regarded local person, he or she should have made a signal contribution as a planner, an agent of change, a visionary (secular), a lawmaker, a forecaster, or the admirable like. Unfortunately, this process could exacerbate local rifts and prove counterproductive.

2. Pinker, Steven "The Moral Instinct." *New York Times Magazine*, January 13, 2008, 32 (32–35, 55–58).

3. Cystic Fibrosis Foundation, Acura, Siemens, Power Plate, The Children's Hospital of Philadelphia, Panasonic, GE, Panerai Watch Company, Drexel University College of Law, Citi, Samsonite, Sodexho, Toyota, Citizens Bank (Philadelphia), Fidelity Investments, Time Warner Cable, SAS, Lexus, University of Phoenix, AT&T.

4. Bradbury, Danny. "Every User to be Part of Move to Green Buildings." *Financial Times*, January 30, 2008, 6. See also Cox, Joe. "The School Building is a Teacher." *Philadelphia Inquirer*, February 22, 2008, B2. "Learning in a green school may prove instructive to the students who will be left to face the consequences and find the solutions to future environmental concerns."

5. Early in the design stage, the Futures Committee should look into the example of an exciting New York City high school project. It enables students to collaborate with professional architects and designers on improving their own world.

Teenagers plan future-shaping renovations of their *own* classrooms, school halls, and school offices. Sponsors believe the youngsters not only get a chance to preview related careers, but they also get valuable insights into how a physical environment can and does help shape the future. Fried, Joseph P. "School Renovation as a learning Experience." *New York Times*, November 25, 2007, 19-BU.

6. In 2007, over 7,000 small wind turbines were purchased in the U.S.—defined as those that have a capacity of up to 100 kilowatts, roughly enough to power a large school. Sales are expected to top 10,000 in 2008). Shevory, Kristina. "Homespun Electricity, from the Wind." *New York Times*, December 13, 2007, F4 (I, 4).

7. Typical of upgrades would be computerized controls for air conditioning and heating. A console on a single screen would enable building managers to check and adjust occasionally. Located in the front lobby, and also available on the computer screens of administrators and Future Committee members, the screen would tell all what the energy consumption was, what it should be, and how to get there. Sensors in every room would tell the console if a room was empty, and, adjust the lights and temperature accordingly.

8. Lacayo, Richard. "Curveballs Are in Play." *Time*, March 20, 2006, 98.

9. Decisions about which simulation to create—if any—would be reached by a teacher whose students felt their views had been respectfully considered. Some classroom simulations might be preserved for years on end, updated and improved with every passing school term. Others might be replaced more often, especially after a new teacher with different interests appears.

10. van Notten, Philip. "Scenario development: A Typology of Approaches." OECD. *Think Scenarios, Rethink Education*. Paris, OECD, 2006, 88 (69–91).

11. Hu, Winnie. "Students Click Answers, and a Routine Quiz Becomes a Game." *New York Times*, January 28, 2008 A22.

12. Developments cited with admiration by Terry Holliday, Superintendent of the Iredell-Statesville School District in North Carolina, in his essay, "My Inner Conflict between Logic and Creativity," *The School Administrator*, February 2008, pp. VV-BB.

13. Wingfield, Nick. "Wii Fit, Other Innovations Unveiled." *Wall Street Journal*, February 20, 2008, D6.

14. Richard Garriott, as quoted in Schiesel, Seth. "An Online-Gaming Pioneer is Back, and This Time He's Banking on Sci-Fi." *New York Times*, November 2, 2007, E24.

15. Spence, Anne. "Closing the Science Gap by Hand." *Education Week*, February 6, 2008, 25 (25, 27).

16. Noddings, Nel. *Happiness and Education*. New York: Cambridge University Press, 2003, 35.

5

Required Courses: Fundamentals

"Thus, the task is not so much to see what no one else has seen, but to think about what nobody yet has thought about that which everybody sees."

Schopenhauer

A youngster graduating from a high school of the future should be able to, and, more importantly, care to converse intelligently about such consequential matters as artificial intelligence; biotechnology; "black" biotechnology (weaponry); climate change; conflict resolution and mediation; disaster relief; environmentalism; fundamentalism; gerontology; globalism; governance; informatics; nanotechnology, the singularity; space issues; spirituality; sustainability; terrorism; and war and peace . . . and many more such mind-stretching matters.

Each topic involves high probability/high impact developments, and poses many tough questions, only tentative answers, and fairly invigorating debate . . . the stuff of a first-rate high school education. Each would have a teenager interrogate the nature of human volition, and ponder the sorts of visions that animate us.

We explore below a plausible basic curriculum designed to promote such familiarity, assigning to the next chapter the school's implicit curriculum (its nonclassroom aids to education) and cocurriculum (its noncredit aids to education). Required courses novice futurists are now old enough to tackle are discussed hereafter in three clusters, arranged in a progression that might help students make more of them: Naturally, other elective courses that arise from both the special interests of teachers and requests from students should help make the entire learning experience more engaging.

FUNDAMENTALS

 1. History (learning from the past)
 2. Methods ("How To" do futuristics)
 3. Science Fiction (other worlds)
 4. Film (learning from the Silver Screen)
 5. Slighted Futures (neglected cultures)
 6. Assessment Processes (testing large systems)
 7. Claims (testing small boasts)
 8. Community Service (chipping in to help)
 9. Disputes (taking sides)
10. Limitations (facing up to the field's shortcomings)

PERSONAL MATTERS

 1. Social Competences (self-esteem aids)
 2. Love and Human Sexuality (reaching out to one another)

FORECASTING

 1. Collapses (*post mortem* on failed societies)
 2. Crisis Anticipation (dangers ahead)
 3. Cross-Cultural Relations (getting along)
 4. Reforms (doing better)
 5. Possibilities (reward options)
 6. Utopian Ideas/Projects (reaching beyond)

Exact titles (and much better subtitles) should be chosen by the school's Futures Committee in collaboration with school administrators, another of many customizing opportunities that can make a significant difference in promoting a national K–12 futurizing campaign.

Cluster 1: Fundamentals

Our goal with these ten courses is to help assure a graduate has more than a passing familiarity with the art of futuristics and can explain much of it to inquiring minds. If we are especially successful with some of the students we may even learn ways they can contribute to, and help improve the art form.

1. *History*

Studying the origins of familiar things offers the excitement of complexity, and apprentice futurists cannot get good enough at this. History is ever-present in the moment (Faulkner famously maintained "the past isn't dead and buried. In fact, it isn't even past").[1] It casts a long shadow over the future. Its many lessons are the foundation of solid forecasting.

Here, as with every subject, the approach should stand on the shoulders of giants (highly-regarded historians), but also go far beyond to make exciting use of computer simulations, computer-based games, virtual visits to digitally-created long-gone sites, and high-quality teleconferences with authorities and students in distant lands. Proto-futurists should feel like a Woody Allen "Zelig" passively "attending" critical moments in the past.

Histories that are difficult to share, histories of the grievous crimes some humans have committed . . . ethnic-based genocides, massacres, and the shameful like . . . must be analyzed for the light they can shed on our ability to avoid repeating such disasters. Fortunately, dedicated groups of teachers have tested and improved classroom material dealing with the killing fields of Cambodia, ethnic cleansing in Darfur, the tribal warfare in Rwanda, the European Holocaust, and other "Never Again!" crimes against humanity. Youngsters need to learn that "an understanding of human nature entails knowing both the shining city on the hill and its darker neighborhoods."[2]

In a futures-focused history course, special attention should be paid to "touchstones," such as Moore's Law, which has accurately forecast the doubling of computer power since it was formulated in the 1960s. These "rules of thumb" use history as a basis for valuable extrapolations, many of which initially appear "too fantastic for words on the one hand, yet are reasonable projections of where we might be in the future."[3]

Proto-futurists should study historic efforts by societies to recover from devastating criminal acts. These efforts to claim a better future include creation of the Truth and Reconciliation Tribunals in South Africa and Rwanda, improvement of the International Court of Peace and Justice (and its ongoing trial of Serbian and Croatian war criminals), worldwide use of the U.N. "Blue Helmet" peacekeeping military, and the inspiring like.

Above all, attention should go to assessing yesteryear's methods of "foretelling" the future. Given our historical amnesia, it is all too easy to overlook past tools, including astrology, legendry, magic, mysticism, shamanism, theology, wizardry, and so forth. Today's proto-futurists should get clear about their irredeemable flaws, put these limitations in their historic context, appreciate how far we have come, and acknowledge how far we have yet to go.

2. Methods

An energizing course should focus on the "how to" mechanics that sets futuristics apart and above fortune-telling, mysticisms, and pop culture nonsense. Youngsters should make hands-on age-appropriate use (*a la* John Dewey) of such challenging tools as chaos and complexity theory; computer modeling; cross-impact analysis; Delphi poll techniques; environmental scanning; expert interviews; futures wheels; games; relevance trees; scanning; scenario writing; science fiction; simulations; technological forecasting; trend analysis; trend extrapolation, and visualization.

A case study could be made of an especially popular method—the polling of professional forecasters. TechCast, for example, a unit of George Washington University, regularly processes the forecasts of one hundred futurists polled as members of a TechCast Expert Panel (www.techcast.org). *[Full Disclosure: I am a Panel member]*. They are asked when a particular cutting-edge technology might command as much as a third of its potential market, how large in dollars that market might be, and what degree of confidence they have in their forecast. They are also given an opportunity to explain their reasoning. Classroom attention could focus on especially intriguing TechCast components (such as forecasts concerning artificial intelligence, nanotechnology; etc.)[4]

Likewise, attention could go to tests of the so-called "wisdom of the crowd," an increasingly popular method of forecasting. InTrade, for example, is a Web site where people buy and sell contracts whose price is tied to likely changes in the real world. It has surprised many with the accuracy of its election forecasts since 2004. Academic studies show its record is "better than that of any single poll or any single pundit."[5] A miniature version of the stock market, where the collective forecasts of millions shapes stock prices, InTrade would seem to warrant close exploration by apprentice futurists.

3. Science Fiction

The special world of science fiction literature can barely be introduced in only one course, but an attempt should be made nevertheless. Its extrapolations can serve as a lens with which we can examine the human condition. Dedicated to conceiving the inconceivable, the genre is entertainment, but much more. It requires that we use our imagination, and sharpen our ability to speculate. It provokes curiosity like almost nothing else.

A portal to many futures topics, science fiction is a rich source of stimulation; for example, the biotechnology future, as imagined by some authors, includes interstellar genetic engineers pod-gestated babies, and secret government research laboratories, among 101 other provocative matters. Futurists—young and old—find this literature an endless source of imagination and insight.

4. Film

Nearly every course in a high school of the future would at one time or another draw on such films as *AI, Alien, Blade Runner, Brazil, Children of Men, Close Encounters of the Third Kind, Colossus: The Forbin Project, Cloverfield, Fahrenheit 451, Forbidden Planet, Futureworld, Gattaca, Independence Day, Martian Child, Metropolis, Outland, Planet of the Apes, Star Wars, Solaris, The Postman, The Sum of Our Fears, Things to Come, THX 1138, Waterworld, Westworld, 12 Monkeys, 2001, 2010,* and scores of others.

Remarkable for their creative richness and moral weight, the best of these films are not absurd or childish. Rather, they can help sensitize viewers to the confounding potential for violence in the most tranquil settings, and to a timeless quest for order in chaotic settings. Young futurists can learn how large abstract forces (like ever-fiercer competition for affordable oil, or deadly pandemics innocently spread by global travelers) can bear on their individual futures, and of those of us all.

5. Slighted Futures

Teenagers should learn about the future of overlooked peoples in the Adriatic countries, Africa, the Baltic nations, Central America, the Pacific Isles, and South America. Schooling in America remains primarily Eurocentric, though China and the Middle East are finally getting overdue attention: "We're moving into a very new world, one in which countries from Brazil to South Africa to India and China are getting richer, stronger, and prouder. For America to thrive, we will have to develop a much deeper, richer, more intuitive understanding of them and their peoples."[6] High schools for the future can help remedy this imbalance in attention.

6. Assessment Processes

Students should gain familiarity with major techniques for assessing large-scale social systems. The background, formulas, strengths, and limitations of Social Impact Assessment, Social Indicators, and Technological Assessment warrant close study, as these tools are critical in taking the measure of an organization or social system that purports to help change our future.

A case study could be made of the federal government's now-defunct Office of Technology Assessment (OTA), once a key adviser to the Congress about proposed future-shaping matters seeking federal support (funding, legislative, etc.). OTA was expected to help Congress differentiate between the bleeding edge and the leading edge of proposed technological advancements, a service of critical importance, as fragile proposed technologies could be seriously setback or substantially boosted by an OTA Report . . . thereby helping shape the future.

A related case study could be made of leading social indicators like the annual Index of Economic Freedom, the Corruption Perception Index, the Human Development Index, and the Calvert-Henderson Quality of Life Indicators.[7] Also, a new Index of Sustainable Economic Welfare (ISEW) championed as a replacement for the old Gross Domestic Product metric (GDP). All are good examples of efforts underway to capture "soft" or subjective intelligence which, while it may lack many hard numbers is no less valuable for helping guide judgments about going this way or that in shaping the future.

7. Claims

It is vital to consider how we might test claims for items too small to warrant a technology assessment, items promoted as significant future-aiding matters. The market, for example, is now being flooded with new "Green" products (and old repackaged ones), hyped as good for the environment. With foods labeled not only as good for your health, but as capable of preventing illness. With new coiled light bulbs hailed as better for countering climate change, and so on.

Proto-futurists should get help in class asking—*Are they?* In this connection, they should study popular resources, such as the magazine of the Consumers Union, for insights into methods for testing PR hype. They should learn the answers one gets depends partly on what one asks, and that hinges on your purpose and place in the class structure. They should learn how to become "crap detectors," independent learners who can sift through arguments and evidence, make reasoned judgments, and know how to learn.[8]

8. Community Service

Apprentice futurists should spend considerable after-school time helping, but also studying any organization trying to make a positive difference. Placement in assisted-living facilities and nursing homes is especially desirable, as teenagers have much of value to learn from oldsters eager to share accumulated wisdom. As helpers aspiring futurists should be available for almost any role; for example, dishing out meals in a food kitchen for the homeless, washing floors in a center for abused women, and so on.

After having settled in to their service assignment, the student should seek to learn if the organization has a long-range plan for its future. If so, when was it drafted, how, and why? What controversies did it resolve, and with what effect? How much use does the plan actually get, why, and with what effect? How is it kept up-to-date? And, how could explicit use of futuristics possibly help improve the organization and its long-range plan?

Use might also be made of the Generation Y Model, up and going since 1985 in over 500 schools. It starts by listening to students who, for example, may want to help a local nonprofit day care center add solar panels for hot-water assist, and/or create a TV spot to recruit enrollees and new staff for the center. As part of a futures-oriented education, the students would learn about the solar industry, actually apprentice with skilled installers, and possibly later take post-high school courses in creating computer animation for TV spots.

9. Disputes

Controversies in forecasting warrant close attention, as they give an opportunity to broach matters unsatisfied by trite answers. Students who aspire to be futurists should learn to adopt a healthy sort of skepticism where high-profile disputes and disputants are concerned. A case study, for example, could be made of the clash between glaciologists who, looking at the same melting phenomena, do or do not forecast a rise this century in the world sea level. Some expect a three-foot rise—thereby threatening extraordinary coastal damage, and the relocation of hundreds of millions, with much ensuing hardship. Others, however, warn of six feet. And a few scoffers expect only a six-inch rise.[9]

Another dispute worth study concerns current preparation for the next flu pandemic. Some states are spending millions purchasing antivirals through a federal discount program that cuts costs to $20 from $80 for one person. Other states, noting a shelf life of only five years, decline to make any purchases. Each side has its emotional supporters. As if this wasn't difficult enough, states that do buy the drug expect to have enough on hand for only 25 percent of their population should a pandemic break out, leaving open to heated dispute the grounds for eligibility to receive life-saving medicine. Controversy here abounds.[10]

Coming closer to home aspiring futurists could study the ongoing fight over whether fast food chains should be required to post caloric counts, since patrons routinely underestimate the number of calories when they eat out. In 2008 over twenty cities were weighing bills similar to New York City's requirement.[11]

They could also study open conflicts about the appropriateness of sugary drinks in schools. Full-caloric soda is being forced out, but mid-caloric sugary drinks continue to be allowed (enhanced waters, sparkling juices, sports drinks, sweetened teas). Nutrition advocates insist schools should offer only water, low-fat milk, or 100 percent fruit juices during the school day. Novice futurists could weigh competing claims in both of these controversies, and, through the agency of the Futures Committee, advise school authorities.[12]

Students could ask whether or not the school lunch program should offer milk or meat from cloned animals (cows, goats, and pigs) and their offspring. (FDA approval, after over six years of study, came early in 2008). Some parents can be expected to hail related cost savings and product upgrades (leaner and larger cuts of meat). They note cloning "has the potential to produce products that are safer, healthier, and tastier—bacon that has heart-protective Omega-3, say, or milk produced by cows that are stronger and thus need fewer antibiotics."[13]

Opponents, however, are likely to charge cloning causes suffering to animals, citing a 2008 EU Study Group finding.[14] They may also warn darkly of imagined safety risks from what they call "Frankenfood." After patiently studying both sides, and considering the material offered by such companies as Cyagra, Trans Ove Genetics, and ViaGen, students might ponder why, "like abortion and capital punishment, biotechnology inspires knee-jerk rhetorical passion rather than rational debate."[15] In due course, they might urge school buy-in, or, explain why this is not their recommendation.

Students should learn some people will cheer the same future-shaping products or trends others fear or jeer; for example, "Does a world of a million video channels on your iPhone sound exciting to you, or like a living hell of mindless dreck? Do you think stem-cell therapies will lead to better lives, or just prolong a painful and expensive process of aging and dying?"[16] Teenagers should learn how to either take sides, or find a way between extreme positions, and how to disagree without becoming disagreeable.

10. Limitations

Proto-futurists need to understand why forecasts have often been off the mark. Students need to appreciate the toll taken on the profession of futuristics by today's weak theoretical models of change, reliant as they are on the social sciences, the youngest and least reliable of the sciences. They need to understand why our mathematics and statistics are only as good as data entered, and that even the "best available data" always has critical gaps, is often outdated, and sometimes is flat wrong. They need to be reminded that correlation does not necessarily demonstrate cause (see chapter 1).

Once limitations have been studied, energizing attention can be paid to the many ways forecasting tools are stronger now than just five or ten years ago. Futurists work hard at remedying obvious faults, propping up weak links, inventing fresh tools, and in myriad other ways, trying to pass along a finer art that the one they inherited. The more aspiring futurists learn about these efforts—and the limitations that are their source—the better.

Cluster 2: Personal

Our goal with these two required courses is to surface awareness that forecasters are fellow humans with all that that implies, including their need to upgrade social skills and emotional health as much as they strive to boost their cognitive and creative competencies.

1. Social Competences

The struggle to create an identity and build self-confidence is arguably "the most fundamental chore of high school learning."[17] A required course should promote the arts of conversation, diplomacy, etiquette, and related life management and social skills. For to effectively and efficiently share forecasts with others, one must first have confidence in one's self, as an individual and an intellect.

Accordingly, novice futurists should learn about the art of listening, cultivated taste, politeness, wit, and other skills that add grace and zest to life. They could practice in sophisticated role-plays; for instance, skits that explore how to ask or respond to unsettling questions. Employ sophisticated language with flair. Apologize for an unintended faux pas. Defend oneself against a sharp-tongued critic. As well, more mundane, but no less challenging matters warrant attention; for example, methods for financial, stress, and time management, along with physical well-being. And, students should come to appreciate the anonymous aphorism—"Do something every day you are afraid of."

Special attention could also go to what a film critic identifies as the "underlying message" of a 2008 film about high schoolers: "Empathy and compassion, communication and friendship, have more to do with emotional growth than does striking cool poses on the high school steps."[18] This course might also venture out five or ten years to forecast new social skills—probably just emerging—the better to help youngsters get a head start on acquiring them.

2. Love and Human Sexuality

This course would enable teenagers to upgrade what most have learned primarily from peers or from very uneven sources in our sexually saturated culture. Better still, attention would be paid to the enriching place of caring, dedication, ethics, love, and morality in intimate matters.

The course might have well-schooled volunteer juniors and seniors join their teachers in conducting outreach educational sessions for new students. Skits and interactive activities could deal with the case for abstinence, the case against alcohol/drugs, caring norms in dating, the risks of HIV/ AIDS, the art of sexual decision-making, the case against sexual harassment, and the art of talking with parents about these matters.[19]

Classroom discussion topics might also include the possible impacts of a male "fail safe" contraception pill, guidelines for sexual relations among the first residents of a moon or Mars colony, or the impact of reproductive technologies that make conception and childbirth solely by a female— parthenogenesis—an option (normal fetuses could be conceived extra uteri, and brought far along by equipment originally developed to keep premature babies alive).

As 60 percent of high school students are sexually active by twelfth grade, this course in "Love and Human Sexuality" should add much of value to the lives—and the future—of participants.[20] Its course materials might be available online 24/7 (via a teacher-assigned password), and have hypertext features to help a teenager develop informed, sound, and healthy views about love and human sexuality.

Cluster 3: Forecasting

Our goal with these five courses is to involve proto-futurists with a range of disparate forecasts of varying quality, the better to help hone their skill in assessing leading forecasts, and, daring to advance tentative ones of their own.

1. Collapses

Students could profit from a clearer understanding of why plans to stay on top of the future often fail, that is, why the problem-solving abilities of societies give out? While large social systems, like ours, are inherently unstable, and "complacent oligarchies, like soft cheese, turn rancid in the sun," their fates are largely in their own hands.[21] Thanks now to ongoing advances in information technology we have better-than-ever understanding of the complexities, and vulnerabilities, of social systems.

Particular attention could be paid to the decline and fall of Greece and Rome, the disappearance of Aztec and Mayan civilizations, the ancient African kingdoms, the Chinese "Middle Kingdom" empire, and other classic cases (Stalin's Russia, Nazi Germany, Mussolini's Italy, Japan of WWII, the Comintern [Eastern Europe Communist] nations, Mao's China), about which a good deal is known (and more is always being learned).

Attention might also be directed at the oft-overlooked case of Easter Island. Some 1,500 years ago on one of the most isolated inhabited places anywhere, Polynesians carved over 1,000 statues there to honor their ancestors. They left behind evidence of the entire arc of a civilization—from birth to pinnacle to collapse. Theorists point to deforestation as the likely source of the collapse. Novice futurists—indeed, all of us—have much to learn from pondering this matter of a squandered future.

To bring this more up to date, attention should go to the setbacks suffered by the U.S. occupation of Iraq. Aspiring futurists could study the reasons why the oft-cited State Department-produced "Future of Iraq" Project Report was seemingly disregarded by American military officials in the years immediately after our 2003 invasion. Likewise, students could try and learn why the Report "failed to warn about [the radical cleric Moqtada al-Sadr] in its thousands of pages of projections and scenarios."[22]

On a smaller, but no less informative scale, aspiring futurists could explore the 2008 collapse of the effort in American cities to create affordable Internet access for the masses. Initially hailed by enthusiasts as the answer to the Digital Divide challenge, the excited momentum "has sputtered to a standstill, tripped up by unrealistic ambitions and technological glitches."[23] Efforts persist to help American cities catch up with places like Athens, Leipzig, and Vienna, where free citywide WiFi is already available, thanks to reliance on the public, rather than the private sector.

2. Crisis Anticipation

This challenging course would assess trends that pose more threat than promise for young people—and everyone else. These vertigo-inducing glimpses of a perilous future warrant proactive concern; for instance, "One of the lessons of Darfur, Rwanda, and Bosnia is that it is much easier to avert a genocide ahead of time than to put the pieces together afterward."[24]

A case study, for example, could be made of perils to democracy. There is reason to think it increasingly imperiled, as there is a systematic effort to weaken or even eliminate counterparts of our Bill of Rights in many countries (the former Soviet Union, Middle East countries, etc.). Edicts, "laws," and religious proclamations diminish freedom of assembly, smother civic society, and silence critics.

In 2007 the number of countries judged as free was only 47 percent of all, covering only 46 percent of all people—and this had not changed significantly for the last ten years.[25] Progress made in the 1970s and 1980s has stalled ever since, and a pattern threatens of stagnation in political freedom. (Not surprisingly, there is a related ten-year pattern of stagnation concerning media freedom).[26]

Particular attention might go to "the boundaries any democracy must set to remain true to its values." Given the unease aroused recently in the U.S. by knowledge of our use overseas of alleged methods of torture, "we should be asking ourselves if our democracy is losing its moral boundaries."[27] Aspiring futurists should study these matters in some depth, and explore what the least-worst responses might be and how to promote their likelihood.

3. Cross-Cultural Comparisons

Recognition grows that our planet is more tightly knit than ever before, yet we lag in empathy and "deep" comprehension of one another's culture. Aspiring futurists should take from this course skills sets of lifelong value as they travel, in fact or virtually, and struggle to understand, and make themselves understood in foreign settings.

As well, the course should explore the strengths and limitations of separatism, assimilation, and other options people have as they migrate, or accept temporary residence in lands other than that of their origins. Likewise, attention should go to the challenge ethnic communities are waging to shape a future that would preserve ancient cultural ways even as their offspring feel pressures to "go modern."

Aspiring futurists should pay special attention to educational coursework operating across cultural divides, as much of the future may hinge on successes here. Typical is Heymath!, an interactive math program co-designed by Britain's Cambridge University and some Indian bankers. It serves 250,000 children in thirty-three countries, and is in use in Connecticut, Massachusetts, and elsewhere. Proponents believe it helps students join a global conversation when they grow up.[28]

4. Reforms

This exciting course should focus on actual reform campaigns, as they are arguably second only to methods in importance in the entire futuristic curriculum. Students should learn how to assess reform ideas put forward as future-shaping tools . . . assess, and help improve or disagree with them.

Typical is an effort underway in 2008 in Hudson, New York, to "import" ideas based in the derelict shantytowns of Tijuana, Mexico, as a template for redevelopment of its own low-income area. The plan would feature creating a co-op grocery, communal gardens, playgrounds, an outdoor amphitheater, and "incubator spaces" for arts or job training. Proponents see here "the seeds of a vibrant social and architectural model, one that could be harnessed to invigorate numbingly uniform suburban communities. . . ."[29]

Overseas reforms, especially those seemingly transferable to the U.S., warrant special attention. Israel, for example, announced early in 2008 that it has decided to make the country a laboratory to test the practicality of an environmentally clean electric car. Purchasers will get a subsidized car, and pay a monthly fee for expected mileage, eliminating concerns about the fluctuating price of gasoline.

While only a few thousand are expected on the road in 2009, over 100,000 electric cars should be there by the end of 2010, and 10 percent of all now being driven should be replaced annually.[30] Promoters maintain, "the beauty of [the test] is that you have a real place where you can get real human reactions. In Israel, they can control the externalities and give it a chance to flourish or fail. It needs to be tested . . . and the Israeli government is to be commended for trying it."[31]

After studying such future-shaping reform ideas, native or foreign, students could come up with their own tentative answers, and take these via the Internet to knowledgeable parties here and abroad, the better to learn the strengths and weaknesses of their ideas—and then revise them. If students who at first rejected the reform later admit to a twinge of belief, and if those who rushed to embrace it later admit to a twinge of doubt, much sound learning is likely to have been achieved.

5. Possibilities

This course studies imaginative ideas capable of radically altering the future . . . ideas yet to win implementation, but no less important for that. Students learn how to get past knee-jerk disbelief; suspend judgment; do research; and reach judicious estimates of the desirability, plausibility, and overall merits of proposals some hail as brilliant, others dismiss as far-fetched.

Typical of a "wild idea" worth attention is the American Solar Plan. It proposes a massive solar energy infrastructure theoretically capable by 2050 of providing 69 percent of America's electricity and 34 percent of our total energy needs. A vast area of photovoltaic cells (30,000 square miles) would be erected on otherwise barren land in the Southwest. Excess daytime energy would be stored as compressed air in massive underground caverns to be tapped during night time hours. Large solar concentrator power plants would also be built. A new direct current high-voltage power transmission backbone would deliver solar electricity everywhere.

This project would displace 300 large coal-fired power plants and 300 more large natural gas plants and all the fuels they consume. It would help make us independent of overseas oil (dependence would be cut from 60 to zero percent). It would drop our carbon dioxide emissions by 62 percent of our 2005 figure. As well, this Grand Plan would fundamentally cut our trade deficits, and ease political tensions in the Middle East, lower our military costs, and increase domestic jobs.

Relying on only incremental improvements in solar technology, the project could cost as much as $420 billion in subsidies from 2011 to 2050, but proponents insist this is a bargain in terms of energy and environmental gains.[32] They contend the climate change crisis requires "all of us to think boldly about what should be done, and not be intimidated by the problem's large scope . . . we can't be afraid to think big."[33]

Critics, however, note that as of 2008 solar power cost three to five times as much as coal (depending on the technology used). They doubt it will be cost-worthy soon, especially as it only represents less that one-tenth of one percent of the global energy market.[34] The American Solar Plan, they conclude, gets way ahead of itself—a dismissive judgment that protofuturists could well evaluate.

Another brow-arching example, but one which regards the sun quite differently, involves geo-engineering projects. These would try to compensate for an intensified greenhouse effect by reducing the amount of solar radiation reaching the earth. The idea was once regarded as the province only of kooks, "but as the difficulty of reducing greenhouse gas emissions has become harder to ignore, it is slowly emerging as an option of last resort." Its techniques seem "like pure science fiction," and include using massive orbital mirrors to bounce sunlight back into space. And, fertilizing the oceans with iron to amplify their ability to absorb carbon. And painting roofs white to increase their solar reflection.

Critics point out these options could increase air pollution, would require ceaseless reinforcement, and would cost quite a bit. Proponents reply that "unless the geopolitics of global warming change soon [for the better], the Hail Mary pass of geo-engineering might become our best shot."[35]

A third "wild" idea well worth serious consideration concerns the forecast that in the twenty-first century, VIVOs (voice-in/voice-out computers using visual displays but no text) will make written language obsolete. Should this occur, there would be no compelling reason for schools to teach literacy skills. Talking computers could replace writing for storing and retrieving information. They could do this cheaper, faster, efficiently, and universally, and they would not require users to know how to read and write. By 2050, electronically-developed nations might have become oral cultures; by 2150, a worldwide oral culture could be in place. VIVOs would seem good candidates to transform education, the arts, human relations, politics, and business.[36]

Independent of the specifics of any reform scheme, students should take away from this course an appreciation of the indispensability of bold risk-taking: "We can advantage only when we embrace risky breakout ideas. Our survival depends not on sticking to what works, but on making leaps that let us predict new challenges and seize on new opportunities."[37]

6. *Utopian Ideas*

Young people need help appreciating historic musings about ideal societies, and how to create and maintain new visions. This sort of poetic, yet utilitarian thinking can serve as a welcome antidote to the enervating notion that "this is as good as it can get." Rather, a utopian blueprint can be turned into a real-world project, be embodied in measured achievements, and produce a successor ideology capable of stimulating and justifying still further gains (along with testy diversity and vexing contradictions).

Utopian writers contend, "the age of imagination is not over. Utopias are not opposed to reality; on the contrary, they are one of the elements on which it is built . . . one of its essential components."[38] They insist the enormous scale of the challenges today—climate change, terrorism, looming food and water shortages, and so on—"may require quantum leaps [in reforms] . . . more utopians proposing 'dreams to live by, more public intellectuals issuing impassioned wake-up calls, and more public citizens hungry to foresee and act.'"

Key to assuring success here is informed, passionate, and unfettered public debate, The sooner young minds, especially those of aspiring futurists, wrestle with the ideas of outstanding utopians—Plato, Rousseau, More, Saint-Simon, and more recently, Ernest Callenbach, Paul Goodman, Jacques Fresco, R. Buckminster Fuller, Ivan Illich, Paolo Soleri, Jim Wallis, and the inspiring like—the more likely their minds and spirit are to become as creative and nuanced as they wish.

Naturally, classroom time should include the thoughts of critics, and of recently failed ventures ("New Utopia, an intended sea-based libertarian micro-nation in the Caribbean degenerated with breathtaking predictability into nonexistence and scandal").[39] Attention should go as well to successful modern applied examples of utopian thinking, such as the Farm (Kentucky) and other communes here and abroad, the entire Scandinavian nation complex, and the small Kingdom of Bhutan, where a "Gross National Happiness" Index helps a democratizing monarch measure progress and minimize the toll modernization can take.[40] Of course, the environmental movement worldwide fits in here, especially as key members are busy promoting what they call "Greenopia."[41]

COMMON CHARACTERISTICS

Whatever the subject matter, these eighteen courses should involve a blended learning environment, one that mixes a real-time classroom with online learning materials accessible by password 24/7. Homework assignments in particular should be posted online, the better to help keep parents abreast of the progress of their teenagers, and to help get students accustomed to the sort of hybrid course increasingly common in higher education. As twenty-six states now offer full-time online schooling programs, and as colleges and universities are making this normative, it should be readily achieved.[42]

In all of the courses, the emphasis should be on ratcheting up the quality of questions rather than on a youngster taking satisfaction with coming up with answers. Attention should be paid to novel and even ill-defined challenges that have no simple and clear answer, no "right" answer, though some are better than others.

Aspiring futurists must learn to question classical certainty, reject mechanistic reductionism, and be skeptical of claims of objectivity. They should learn to "stay within the tension of a question or issue, and not rush to assuage our insecurity with easy solutions."[43] The goal is to establish and improve a cycle of inquiry. They should appreciate why a high school physics teacher very deliberately told his students—"At our present level of ignorance, we think we know . . . "[44]

For example, a basic course in Artificial Intelligence could have students ponder such questions as:

> Can you ever be smart enough to build a [machine] copy of yourself, or does the job keep getting harder as you get smarter, always just out of reach? Will it be cruel to tease a [thinking] robot? Should an AI [robot] be held accountable for its actions, or simply disassembled if it does the wrong way?[45]

A course that explored the creation of life forms driven by completely artificial DNA could ask:

> What kinds or organisms should scientists make? What kinds might terrorists or bio-hackers make? How might self-replicating entities be contained, as the danger is not just from bio-terror, but also from bio-error?[46]

And a course that included consideration of genetic enhancement should raise such questions as:

> How much risk should a parent be allowed to take on behalf of a child? What should we do if parents want to eliminate homosexuality in their offspring, or if black parents seek children with lighter skin? What about parents who want

odd, or dangerous adaptations—children with high red-blood-cell counts who could be super-athletes, say, but could also have a far higher risk of heart disease?[47]

The sooner students learn how to wrestle with such tough questions, the stronger their creative problem-solving artistry and rapid cognitive adaptability.

The courses should boast stretching ability. As an ancient wisdom recommends, young people need something to push against in order to grow. The courses should be affable, but difficult; student-friendly, but still a challenge. Alumni should long remember their course work in a high school of the future as rigorous, as the source of many transformative initiatives, and all the more helpful for that.

Finally, the courses should require contributions to a student's electronic portfolio. This would not be a personal home page, but instead have links to examples of course work completed over the years. Contents would include exchanges of comments between the aspiring futurist and peers, teachers, and other futurists. A highlight would be personal reflections on completed work and work in progress.

SUMMARY

With high schools of the future we met our nation's need for a school with tomorrow at its core. Required courses, colorful, cutting-edge, and unapologetically demanding, can add much to the skill set and tool-kit graduates take away with them. As well, these courses should whet the appetite for a post-high school education in advanced futuristics, and thereby show America it has finally gained a first-rate feeder source for well-schooled forecasters.

HIGHLY RECOMMENDED READING

1) *The Future and Its Enemies: The Growing Conflict over Creativity, Enterprise, and Progress*, by Virginia Postrel. New York: Touchstone, 1998. Constructive comparison of two major views, that of dynamists and of stasists. It "celebrates the complexities and surprises of the contemporary world, and of the world to come" (xviii). 2) *Tomorrow Now: Envisioning the Next Fifty Years*, by Bruce Sterling. New York: Random House, 2002. Sterling considers his book "an ambitious, sprawling effort in thundering futurist punditry . . . This book asks two questions: *What does it mean? And how does it feel?*" (Book Jacket)

NOTES

1. Quoted in Noonan, Peggy. "A Thinking Man's Speech." *Wall Street Journal*, March 22/23. 2008, W16. See also Adler, Jerry. "A Big Dose of Skepticism." *Newsweek*, December 10, 2007, 22; Vedin, Bengt-Arne. "Incorporating the Past into the Future." *Futures Research Quarterly*, Summer 2007, 55–64.

2. Schwab, Klaus. "Global Corporate Citizenship: Working with Governments and Civil Society." *Foreign Affairs*, January–February 2007, 107–118.

3. Thornburg, David D., "Foreword." In McCain, Ted and Ian Jukes. *Windows on the Future: Education in the Age of Technology*. Thousand Oaks, CA: Corwin Press, 2006, viii.

4. See Halal, William E. *Technology's Promise: Expert Knowledge on the Transformation of Business and Society*. London: Palgrave Macmillan, 2008.

5. Leonhardt, David. "Testing the Market in Politics." *New York Times*, February 13, 2008, C4 (1.4).

6. Zakaria, Fareed. "The Power of Personality." *Newsweek*, December 24, 2007, 41.

7. Puddington, Arch, et al. *Freedom in the World 2007: The Annual Survey of Political Rights and Civil Liberties*. New York: Freedom House and Rowman & Littlefield, 2007. See also www.calvert-henderson.com/about.htm.

8. Postman, Neil and Charles Weingarner. *Teaching as a Subversive Activity*. New York: Delacorte, 1999, 23.

9. Revkin, Andrew C. "In Greenland, Ice and Instability." *New York Times*, January 8, 2008, E4 (1, 4).

10. Salzman, Avi. "What If a Flu like 1918's Broke Out Now?" *New York Times*, March 23, 2008, NJ3.

11. Nichols, Rick. "Obesity Expert Sides with Chain Restaurants." *Philadelphia Inquirer*, February 21, 2008, F6 (1, 6).

12. Martin, Andrew. "Sugar Finds Its Way back to the School Cafetaria." *New York Times*, September 16, 2008, BU8. A new agreement means only 12-ounce sports drinks can be sold in high schools rather than 20 ounces.

13. McWilliams, James E. "Food Politics, Half-Baked." *New York Times*, February 5, 2008, A23. See also Martin, Andrew. "Fighting on a Battlefield the Size of a Milk Label." *New York Times*, March 9, 2008, 7-BU.

14. Kanter, James. "Europe's Ethics Panel Says Cloning Harms Animals." *New York Times*, January 18, 2008, C4.

15. Zhang, Jane, et al. "Cloned Livestock Poised to receive FDA Clearance." *Wall Street Journal*, January 4, 2008, B1, B2.

16. McWilliams, *op. cit.* Cloning "deserves a fair hearing, one in which impassioned language yields the floor to responsible discourse."

17. Storm, Jonathan. "True Tales from the Halls of High School." *Philadelphia Inquirer*, March 9, 2008, H2.

18. Rhea, Steven. "Prep-school Washout Charms the Hoi Polloi." *Philadelphia Inquirer*, February 22, 2008, W14 (9, 14). To promote self-assurance and savoir-faire, students could learn how to order a meal in an upscale restaurant or a hoi polloi dive. "Go native" as part of a global assignment without going overboard. Read social clues in foreign settings. As well, students could be introduced to the right and

wrong ways of banking, using credit cards, arranging for loans, signing business agreements (co-signing, purchase, rental, etc.), and investing in the stock and futures markets. And, in 101 other demanding situations, do themselves proud.

19. I draw here on the New Jersey Prevention Education Program (PEP), first taught back in 1994, and offered in 2008 in close to fifty New Jersey high schools. See also Sullivan, John. "Sex Education led by Teens Divides Parents." *Philadelphia Inquirer*, February 17, 2008, B1 (1, 9); Robinson, Matthew S. "Scared Not to be Straight: Gay Students Seek Protection from Bullies." *Edutopia*, February/March 2008, 56–58.

20. Basso, Michael J. *The Underground Guide to Teenage Sexuality*. Minn, MN: Fairview Press, 1997, xix. A long-time high school sex educator ruefully notes, "nine times out of ten, young people do not know too much of anything about sexuality," 9.

21. Lapham, Lewis. "Is the United States Bound for Collapse?" *The Futurist*, November–December 2007, 19.

22. Senor, Dan and Roman Martinez. "Whatever happened to Moqtada?" *Wall Street Journal*, March 20, 2008, A19.

23. Urbina, Ian. "Hopes for Wireless Cities Fade as Internet Service Providers Pull Out." *New York Times*, March 23, 2008, A10.

24. Kristof, Nicholas D. "A Genocide Foretold." *New York Times*, February 28, 2008 A25.

25. Puddington, Arch, et al. *Freedom in the World 2007; op. cit.*, 212–213.

26. Karkelar, Karin D. and Eleanor Marchant. *Freedom of the Press 2007: A Global Survey of Media Independence*. New York: Freedom House and Rowman & Littlefield, 2008.

27. Rubin, Trudy. "A Look at the Limits Democracy Must Set." *Philadelphia Inquirer*, February 24, 2008, C1. See also Cetron, Marvin J. "Defeating Terrorism: Is It Possible? Is It Probable?" *The Futurist*, May–June, 2007, 17–20.

28. Anon. "Let's Talk about Figures." *The Economist*, March 22, 2008, 68 (67–68).

29. Ouroussoff, Nicolai. "Learning from Tijuana: Hudson, NY, Considers Different Housing Model." *New York Times*, February 19, 2008, E1, 5.

30. Erlanger, Steven. "Oil-Free Israel Is Set to Embrace Broad Project to Promote the Use of Electric Cars." *New York Times*, January 21, 2008, A7.

31. Wolfensohn, James D., the former World Bank president, and a modest investor in the project, as quoted in *Ibid*.

32. Zweibel, Ken, et al. "A Solar Grand Plan." *Scientific American*, January 2008, 64–74. See also Rennie, John. "Big and Small Solutions." *Scientific American*, January 2008, 8.

33. Richtel, Matt and John Markoff. "A Green Industry Takes Root Under the California Sun." *New York Times*, February 1, 2008, C9 (C1, 9).

34. Walsh, Bryan. "Geoengineering." *Time*, March 24, 2008, 50.

35. Crossman, William. *VIVO [Voice-In/Voice-Out]: The Coming Age of Talking Computers*. Oakland, CA: Regent Press, 2003.

36. Rennie, "Big and Small Solutions," *Scientific American*, *op. cit.*

37. Flichy, Patrice (translated by Liz Carey-Libbrecht). The Internet *Imaginaire*. Cambridge, MA: MIT Press, 2007 ed., 207–8.

38. Belasco, Warren. *Meals to Come: A History of the Future of Food.* Berkeley, CA: University of California Press, 2006, 266. "I doubt very much such problems can be overcome through pragmatism alone."

39. Mieville, China. "Floating Utopias." *In These Times,* October 2007 25 (24–28).

40. Wonacott, Peter. "Smile Census: Bhutan Counts Its Blessings." *Wall Street Journal,* March 22/23, 2008, A1, A7.

41. The Green Media Group. *Greenopia: The Urban Dweller's Guide to Green Living.* Santa Monica, CA: The Green Media Group. 2007, 2.

42. North American Council for Online learning. *Edutopia,* February/March 2008, 17.

43. Peat, F. David. "From Certainty to Uncertainty: Thought, Theory, and Action in a Postmodern World." *Futures,* October 2007, 1007 (915–1007).

44. Anonymous teacher, quoted in Christy, John R. "My Nobel Movement." *Wall Street Journal,* November 1, 2007, A19.

45. Hall, J. Storrs. *Beyond AI: Creating the Conscience of the Machine.* Amherst, NY: Promethus Books, 2007, 36, 266.

46. Weiss, Rick. "Creation 2.0" *Philadelphia Inquirer,* December 31, 2007, E1, 2.

47. Anon. "Conceiving the Future." *The Economist,* February 9, 2008, 89.

6

High Schools of the Future: Learning Aids

"It is good to have an end to journey toward; but it is the journey that matters, in the end."

Ursula K. Le Guin

With the discussion in the previous chapter of the high school naming process, physical premises, and basic curriculum as a foundation, we can proceed to explore here the Implicit Curricula, the Cocurriculum, Career Focus, and Student Forecast components that help make these institutions truly high schools of the future.

1) IMPLICIT CURRICULUM

Certain aspects of the non-credit-granting culture warrant special attention, as they help define the *implicit curriculum,* that is, values promoted by the school system. Elsewhere this has meant such stultifying matters as learning to passively follow directions, show up on time, respect and never question authority, and accept shopworn methods of doing and learning. In high schools of the future, much differs . . . so much that a zesty resulting ambience helps set these schools apart from anything we have at present. Four components discussed below in alphabetical order—Field Trips, Idea Fetes, Musical Events, and Student Government—represent all such enrichment activities.

Field Trips

Aspiring futurists should leave campus as often as possible to study first-hand unique sites that seem an important part of possible tomorrows. Field trips could be made—in fact or virtually via the Internet—to many diverse sites, for example:

1. Arcosanti, a futuristic city under construction near Phoenix.
2. EPCOT (the Experimental Prototypical City of Tomorrow), a world-famous section of Disney World in Orlando, Florida.
3. BP Solar Plant in Frederick, MD, the largest fully integrated solar plant in North America.
4. Kennedy Space Center near Orlando, Florida ("Come see the technology that took us to the moon, and will take us there again").
5. MIT Media Lab in Cambridge, Massachusetts.
6. Smithsonian Air and Space Museum in DC.[1]

The names of many other candidate sites should be invited from teachers, students, and parents. Requests for suggestions could be e-mailed to high schools here and abroad.

A special effort might be made to explore and assess EPCOT (the Experimental Prototypical City of Tomorrow), a world-famous section of Disney World in Orlando, Florida. Updated in the late 1990s, it offers a ride that transports one to the "further reaches of the solar system in a Time Machine vehicle," a futuristic maze at the Space Base, the ability to play with "the toys and tools of tomorrow," and an "imaginative soar on a journey through all your senses."[2]

Proto-futurists should be asked to note what escapes attention at EPCOT, and why this might be so—along with what values are celebrated at the site. As well, students could explore reasons why EPCOT developed at great variance from Walt Disney's vision, a story that reveals much about the chances for building a genuine EPCOT in America.

Sites need not be celebrities like those mentioned above, as seemingly prosaic places nearby can offer rich learning material. WalMart stores, for example, could help novice futurists see at first hand what computer control of inventory makes possible: the largest retail enterprise in history automatically orders a new light bulb every time it sells one, as its cash registers, warehouses, and vendors are all knit together in a seamless web—one well worth experiencing and assessing.[3]

Sites still in planning should also be noted, and followed, both as prospective visit locations, and as case studies should they fail to materialize. Typical are plans to open in the Phoenix area in 2012 one of the world's largest solar-electric generating plants, a three-square mile area of thousands of mirrors to focus the sun's rays and help them run turbines and generators to make power.[4]

If funding is ever permitted, educational sites overseas for field trips, either virtual or actual, could include the mix below of uplifting and also of troubling places, each a sound source of educational and forecasting material:

1. Copenhagen Institute for Futures Studies
2. Concentration Camp Museums (Auschwitz, Dachau, etc.)
3. Dongtan Eco-City (near Shanghai)
4. Dubai (United Arab Emirate)
5. Dutch wind power installations
6. EU Headquarters in Brussels
7. Falconcity of Wonders (United Arab Emirates)
8. Fantasy Island (United Arab Emirates)
9. Genocide Museum (Rwanda)
10. Hydropolis (first underwater hotel; Dubai)
11. Icelandic thermal heat plants
12. "Killing Fields" Museum (Cambodia)
13. Masdar City (Abu Dhabi)
14. Museum of Terror (Budapest)
15. Science Center in Osaka
16. Solar power sites in the Middle East
17. Technion College in Haifa, Israel
18. Tidal power sites, as in Newfoundland

While all could be studied and interacted with via the Internet, the indispensable value of person-to-person contact should not be forgotten . . . and summer field trips abroad (complete with parents and siblings) would help top off an academic year in high style.

After each field trip students can create Webcasts documenting what they have seen and learned. They can practice explaining themselves, and create narratives for their blogs or podcasts. Teachers can facilitate ongoing Internet collaboration projects between classrooms, and aspiring futurists can learn in that way from one another's real or virtual fieldtrips.

Your Futures Committee could discreetly help validate the communications channels for privacy and safety. As well, it could help secure backup equipment (Moodle, ThinkFree, YackPack, and VOIP tools, such as Skype, with which to exchange photos, videos, and more).[5]

Idea Fete

Every year certain writers and/or themes could help knit a student body together as a focused community-of-concern. ("Imagine a year of medical school revolving around the liver; or a car repair course centered on the Chrysler LeBaron.")[6] Proto-futurists would in this way develop a "search image," to borrow a term from field biologists, that would have them sensitized to see trends.

Attention, for example, could go to the ideas of contemporary female writers of science fiction, like Margaret Atwater or Ursula K. Le Guin, or writers of color, like Walter Mosley. After their ideas had been processed, some might be asked to actually speak at the school—or via a teleconference.[7]

Likewise, invitations could go to other prominent contemporary forecasters, such as Daniel Bell, Joseph Coates, Hazel Henderson, Ray Kurzweil, Timothy Mack, Gary Marx, David Pearce Snyder, Alvin Toffler, and so on.[8] Contemporary writers of science fiction might get special consideration; for example, Greg Bear, Ernest Callenbach, Orson Scott Card, Michael Crichton, William Gibson, Neil Stephenson, Bruce Sterling, Vernor Vinge, and so on. Other giants no longer with us could have their contributions celebrated; for instance, Octavia Butler, Philip K. Dick, and Frederick Pohl, to name a few.

As the world of forecasting has been and is now dominated by Western white males, the search should be widened to include the globe and all time past. Attention, for example, should be paid to role models of color, such as African-American writers of science fiction, such as the late Octavia Butler, Samuel Delany, and Walter Mosley. Also, to women writers of science fiction, including Margaret Atwood, Wilhelmina Baird, Ursula L. Le Guin, and so on.[9]

A topic could be explored from A to Z, thereby involving many school courses across the curriculum. These might focus on Accelerated Climate Change: Facts and Implications; China and India: Tomorrow's Competition; Solar Panels in Space: Pro and Con, Teenagers in 2020, or Tomorrow's Extreme Sports: Pro and Con. Alternatively, the organizing topic might be phrased initially as a provocative question, for instance, National Service: Yes or No? or What Might Happen After ETI Says "Hello"?

Here, as in the case of the basic courses (chapter 5), the emphasis should be on transferable learning, on lessons that have lifelong general value on and off campus. (Nearby schools might be invited to send busloads of interested students to join in particular high-profile sessions).

Musical Contributions

The school's student orchestra could experiment with the novel musical works of John Cage, Philip Glass, Steve Reich, Terry Riley, and other controversial composers. All the groups could offer avant-garde compositions (electronica, jazz-fusion, metal, etc.), including some that use dissonances, surprise with interludes of near or total silence, and challenge with atonal irreverent sounds. And pieces by the late Karlheinz Stockhausen might be tried, especially those that require musicians to wear Star Trek costumes.[10]

Some performances might eliminate traditional instruments altogether in favor of using barcodes and a bar reader to play sequences recorded earlier by someone else. Likewise, attention could be paid "to a 'virtual' piano which uses a laser projection of a keyboard instead of real keys (as is already done with computer keyboards), and which feels like a real keyboard when you wear "haptic gloves." It is possible that the training of fingers for piano, organ, and guitar might someday be done with such "gloves." A student could start out running the gloves at a slow speed, and eventually, for example, get used to the feel of playing a Chopin concerto."[11]

Care should be taken to look back in time as well as abroad. The school's orchestra and choral group, for example, could offer a concert of Russian "Future" compositions, from a long ago betrayed period (1917–1940) when composers (Mosolov, Popov, Shostakovich, etc.) envisioned a future of bold innovations embraced by a tolerant society. Mosolov's "Iron Foundry" symphony, intended as a paean to the utopian potential of mechanized industry and human ingenuity, would seem especially apt for student appraisal.[12]

Student Governance

The school's student government should break with a self-deprecating historic precedent for such organizations and actually help govern. Most such bodies are the locus only for a superficial popularity contest at annual elections for officers, or worse yet, a mean-spirited battleground between rival factions (Goths vs. Mods; Blacks vs. Whites; Blue-Collar vs. Others, etc.). This student government could differ in daring to become the site of creative and mature deliberations about possible student contributions to the school's mission.

Aided by a faculty member of the school's Future Committee, the government could serve as the constructive voice of the student body, and, when helpful, speak Truth to Power (an energizing Quaker precept). It could vett proposed course evaluation forms to assure they include student issues, vett proposed school PR publications for authenticity, offer opinions about candidates for teacher slots, and in a multiple of other significant ways, bring the mind and soul of youngsters to the explicit aid of the school.

On a related front, linked in cyberspace with other student government organizations here and abroad, this high school's student government could help spread word about what a futurizing campaign has meant, and continues to mean for its well-being. In turn, using these communication channels, an empowered student government could seek fresh ideas to import and adapt from future-oriented school projects elsewhere.

2) CO-CURRICULA

In tandem with its name and physical features (chapter 4), its basic curriculum (chapter 5), and the Implicit Curriculum above, a High School of the Future should be distinguished by many co-curricula strengths. Before turning to a mainstay here, student clubs, we should note how certain unexpected resources can contribute to the school's mission, provided they are reframed as pro-future learning aids.

School cafeterias and lunchrooms, for example, can be distinctive sources of learning, as "one of the most intimate moments we share with our planet is when we're holding a fork. The food we eat comes from the earth, and turns into the stuff we're made of."[13] Young futurists could begin by exploring the history of recent food fads; for example, beta-carotene, green tea, "low-carb" foodstuffs, soy, and vitamin E. With this as background, they could next study future-shaping matters like "digestive health" favorites, "functional" foods (stuffed with heavy doses of antioxidants and vitamins), immunity-enhancement foods, macrobiotic diets, raw foodism, science-based nutrition standards, and veganism.

Attention could be paid to the National Farm to School Network, as it is imbued with a special vision of a desirable future. The Network connects area farmers to nearby school cafeterias, and in 2008, enrolled nearly 11,000 schools in 39 states. Proponents want "to make sure kids get produce, meats, and dairy from area farmers who have it fresh—and who need the business."[14]

As a case study, students could weigh the future-shaping prospects of the steadily growing Slow Food Movement, which urges us to become informed coproducers of what we eat (e.g., create vegetable gardens, become lovers of healthy low-cost ethnic cuisine, etc.).[15] Samples of tomorrow's foods could be offered and explained. Major food companies could be invited to preview healthy candidates for sale several years hence. Above all, proto-futurists should look to school dieticians and other food staffers for help in finding (tentative) answers to the BIG question—*How can our future have us feed more people more equitably and do so within ecological limits?*

Student Clubs

These remarkable aids to education—commonly eclectic, fragile, and vibrant—cannot be encouraged enough, supported enough, and given enough breathing space to permit age-appropriate risk-taking, self-governance, and resultant pride in accomplishment. They are listed below alphabetically, as they are all equally valuable.

Members of a *Car Club* could model theirs on the remarkable West Philadelphia High School Automotive Academy (one of 24 different academies in the city's school system). After school hours its 140 inner-city student members have built and competed successfully in alternative fuel vehicle competitions since 1997. The Academy's prize-winning hybrid car burns fuel made from soybeans, gets 55 mph, and a great source of student pride: In 2008 they entered a competition to build a car that gets 100 mph, and had to provide a business plan to produce 10,000 vehicles per year. Admirers believe that "in addition to learning skills, the urban teenagers expand their view of the future, discovering, often for the first time, how exciting their job options may be."[16]

A *Chess Club*—drawing extensively on the Internet—could engage in tournament play with youngsters around the world (and especially in nearby inner-city schools—much as is done by the San Francisco school attended by my grandson Benjamin). It could tutor anyone in the school eager to take advantage of the game's mental exercise. The most venturesome of members might try out a new type of chess that has 80 squares on the board instead of 64 (www.GothicChess.com).

Computer Club members might volunteer to cordially, discreetly, and privately tutor those eager to raise their skill level, people ranging from crossing guards through teachers, staff, and parents. It could sponsor forums, including one about edgy Web sites on the blogosphere of likely interest to young people. Or hold workshops on how to join the open-source community using free resources (Wordnet, the CYC ontology, and the Open Mind ontology).[17] Especially valuable would be the club's help in redressing a serious gender imbalance: In 2006, high school girls comprised less than 15 percent of students who took the AP computer science exam.[18]

Dance Club members could explore learning links between movement and insight: "students can use their bodies to connect elements of dance (such as weight, time, force, energy, and transformation) to concepts in science. . . . Imagine dancing the water cycle—moving through the stages of liquid flow, evaporation, condensation, and rainfall—as a way of learning in the classroom."[19]

A *Film Club*, in addition to offering panel discussions of major future-oriented films (see a list in chapter 3), could encourage students to create and show their own future-oriented digital films. These, in turn, could be shared with comparable schools around the country—and the world—with a Cannes or Sundance-like film festival held perhaps the week before the Annual Meeting of the World Future Society (see chapter 2), the better to facilitate attendance by distant student futurists and others.

A *Futures Club* could tackle three special challenges: First, it could devote time to ideas on the Web site of the WFS, and also to articles featured in The Futurist, annotated bibliographic notes in *Futures Survey*, and essays in *Future Research Quarterly*, three invaluable publications of the WFS. Second, it could hold high-quality meetings on unorthodox topics, and thereby fill a valuable educational niche. And third, once a year it could offer a rollicking spoof on all in futuristics that begs for good-natured teasing, and warrants a good laugh.

As for helping to take inquiring young minds where the official curriculum has reasons to keep its distance, one such event might responsibly discuss edgy comic books focused on the future; for instance, a six-year long dystopian comic book series, *Y: The Last Man*, "consistently surprises with imaginative concepts of a manless world run by women."[20] Or hold a panel discussion of the cutting-edge ideas of physicists who maintain the past, present, and future exist simultaneously, as we all live in parallel universes. Young futurists would profit from early consideration of this mind-boggling idea's awesome implications.

A *Game Players Club* might facilitate learning from games that are very future-focused; for example, BioShock, a noir thriller set beneath the Atlantic Ocean, offers a complex story underpinned by a sophisticated interpretation of Ayn Rand's controversial philosophy of Objectivism. Gamers, if over eighteen, might bet their skills against one another in legal (skill-based) "tournaments" and wager on the outcome. And teenage golf players might enjoy "World Golf Tour," a game still only in demo early in 2008, but already hailed as the Killer App. ("You've been warned.")[21]

Members of a *Green Club* could become knowledgeable about the multiple ways their parents could revamp matters at home and work to save energy, reduce unnecessary consumption, eliminate waste, and promote "Green" causes. They could help assess many new products claiming to make a pro-earth difference, such as new hybrid electric bicycles that can reach 25 MPH, allowing riders to travel farther and faster than ever before. After a pro bono consultation with lawyers contacted by your school Futures Committee, the Club could share its evaluations far and wide.

Using a hypothetical starting sum, say, a million dollars, a student *Investment Club* could experiment with applying insights from futuristics to stock markets, here and abroad. Club members could choose a favorite sector to monitor (Agriculture, Banking, Communications, Entertainment, etc.), and trade in the stocks of relevant companies as part of the Club's portfolio. Over time the students could test their ideas about consumer trends, product competition, rising companies, and other key aspects of the economy.

Members of a *Robotics Club* could draw on Lego Mindstorms opportunities, and related products, to learn about the building blocks of computer logic and demystify the world of mechanical/computer processor interface (much as is done at the San Francisco school attended by my grandson David). They could design robots to perform specific tasks, and enjoy the real physical problem solving and troubleshooting involved. Linked with course work in artificial intelligence, club products could provide "edutainment" gains for all.

A *Science Club* might wrestle with some topics suggested by my brother, Stan Shostak, a university biologist: "Climate change; climate change; climate change. You might add enhancement (enhancing human capabilities via drugs and gene replacement), curing ALL diseases, and reversing aging. I would add diet reform (vegetarianism) and animal rights (humane treatment), but bionics, cryonics, and expanding the biological interphase with technology are further down the list—let's not replace Mozart with a pill or a plunger!"[22]

Finally, *Sport Clubs* aiming to help enrollees gain some mastery of their bodies could explore tamer adaptations of the hard-contact game called "Rollerball" (of film fame). Or quixotic adaptations of the "Harry Potter" game known as "Quidditch," possibly complete with a tournament match between broom-riding "Wizards." Or try free sledding, and other creative updates of winter sports. Or modern adaptations of yoga to help improve flexibility, mental grit, and strength.

Particular attention might be paid to WiiFit, a 2008 Nintendo fitness program predicated on the use of a balance board you stand on in front of your TV set. It offers dynamic training exercises for aerobics, muscle conditioning, and yoga—an eclectic mix of likely appeal to teenagers. (The ski simulation recreates the sensation of leaning to the left and right as you ski your way rapidly down a mountain slope).

Career Preparation

Along with the future jobs material included in chapter 3, students should study the specialized work world of forecasters—its range, strengths, limitations, and prospects. Here, and only here, across the spread of the nation's many high schools, teenagers would be able to weigh whether or not professional futuristics is a desirable career choice for them.

Annotated lists of relevant job titles—jobs available after one has earned a college degree, and probably an advanced one at that—could be posted in a conspicuous display case, updated weekly, and cited in senior year counseling sessions. The list might include such titles as: academician, builder, business planner, city planner, consultant, corporate planner, epidemiologist, forecaster, innovation manager, investment counselor, marketing specialist, journalist, public relations specialist, science reporter, science fiction writer, screen writer, teacher, traffic planner, trend analyst, speech writer, venture capitalist, urbanologist, and so on.

Attention should also be paid to other employment possibilities less often thought of, such as artist, clergy, counselor, designer, graphic computer designer, lawyer, military officer, novelist, playwright, politician, and so on.

Teenagers would be expected to participate in credit-granting practicums (sometimes known as Co-op jobs) to experience what futurists do, why, and how. This career preparation course would ask, "What is life like for professional futurists?" Interviews with such men and women, exceedingly frank and constructive events, could help teenagers get at some valuable truths. Guided by a subcommittee of the school's Futures Committee, an individual student, using a teleconference format, could ask a futurist somewhere around the world about the profession five, ten, and more years from now—the better to help guide their own decision about whether this Calling is for them.[23]

Before graduating the seniors might be urged to consider taking a year off between high school and college. A well-earned breather, the time could be usefully spent exploring vocational possibilities, as well as aiding a socially-oriented NGO create a Five Year Plan, or in some other way, gain from what an aspiring futurist can offer.[24]

Student Forecasts

In the closing term of a senior's graduation year he/she might work in a small team to prepare a required presentation of forecasts to the entire student and faculty body (along with outsiders, including parents and school board members, who appreciate the valuable learning possible from earnest attendance). Each team might share three or more forecasts in a full day set aside for this event. Half of the time could go to didactic material, and half to freewheeling, good-natured Q and A.

In this way, the oldest students can model what an education at the school makes possible (attitude, creativity, maturity, sense of humor, trade craft, etc.). In addition, given the strong likelihood some forecasts will conflict with others, they can model how to disagree while not being disagreeable.

This "gift" to the school of a cache of thoughtful forecasts can be drawn on by following graduating classes. Seniors can search for valuable insights into how and how not to look ahead. Admiring media attention could be sought for the forecasts, and over time, a (hopefully flattering) Index of Sound Forecasts (good vs. poor ones) could be leveraged to help the school secure scarce outside financial support (especially public and foundation funds).

SUMMARY

In high schools of the future, we are seeking to achieve a very special culture: To paraphrase Peter Senge's famous 1990 definition of a learning organization, these schools would be places "where people are continually discovering how they create their reality [in response in part to their images of tomorrow] and how they can change it [on behalf of helping to achieve a finer future]."[25] They would be capable of continuous transformations, much as reading road signs gives way nowadays to listening to your car's GPS guidance system.

For far too long no high school has put an emphatic and rewarding focus on the future—its probable, possible, preferable, and preventable aspects. Nor have any offered youngsters a chance to test out whether careers as forecasters were their "calling." This continues to undermine our ability to have futurism serve as everyone's "second profession."[26] We need many high schools of the future as "boot camp" training grounds to help prepare guides for tomorrow's decision-makers.

HIGHLY RECOMMENDED READING

1) *Creating Learning Communities: Models, Resources, and New Ways of Thinking about Teaching and Learning*, edited by Ron Miller. Brandon, VT: The Foundation for Educational Renewal, Inc., 2000. Essays from an ad hoc coalition for self-learning. Explores "the future of learning and the potential impact on society of the cooperative community lifelong learning centers that are emerging and self-organizing from the rapidly growing home-schooling and other self-learning movements" (3). 2) *Radical Evolution: The Promise and Peril of Enhancing Our Minds, Our Bodies—and What It Means to be Human*, by Joel Garreau. New York: Doubleday, 2005. Explores the implications of our efforts to "alter our minds, our memories, our metabolisms, our personalities, our progeny—and perhaps our very souls . . . [For] it is only by anticipating the future that we can hope to shape it" (Book Jacket).

NOTES

1. DNC Parks and Resorts. Kennedy Space Center. Orlando, FL: Delaware North Companies, 2007, 1.

2. Magic Kingdom Productions. *The Guide to Everything Disney.* Lake Buena Vista, CA: 2008, 9.

3. Shachtman, Noah. "What Went Wrong." *WIRED*, December 2007, 241 (240–249, 282).

4. Smith, Rebecca. "Solar Project is Set for Arizona." *Wall Street Journal*, February 21, 2008, A14.

5. Nussbaum-Beach, Sheryl. " No Limits." *Teaching & Learning*, February 2008, 15–18. "Classrooms in the 21st century need to be collaborative spaces where

student-centered knowledge development and risk taking are accepted as the norm, and where an ecology of learning develops and thrives" (18).

6. Wakin, Daniel J. "What's in a Beethoven Quartet? A Full Curriculum." *New York Times*, February 12, 2008, E1.

7. Other female science fiction writers worth the attention of high schoolers include, but are no means limited to, Lois McMaster Bujold, Elizabeth A. Lynn, Laura J. Mixon, Melissa Scott, Joan D. Vinge, and Kate Wilheim.

8. I recommend in particular *Neuromancer*, by William Gibson; *The Diamond Age*, by Neil Stephenson; and *Ecotopia*, by Ernest Callenbach. The first foreshadows the evolution of the "World Computer System." The second, a world suffused with nanotechnology applications. And the third, an America in industrial disarray, save for a rococo segment rich in Green achievements, this, the most popular science fiction book I employed over nearly thirty recent years.

9. See Barr, Marleen, ed., *Envisioning the Future: Science Fiction and the Next Millennium*. Middletown, CT: Wesleyan University Press, 2003. "Feminist science fiction asserts that outer space is a logical venue for feminist ideals and hence, critiques the need for future war, forever war, and starship troopers," xviii.

10. Anon. "Obituary" *The Economist*, December 15, 2007, 95.

11. E-mail from Bob Shilling; February 24, 2008.

12. Smith, Steve. "American Symphony Orchestra." *New York Times*, January 28, 2008, B6.

13. The Green Media Group. *Greenopia: The Urban Dweller's Guide to Green Living*. Santa Monica, CA: The Green Media Group. 2007, 2.

14. MacDonald, G. Jeffrey. "'A' is for Farm-Fresh Apples." *USA Today*, March 24, 2008, 4D.

15. Steinhauer, Jennifer. "A Spoonful of Immunity?" *New York Times*, February 17, 2008, ST1, 10.

16. Phillips, Ginny. "Auto Motive." *Edutopia*, July/August 2008, 25 (24–27).

17. Dodd, Scott. "Making Space for Time." *Scientific American*, January 2008, 26 (26, 28).

18. Rosenbloom, Stephanie. "Sorry, Boys, This is Our Domain." *New York Times*, February 21, 2008, G8 (G1, 8).

19. Daft, Marcia. "Artists as Education Consultants." *Education Week*, February 13, 2008, 32 (31–32).

20. Weinberg, Bob. "The Last *Last* Man." *City Link*, January 23, 2008, 53.

21. Quittner, Josh. "World of *Fore!*-craft." *FORTUNE*, January 21, 2008, 34 (32, 34).

22. E-mail, February 8, 2008. Stanley Shostak is a retired biologist, formerly on the faculty of the University of Pittsburgh.

23. Every level of local, city, state, regional, and federal government, along with NGOs and profit-seeking businesses, could be asked if students could shadow, or better yet, apprentice with key forecasters and others with aligned responsibilities. Students could also assist area nonprofit organizations develop sophisticated long-term plans, great Web sites, effective Futures Committees, and other similar aids . . . all of this attached to a formal credit-awarding course.

24. Newmarker, Chris. "Service Before Starting College." *Philadelphia Inquirer,* March 9, 2008, B7. More and more colleges and universities are encouraging a Gap Year, and some, such as Princeton University, are subsidizing it. See also Williams, Alex. "A Cure for the College-Bound Blues." *New York Times,* March 9, 2008, 2-ST.

25. Senge, Peter. *The Fifth Discipline: The Art and Practice of Learning.* New York: Doubleday, 1990, 13.

26. As quoted in an editorial, "Futurism is Not Dead," www.wfs.org/ futurism.htm.

III

Educational Futures "GPS"

We live in a world that is lit by lightening. So much is changing and we will change, but so much endures and transcends time.

Ronald Reagan

In Part III, the book's closing section, we begin with a colorful adaptation of an old-fashioned County Fair. At this happy event the fruits of a futurizing process are put on proud display, the better to encourage adoption by nearby school districts (chapter 7). Ideas are shared about variations in what youngsters might chose to display, the role of the school per se, the part vendors might play, and the many gains possible from the fun-and-learning focus special biannual event.

The following chapter explores what school systems can expect soon—both of the appealing and also of the alarming variety. I am guided here by the contention that "the future of education hinges on our ability to take a good, hard look at the realities facing the students we'll be called upon to educate in the future."[1]

The first high probable/high impact matter concerns our need to close the Digital Divide between teachers who use computers with creative savoir faire and all others. Given the eerie ability many youngsters have to master new computer challenges without so much as a glance at a manual, and their ease in helping one another get up to speed, teachers can fall further and further behind (one of many reasons I retired when eligible). Unless and until your school Futures Committee makes progress here, trouble brews.

The second over-the-horizon matter concerns the nation's human capital needs. I contend that we are under-supporting aspects of the social order vital to helping us create the high-quality labor force (agile, creative, collegial, and dynamic) we need to stay competitive in the world markets. I suggest several pragmatic and affordable reforms, fully understanding how controversial is the whole matter. A role is nevertheless suggested for your Futures Committee, as, to draw on a favorite disclaimer of mine, I never "promised you a rose garden."

Two more far-out matters round out chapter 8: First, I explore the remarkable challenge posed by steady gains in intelligence acquisition being made by robots, and I share a "calendar" which has them our intellectual equals as soon as 2035, give or take five years. After noting the havoc this could mean for our job market, I dwell on a greater challenge, namely, the question of whether we can become smart enough between now and then to engineer traits into "smart" machines likely to save us from them, and, vice versa. As exotic as this may sound, I suggest a research role here for your Futures Committee.

The last of the forecasting challenges concerns the oncoming "civil war" I expect between diehard Greens and their various opponents (doubters, financially-strapped citizens, libertarians, etc.). I explain how K–12 school systems are likely to be caught in the cross-fire, and I urge your Futures Committee to try and get out ahead, the better to lower the temperature of the debate, and try and find civil compromises.

Finally, an Epilogue explains where I finally come out concerning the prospects for futurizing K–12 education. Given my propensity to opt for action when in doubt, it ends with a long list of programmatic thoughts about next steps we might take in advancing our national futurizing campaign. I call for development of a national campaign-directing committee (an Education for Tomorrow organization), and offer several other such "roll-up-our-shirtsleeves" ideas.

It is time K–12 graduates knew how to trace future-shaping pathways; identify significant preferences; and imagine possibilities and perils beyond the obvious. As a nation we take great risks in our casual approach to teaching the future. We devalue or exclude it from the curricula, much as if students could somehow absorb it from the air or drinking water. Education, we must never forget, "is not oil, or electricity, or soybeans or gold, but it represents something more important than any of those: the future."[2]

NOTES

1. Bowers, Reveta. "On Schools and Education." In Buckingham, Jane, ed. *What's Next: The Experts' Guide.* New York: HarperCollins, 2008, 21 (21–23).
2. Owen Edwards, "Editorial," *Edutopia,* February/March 2008, 26.

7

Futures Fair: Come, Let Us Celebrate!

"Every day we lead the nation into the future with our words and actions simply because we are teaching the future of our nation."

Chip Wood, *Time to Teach, Time to Learn*, 1999, p. 286.

Imagine a time—not too far off—when your Futures Committee has enjoyed many well-earned successes. When it has become a cohesive and reliable learning community. When that time arrives, it may be ready to tackle its most ambitious project to date—one uniquely capable of winning many new supporters, impressing skeptics, and even disarming some critics. Just as (nearly) everyone loves a County fair, and, in K–12 education, a Science Fair, so can your Committee introduce your school and thereby, your school district, to the many rewards of an unprecedented Futures Fair: "just for a hoot we might proceed on the assumption that human beings actually enjoy learning. . . ."[1]

GETTING STARTED

As with every activity mentioned in this book, so with the Futures Fair: Listening is the prime first step. Members of the Futures Committee could fan out and enjoy having focused, though also informal talks with a representative sample of the school community (complete from aides through the ranks on up to the principal). Questions should solicit ideas, however off-the-wall, about what would add value to a Futures Fair (defined for those put off initially by its novelty).

Student members of the Futures Committee have an especially key role, as they should bring back scores of exciting ideas from peers in every grade. When students are the source of ideas they are far more inclined to take ownership of their actions and goals.

Then, the fun begins—as a subcommittee of volunteers can review all of the ideas, and begin creating a pamphlet of recommended ideas to share with curious grade and specialty teachers (the subcommittee should also agree which ideas have not made the cut, many of which should be considered the next time around).

Even while the selection process is underway, attention should go to the calendar, both to assure the event is well scheduled, and to protect the longest possible time for youngsters to complete their Fair preparations. A biannual event, your Futures Fair might be scheduled on two consecutive weekdays, and a Saturday (day and evening). This allows the entire community to attend, but does not overdo the matter.

Every K–12 grade could be expected to operate a booth in which it offers Fair attendees a creative learning experience. Busloads of students from adjacent schools in the district could attend, and not incidentally, take back to their schools the energizing question—*Can we also begin to enjoy learning more about tomorrow?* A DVD of the event could be offered to adjacent schools, and be archived for study when planning begins for the next go-around.

ON DISPLAY

Early grades could offer visually arresting drawings of the kind of spaceships they imagine they may get to use as adults to reach space colonies. Or the kind of communities they envision on space colonies. Or the sort of aliens they suspect are out there . . . good, bad, or ugly.

Coming closer to home, the students could create large colorful replicas of their favorite future-linked fictional characters (e.g., *Star Wars*'s Yoda). Either as puppets or even full-sized costumes the replicas could be used to realize with pleasing verve what children expect of these over-the-horizon characters.

Middle school youngsters could share balsa wood models of ultra-Green housing only five to ten years off (housing modeled on actual buildings in the area, including some of their own homes). Or they could act out short skits devised to share ideas about life in 2025 here and abroad. Or they could feature models of alternative energy sites (fields of windmills, solar panels, geothermal plants, biomass installations, etc.), and stand by to explain all to wandering Fair attendees. Or they could demonstrate the rewards of drawing on Rainforest Math, a popular computer program that combines environmentalism and math.

High school students could show experimental videos, web sites, and virtual reality tapes designed to both thrill and teach. They could offer to introduce attendees to the wonders of cutting-edge computer uses, either practical or entertaining in intent. Various student clubs could highlight their preoccupations, such as imaginary investing in the stock market, creative play of chess game variations, and advanced lab experiments with biotech and/or nanotech materials (see chapter 6).

A booth operated by students from different grades could highlight future-shaping reforms the youngsters want to call to the attention of their folks and neighbors. For example, the youngsters could offer a model of a before/after approach to improved home lawns. The "before" lawn would replicate the norm (mowed grass), while the "after" lawn might feature a vegetable garden or a cover of pebbles, the former to reduce reliance on plants grown far away, and the latter to reduce watering. Far more ambitious would be a scale model of what the school itself might resemble were it to become a carbon-neutral, zero-emissions showcase.

A related booth, also operated by students of different ages, could salute early neighborhood adopters of future-shaping innovations. The first few homes close to the school to add solar to the rooftop, or paint a roof white, or cover a roof with plants, might be photographed by the students (operating with the homeowners' permission) and awarded a Future Fair prize ribbon. Families that have switched to a hybrid or electric car, or energy-proofed their home, or gone back to drying clothes on outside clothes lines, or have sought to reduce their carbon footprint, might find their names proudly emblazoned on a student-created Future Honor Roll.

Another booth, also hosted by students from different classes, could offer a book swap, VHS/CD/DVD Swap, and gadgets and memorabilia swap—all the stuff clearly linked to futures themes. The entire school community—teachers, students, professional and nonprofessional staff—could be invited to clean the attic and basement, bring in extras and duplicates, and enjoy swapping for more desirable links to tomorrow. (To head off awkward matters, a volunteer from the Futures Committee should vett everything beforehand.)

Elsewhere around the school, Fair attendees could spend time in classrooms with the "feel" of an extraterrestrial base. Or a domed colony on Mars. Or an advanced "Starship." The school lunchrooms could offer and explain samples of tomorrow's foods. The workshops for auto repair, computer repair, or electronics could show off the latest materials and tools, even as the school athletics program could demonstrate candidates for tomorrow's leading sports (see chapter 4).

OUTSIDE HELP

Area businesses could be invited to use Fair booths to boast about products and services hopefully available five to ten years out. They could highlight their near-future job openings, and explain upgrades in entry-level educational requirements. Company spokespersons could answer questions about their "Greening" efforts, their R&D programs, their corporate "good citizen" projects, and like matters.

Local auto dealers could be asked to show an object of likely great interest to teenagers, the driverless (automated) car of the future. Featured at the January 2008 Consumer Electronics Show, the driverless car can navigate a (protected) urban landscape, and complete with traffic, unmapped obstacles, and even gridlock caused by broken-down competitors, all of this consistent with local traffic laws. Common perhaps by 2020, these "smart" cars, guided by artificial intelligence, may save over 20,000 lives a year, and give us the leeway to look around as our automated cars get us around.[2] Models are available to spur interest, even if sales are still years away.

Area restaurants could offer samples of foods of tomorrow, and have representatives to answer questions about caloric diet aids, ethnic cuisine, nutritional gains, wellness foods, and the like. Particular attention could be paid to regional favorites as they might be varied out five or ten years hence; for instance, with tofu substituting for meat.

Approved vendors could sell educational games and toys that boost knowledge of future-shaping matters (biotechnology, climate change, environmentalism, nanotechnology, etc.), all sensitively geared to different learning abilities and styles. Local travel agencies and/or airlines could be invited to take a booth promoting tourist visits to sites here and abroad of special relevance to the future (see CCPA Education Project, chapter 4). Local and chain bookstores and relevant publishers (such as Center for Teen Empowerment, Educators for Social Responsibility, and NSTA Press) could be invited to show their wares, and offer a Fair discount. Booth rental fees, by the way, could help underwrite any costs entailed in assuring a high-quality event.

A film festival might round it all out, one that could have an entire school, including parents and siblings of enrollees, watch and later discuss future-oriented films, both feature films like *AI*, or *E.T.*, and some made by the students themselves. Outstanding student productions could later be shared with schools around the country and the world. (In due course, a biannual national or even international Sundance-like Film Festival might be hosted by a high school that takes filmmaking as a central focus).

HAPPINESS AS A GOAL

While education is the Fair's primary concern, providing reasons for happiness should be a close second. A Futures Fair should not be as anxious and uptight as are all too many Science Fairs. It should feature, instead, an undervalued lesson: "Happiness and education are, properly, intimately related. Happiness should be an aim of education, and a good education should contribute significantly to personal and collective happiness."[3] Future Fair organizers should pause often and ask if they and other attendees are having fun; if not, creative adjustments are in order.

Happiness, of course, is not the Fair's prime aim (or, for that matter, the prime aim of education or of life). To make too much of it "is to become inauthentic, to settle for unrealistic abstractions that ignore concrete situations."[4] A balance should be struck between the poles of hope and worry, of happiness and unease. The Fair should have a sound representation of problem-focused material linked to the grayness of doubt, challenging material that hints at unintended troubles we must prepare to meet: "The world does not exist to give us a hedonic buzz . . . but because of the opportunities for insight and transcendence it supplies."[5] While we can set knowledge aside happiness, the two do not always coincide.

Allowing for this difference, smile-earning material remains a sound evaluative screen with which to help judge a Futures Fair (and everything else we help create): "If our means are to be compatible with our ends, the quality of life in schools must yield some happiness."[6]

SUMMARY

A Future Fair enables a school or school system to brand itself as soundly futuristic. This can help it forge valuable links with influential members of the community (office-holders, leading business people, reporters, clergy, etc.). Much like a memorable movie poster, catchy ad slogan, or jingle you cannot get out of your head, a positive brand identification is highly desirable—and a school or school system Futures Fair appears a sure winner.

Futurizing campaigns can top off a successful year or two by sponsoring a unique and overdue celebration of tomorrow's possibilities, along with age-appropriate warnings about tomorrow's perils. Packaged in the familiar, and always welcomed form of a full-scale County Fair, the event can help establish the host school as one that is clearly "with it"—a brand of considerable merit in our warp-speed times. Not incidentally, it can help replenish the energies of your Futures Committee, and invigorate the campaign.

HIGHLY RECOMMENDED READING

1) *The Playful World: How Technology is Transforming Our Imagination*, by Mark Pesce. New York: Ballantine, 2000. Explores in a most engaging way how a new kind of knowing and a new way of creating are transforming our culture: "Our children will know how to make sense of the playful world, an important lesson they will be happy to share with us, if we were willing" (272). 2) *Youth Futures: Comparative Research and Transformative Visions*, edited by Jennifer Gidley and Sohail Inayatullah. Westport, CT: Praeger, 2002. Nineteen essays that explore how youth (15 to 25) think about and envision the future: "Ultimately, youth futures, like futures studies generally, is about empowering individuals to critically reflect on the futures being created for them so that they can actively create their preferred futures" (xii).

NOTES

1. Weisbuch, Robert A. "Creating a Third Culture." *Chronicle of Higher Education.* February 29, 2008, C2 (2–3).

2. Jenkins, Jr., Holman W. "Decaffeinated." *Wall Street Journal*, January 9, 2008, A14. The car draws on lessons learned earlier from college student and corporate entries in the 2007 first-ever Pentagon-sponsored "Urban Challenge" competition. Driverless features are already part of upscale car models in showrooms: Some cars can sound off when another car enters the driver's blind spot. Let a driver know when they have wandered out of lane. Signal when tires are about to fail. And not only warn of an impending collision, but immediately tighten seat belts, roll up the windows, and adjust the seats.

3. Noddings, Nel. *Happiness and Education.* New York: Cambridge University Press, 2005 Ed. "It doesn't hurt to pause now and then and ask children and ourselves: How much fun are you having?" (38).

4. Wilson, Eric G. "In Praise of Melancholy." *The Chronicle Review*, January 18, 2008, B11 (11–14).

5. McGinn, Colin. "Please Don't Have a Nice Day." *Wall Street Journal*, February 8, 2008, W5.

6. Noddings, *op. cit.*, 5.

8

Future Possibilities: World 3.0

"Hope is not a feeling or a mood or a personality type. Hope is a choice."

Jim Wallis, *The Great Awakening* (2007)

Matters of consequence are changing more rapidly than ever. Our world is undergoing a rate of change arguably greater than ever before. Seeking in 2008 to make this point, a major investment firm noted in a newspaper ad—"Corn is the new oil. Rich countries are debtors to poor ones. Tomorrow, you may be plugging in your next car instead of filling it up."[1] Similarly, a computer hardware boasted, "On the human network, people everywhere are experiencing a new kind of day. Encyclopedias update themselves every minute. Movies appear wherever there's a screen handy. And a phone can double as a train ticket or a lift ticket. . . . Welcome to a network where anything is possible."[2] To which I would add—you haven't heard the half of it yet! Some future possibilities exceed our ability to even imagine them—though the best science fiction writers help.

Just imagine—as soon as 2015 the U.S. Internet may be 50 times larger than in 2008, or, equal then to 50,000,000 Libraries of Congress.[3] Bill Gates, among others, never tires of sharing a vision of a "digital decade" wherein computers will change everything: "In a world where greeting cards talk to you and shopping carts have display screens, there isn't a Luddite left who doesn't understand this."[4]

While tomorrow seems to raise tougher questions than we can remember from our years in K–12 schooling, "the very knowledge that makes it more difficult to face tomorrow makes it morally imperative that we do so," and, do so with ever more "smarts."[5]

AND NEXT?

Major changes, once begun, generally progress as momentum builds, imagination kicks in, and successes begin to outnumber disappointments. With this in mind, I share below some thoughts about four near-future matters that may especially challenge your schools' Futures Committee, the better to support its proactive planning and action-taking.

The first two are relatively familiar matters—staff re-education needs and also human capital investment needs. The next two are less conventional, but no less vital for that: the Artificial Intelligence Challenge and the Climate Change Challenge. All four are examples of many such matters your Committee should explore now—long before others in the school system and general public do so—to the likely benefit of all.

Had space constraints not pressed on me, we could have also discussed what your Futures Committee might consider regarding alternative energy, biotechnology prospects, e-Government, fundamentalism, nanotechnology, space settlements, terrorism, and many other such intriguing matters. But the four below can stand in to make the larger point: your school Futures Committee has a larger responsibility than might be clear at first glance. For it should serve much as did the canary in the mine—to warn, alert, and help prevent avoidable losses.

1. Learning Curve

An elementary school principal at a 2007 Education Conference explained plaintively, "The only people ready to use all the technology all the time are the students."[6] And these tech-savvy youngsters want to communicate as they learn, get answers rapidly, create information, and rush to share it with valued others. Many of these youngsters exchange information at a much higher level than any previous matched cohort.

Germane is a list of characteristics of twenty-first-century youngsters gleaned from a variety of sources by two education writers: They are not looking for one right answer. They have electronic friends. Have less fear of failure. Are nonlinear risk-takers. Enjoy multitasking. Prefer electronic environments. Share a common language. And feel a sense of entitlement.[7] Youngsters of this ilk, all of them "digital natives," are likely to prove digital innovators. They may convert classrooms into "interactive research and discovery labs supporting a generation of creators, publishers, inventors, and consumers of information."[8]

Communication networks used as recently as ten years ago are already obsolete. By 2010 some 80 percent of Americans ages 5 to 24 are likely to own cell phones—far in excess of those owned by 53 percent in 2005.[9] We rush toward use of Web 3.0, along with other open source and participatory

Web venues. A new generation of information appliances, voice-activated, voice-responsive, and ever more powerful and adaptable than their predecessors, are just over the horizon.

Teachers, especially those still uneven in their employ of computer assets, may face an ever-greater learning curve: "A new digital divide is in our future, one that is largely generational. At its heart will be the fundamental questions of what 'school' really means, and whether digital 'immigrants' [those born before 1984 when the personal computer appeared] can ever really get comfortable with user-generated paradigms."[10]

At issue, then, is the ability of teachers to move from "Sage on the Stag" to "Guide at Your Side," one of "the greatest identity changes in the teaching profession."[11] This is likely to raise the bar concerning the public's expectations of the visual media communication skills of teachers. In combination with the steady rise of student-generated content, this trend underlines the necessity for helping find the funds and free up the time to re-educate many K–12 educators.

2. Human Capital Development

America must face up to a painful realization—its workforce is not keeping up with technological change. If this is to rapidly change—and our future progress requires nothing less—the Future Committees of schools coast-to-coast might want to join with others in championing several education-related reforms.

First, to raise low education outcomes we must help strengthen family life (married men earn 10 to 40 percent more than single men with similar skills, and their children are much more likely to graduate from high school). A tax credit applied against the payroll tax, along with a larger child tax credit and increases in the Earned Income Tax Credit would help reduce economic stresses on low income households.

Second, to create a workforce of superior information-economy workers we must first boost early-childhood education. This means nurse-home visits for children in chaotic families so that they can gain some esteem-building authority in their lives. Preschool should be radically expanded and accountability programs put in place. Likewise, we might end the practice of allowing teenagers to drop out on reaching age 16, as many are not yet mature enough to make so consequential a decision.

Third, taking note of such practices overseas (Israel, etc.), teenagers might be required on graduation from high school to serve a year or two in a National Service Corps before pursuing matriculation at a college or trade school. Some Corps members could learn quickly how to mentor K–12 students, and in "win-win" relationships, help bring everyone along.

Other related reforms beckon, especially creation of high-quality retraining accounts and portable health insurance, but the point by now is clear: The U.S. needs new lifetime policies to assure a future wherein for generation after generation our workforce is "better educated, more industrious, and more innovative than the ones that came before."[12] Futurizing K–12 schooling can make a major contribution, especially if part of a Human Capital Improvement package.

3. Artificial Intelligence

One measure of where we are here is available in the fact that since 1997, when Deep Blue defeated Garry Kasparov in a six-game match, we have reached a point in just one decade when "no human would dare to take on a chess program at even strength. The premier chess engine, *Rybka*, is estimated at 3100, or 300 points higher than any human player."[13]

In another decade or two robots should be able to "operate safely and reliably in any environment that an adult human could, and many more besides."[14] They are en route to do human-level tasks a thousand times faster than you or me; for instance, be able to read an average book in one second with full comprehension.

By about 2015 they should be able to drive, clean well-laid-out buildings, and so on. By 2025, they should be able to handle most human tasks that do not require creativity and flexibility. By 2035, they could be called a human equivalent (a development some futurists call the *singularity*), though we would "still be more flexible and capable of comprehending new kinds of things better."[15]

Capable soon of running our organizations, they may even yet prove able—far down the line—of doing what an expert considers the "one really valuable thing" we cannot do—and that is help solve our moral problems.[16]

At this rate, a time is likely when we humans may have been trumped in almost every way: "In the new ecology of the mind, there will be carnivores and there will be herbivores. We'll be the plants."[17] To defend ourselves is to work *now* to assure "smart" machines evolve into moral agents capable of "knowing" right from wrong, doing right, and being legitimately held responsible for their actions: "Being a set of formal rules is becoming less and less an excuse for being stupid. Neither should it be an excuse for being cruel."[18] Humans must see to it that "smart" machines, each with an artificial version of our mind, exhibit a counterpart of such human traits as conscience, emotion, and empathy.

Accordingly, we need to learn how to build moral character into "smart" machines (robots) as they are likely down the road to take a very large hand in their own further development. And this is where futurizing education comes in: either we quicken the pace of preparing forecasters, some of whom may be expected to specialize in studying advances in artificial intelligence, or we fall farther and farther behind this curve . . . an ominous prospect. In this same vein, we must begin now to discuss the implications of AI augmentation: "The debates of yesteryear about whether to allow students to use calculators on math tests will seem quaint when native intelligence can be enhanced by neural implants and ambient computing" (Rhea, 2005, 47).

4. Climate Change

This challenge in particular sets our era apart and exacerbates anxiety. Climate change would seem well underway, and we fear its worse effects can only be slightly mitigated. It "will eventually be recognized as the most crucial problem facing America and the world—maybe not today, and maybe not tomorrow, but soon, and for the rest of our lives."[19]

Polar bears may soon have much company on an expanded list of endangered species—possibly even including huge masses of bewildered people who find themselves in the wrong climate zones at the wrong time for whatever reason. The Artic Ocean, which experienced record melting in 2007, "could be ice-free in the summer as soon as 2013, decades ahead of what the earlier computer models, told us."[20] The last time the Artic and the Antarctic were warmer than today for an extended period—before the last Ice Age—global sea levels were at least 13 feet higher.[21] The melting "appears to be an accelerating trend with no apparent end in sight."[22]

While not getting the attention it merits, there is a positive side to this harrowing matter. Recognition grows that climate change reforms can prove a unifying issue. Aspiring futurists should study preparations underway to replace the Kyoto Treaty on its 2012 expiration with a robust and far-reaching one quite superior to its controversial precedent. Some experts are forecasting the necessary development of a new global system capable of policing global energy saving measures: "For the first time in history, humanity must make political decisions of a normative and legislative character concerning the species and its future. It cannot do so without principles of an ethic of the future, which should become the concern of all and a cornerstone of democracy."[23]

This appealing possibility notwithstanding, where your school's Future Committee is concerned, endless controversy lays ahead. To reduce emissions of carbon dioxide requires significant, disruptive changes. Disputes here are likely to divide people of good will into two antagonistic blocs, one of which will contend "dangerous climate change is the avoidable catastrophe of the twenty-first century and beyond," while the other will emphatically deny this, and decline to sacrifice on its behalf.[24]

Questions are highly likely to be raised about whether or not to permit the cars of parents waiting to pick-up students to idle in a school driveway or lot. Or to continue to use disposable plates and utensils in the cafeteria, recognizing how much water this saves in recycling reusable stuff. Or to convert to the new light bulbs, despite the mercury hazard they pose when discarded.

Other disputes are more complex, as in what to do about school-owned cars? Calls will be heard for rapid conversion to the use only of the new hybrid models. Critics, however, insist when you "calculate all the energy needed to produce and recycle a hybrid (double engine, batteries, electronics, etc.), the energy efficiency during the car's life turns out to be negative compared to a technologically up-to-date "normal" car (not an SUV)."[25]

Others claim electric cars are superior to cars that run on ethanol, the substitute for gasoline now being urged by many governments. An electric automobile would result in lower carbon emissions than an ethanol one, lower overall energy consumption, and therefore lower cost as well. Rather than have ethanol shipped on trucks to a vast network of car fueling stations, they recommend ethanol be used to generate electricity, and it be sent as electrons to power cars.[26] Opponents, however, point out that almost all electricity comes from coal-burning utility plants, many of which produce much carbon dioxide.

A new option, high-tech "clean air" diesel-powered cars from Europe, can allegedly provide at least 30 percent better fuel economy than cars running on gasoline. They can get more than 40 mph in combined city-highway driving, compared to the mid-20s of the gas versions, and they will meet air-pollution standards.[27] But, they are not made here, and have their doubters.

The car question falls in with similar quandaries under the larger question of what do we mean by "Green"? Some auto makers, for example, want to argue that "the least efficient way to reduce carbon dioxide is doing it through the vehicle. Reducing how much people drive, and cutting the energy consumed in houses, is a better way to cut the amount of carbon we consume."[28]

Your school Futures Committee can expect delegations soon of parents championing all sorts of novel changes; for instance, Green roofs are increasingly popular overseas. In Switzerland, new construction must relocate to the roof the Green space covered by the building's footprint. There are similar regulations in Germany. The idea of a living roof on school buildings (as one exists now on the Pentagon roof) is hailed by proponents as "the essence of poetry and practicality," a highly likely piece of an emerging Green future.[29] Opponents scoff, and point to costs of propping up the load, waterproofing the ceiling, protecting against the elements, and so on.

Only this much is presently clear: "Greening" is likely to generate far more riffs than its backers anticipate, especially as related costs get better known. Backers, however, will fervently argue that "to continue on our current path because the alternative seems too much effort is not just shortsighted—it is suicidal."[30] Your school's Future Committee cannot begin to prepare for the debate soon enough.

SUMMARY

Many of us reel from what Alvin Toffler in 1970 accurately labeled "future shock," a "dizzying disorientation brought on by the premature arrival of the future. . . . It is culture shock in one's own culture," and there is no letup in sight.[31] What is in sight is a major balm for our spirit—the option we have to help our children prepare in far better ways than we can remember of our own K–12 years. To be sure, "we must not mistake a clear view for a short distance."[32] But neither can we dawdle.

HIGHLY RECOMMENDED READING

1) *Beyond AI: Creating the Conscience of the Machine,* by J. Storrs Hall. Amherst, New York: Prometheus Books, 2007. A bold and engaging exploration of the AI challenge, particularly our need for the implementation of morality in it. Hall holds out the possibility that with our aid our future super-intelligent colleagues in the mechanical kingdom may develop superior moral instincts. 2) *2025: Scenarios of US and Global Society Reshaped by Science and Technology,* by Joseph F. Coates, John B. Mahaffie, and Andy Hines. Greensboro, NC: Oakhill Press, 1997. A bold and provocative 500-page exploration, via fifteen scenarios based on 107 assumptions, complete with charts, data, and mind-enriching discussion.

NOTES

1. National City ad. *Wall Street Journal,* January 23, 2008, B3.

2. CISCO ad, *New Yorker,* October 16, 2006, 108.

3. Gomes, Lee. "The Year in Technology: Pirates, Flash memory and Hobbies—Oh, My!" *Wall Street Journal,* January 2, 2008, B1.

4. *Ibid.*

5. Schwartz, Peter. *The Art of the Long View.* New York: Doubleday Currency, 1991, xi.

6. Kim Finch, as quoted in "Quotes of the Month." *Technology & Learning,* March 2007, 6.

7. McLester, Susan and Diane Beaman. "Characteristics of a Digital Native." *Technology & Learning*, March 2007, 20.

8. Bowers, Reveta. "On Schools and Education." In Buckingham, Jane, ed. What's Next: The Expert's Guides. New York: HarperCollins, 2008, 21 (21–23).

9. Holson, Laura M. "Text Generation Gap: U R 2 Old (JK)." *New York Times*, March 9, 2008, BU9 (1, 9).

10. McLester, Susan. "The MySpace Gap." *Technology & Learning*, March, 2007, 22 (4, 22).

11. Rhea, Marsha Lynne. *Anticipate the World You Want: Learning for Alternative Futures*. Lanham, MD: Scarecrow Education, 2005, 49. See also Young, Jeffrey R. "YouTube Professors: Scholars as Online Video Stars." *The Chronicle of Higher Education*, January 25, 2008, A19. In 2008 a Web site, "Big Think," began to offer bite-size interview segments of a few minutes each with academics, authors, politicians, and other thinkers. Another site, FORA.tv, streams lectures and debates featuring noted scholars and intellectuals.

12. Brooks, David. "Fresh Start Conservatism." *New York Times*, February 15, 2008, A23. I draw in this section heavily on this column, and disagree only with the call in it to "loosen the grip of the teachers' unions." I would rather they be on board than behind barricades resisting change. I worry that merit pay undermines morale, though I do agree with Brooks that certification rules can be improved.

13. Benjamin, Joel. "Computers are Ever Mightier, But Still Flawed." *New York Times*, February 17, 2008, 32. See also Kay, John. "Business Lessons from the Chess Grand Masters." *Financial Times*, January 30, 2008, 9.

14. J. Storrs Hall, PhD. *Beyond AI: Creating the Conscience of the Machine*. Amherst, New York: Prometheus Books, 2007, 37.

15. *Ibid.*, 258. "These dates are highly speculative at best, and more important, they assume that the amount of effort put into AI remains at about the level it is now."

16. *Ibid.*, 329. "Their moral sense, just as much as their physical sense, must be able to learn and grow" (p. 329).

17. *Ibid.*, 26. "As the computer becomes less like the dog and more like the butler, it becomes more and more accountable for its actions."

18. *Ibid.*, 27. "This book is about how we might go about achieving that."

19. Ingrassia, Paul. "Detroit's (Long) Quest for Fuel Efficiency." *Wall Street Journal*, February 19, 2008, A19.

20. Walsh, Bryan. "Geoengineering." *Time*, March 24, 2008, 50.

21. Kolbert, Elizabeth. "Hot Topic." *The New Yorker*, February 12, 2007, (27–8).

22. Revkin, Andrew C. "Melting Pace pf Glaciers is Quickening, Study Finds." *New York Times*, March 18, 2008, A8. "The long-term trend was clearly toward a warming world with less mountain ice—and related water troubles, including both floods and shortages, from the Andes to the Himalayas."

23. de Cuellar, Javier Perez, as quoted in Binde, Jerome, *ed. Making Peace with the Earth: What Future for the Human Species and the Planet?* Paris: UNESCO, 2007, 136. Mr. DeCuellar is a former UN Secretary-General.

24. UN *Human Development Report 2007/2008*. New York: Palgrave Macmillan, 2007, 3.

25. Graf, Hans C. "Smaller Cars for Real Efficiency." *The Futurist*, November–December 2007, 4.

26. Granoff, Michael J. "Electric Cars Are Better." *New York Times*, January 22, 2008, A20.

27. *Ibid.*

28. White, Joseph B. "Will Inertia Slow the Green-car Drive?" *Wall Street Journal*, March 18, 2008, D6. "It is wrong to say that the climate change argument is over; there is a large cadre of people who don't accept that man-made CO_2 is a real problem."

29. Rumage, Tim. "Green Roofs: Essence of Practicality." *Positive Change*, November 2007, 78.

30. Kolbert, "Hot Topic," *The New Yorker, op. cit.,* 28.

31. As quoted in Anders, Lou, ed. *Futureshocks*. New York: ROC Book (New Amsterdam Library), 2006, 3.

32. As cited in Thornburg, David D., "Foreword." In McCain, Ted and Ian Jukes. *Windows on the Future: Education in the Age of Technology*. Thousand Oaks, CA: Corwin Press, 2001, viii.

Epilogue

"Put just a spark. If there is some good inflammable stuff, it will catch fire."

Anatole France

What is the takeaway message? In the spirit of a bumper sticker, it might read: "Schools need more of the future, and, vice versa!" More seriously, it can start with two key definitions of mine:

Futuristics is the art of exploring probable, possible, preferable, and preventable tomorrows—with an eye toward increasing our power of choice.

Futurizing education is a process whereby we upgrade the use of futuristics in education—with an eye toward increasing the value of both art forms.

The goal of our campaign is to help "futurize" school systems—that is, make the art of futuristics a comfortable and constructive part of our schools' learning culture. Why? Because futurism should be everyone's "second profession."[1]

SETTING AN AGENDA

To move this along is to first recognize formidable challenges, for we must "never mistake a clear view for a short distance."[2] At the top of a long list is a society-wide lack of information about future-shaping possibilities. More is being learned daily about how to alter our brain, our body, our memory,

135

our life span, and our personalities. More power goes all the time into our computers, our World Wide Web, our use of the Internet, and 101 related technological wonders. In combination this suggests tomorrow is going to differ, far more than resemble, today . . . but you would not necessarily know this from the way school people and the parents of school children envision the future.

To cite just one example from scores I have accumulated over the years, in March of 2008 I joined a half-day seminar that had twenty suburban school superintendents tackle the question, "What might K–12 education resemble in 2016?" The answers these professional educators came up with were achingly prosaic. No one thought to mention any of the high probability/high impact possibilities that make likely radical changes in schooling, things like incredible IT changes, far-reaching adaptations to climate change, and other "gee whiz!" matters racing towards us . . . challenges any such discussion should have included.

Likewise, a week later I attended a half-day conference called by an upscale school district to get future-shaping ideas from over two hundred suburban parents. For quite some time in small groups well-educated men and women shared their wishes for a still-better school system. Once again, however, the reported out feedback was risk-free and conventional. Only very familiar matters surfaced—a call for smaller classes, for adequate recess time, etc. (I was reminded of a gray thought of playwright Eugene O'Neill about Ireland: "There is no present or future, only the past happening over and over again").[3]

Unless and until school superintendents think enthusiastically about possibilities cited throughout this book, we cannot futurize K–12 schooling. We must reach them where many start—in the nation's teachers colleges. Unless and until parents weight the same exciting possibilities, we cannot futurize K–12 schooling. We must persuade teachers to inform parents of the gains possible from futurizing efforts.

Linked with these efforts, we must help state authorities find room for futuristics in the state-required curriculum, as only then will many teachers take notice.[4] We must help school boards look with favor on adaptations of futuristics, as only then will school superintendents do so. We must devise measuring devices, as only that which is counted nowadays gets rewarded. We must help PTAs and other school parent bodies understand what our futurizing campaign is about, and rally them to our side. We must . . . but by now you clearly get the idea: *Much to do!*

REASONS FOR HOPE

For one thing and as briefly noted early, we are in a friendly competition here with comparable nations, one we cannot afford to fall behind in, or worse yet lose. Other nations are busy even now exploring variations on ed-ucational futuristics: Australia (Sustainability Project); Canada ("Vision 2020"), England (FutureSight Project), Holland (Slash/21, etc.), and New Zealand ("Secondary Futures" Program) have ongoing campaigns. We ought to be exchanging notes, adapting their best ideas, and taking care not to fall behind.[5]

Second, we are learning more about how to promote good ideas. For ex-ample, proponents "selling" Green ideas to a skeptical public explain that "in the last few years, we environmentalists have learned how to adapt. Rather than change others, we changed ourselves. We learned to speak the language of sustainability, and this has made all the difference. We now speak of solar panels as an 'investment,' of healthy materials as 'best prac-tices,' and of energy efficiency as a 'bottom line benefit.' Following this ex-ample, the world took notice and Green buildings reached the tipping point we all knew would be inevitable."[6]

A third source of hope involves our need not only to stay abreast, but also try and get ahead of change. Given extraordinary global uncertainties (climate change, China, India, oil shortages, terrorism, water wars, etc.), school systems must help young learners employ the art of horizon scanning, in all of its em-powering aspects. In our bold new world of "wow!" educational aids . . . com-puters as wearable items, exotic virtual reality labs, ubiquitous computing, ver-satile electronic books, and so forth, Generation Next and the New Teachers (see the Introduction) expect nothing less than a futuristic education.

Our century is arguably the most challenging, dangerous, and exciting time in human history. As change, rather than a stable environment, is the norm, futuristics has become a thinking person's natural ally. Every day, new developments have people around the planet asking where this dizzy-ing one fits? And, what does it mean for my life, and that of my offspring (especially, my grandchildren)? As future technologies, related ethical quandaries, and shifts in power continue to change our world, "the biggest questions have yet to be asked."[7] The case for a vastly more future-oriented K–12 educational system gets stronger daily.

A fourth source of hope involves the arrival of a new influential Genera-tion, a post-9/11 cohort that has learned the hard way the future has "wild cards," and is best taken seriously—that is, thought long and hard about, and acted on as creatively as possible. Typical are "EcoMoms," who are pre-occupied with "preparing waste-free school lunches; lobbying for green building codes; transforming oneself into a 'locavore,' eating locally grown food; and remembering not to idle the car when picking up children from school (if one must drive there). [Their] small talk is about the volatile com-pounds emitted by dry-erase markers at school."[8]

These parents "tend to be keenly aware of the vicissitudes of economic success and the fragility of the planet in general. [They] want to give [their children] the best possible chance of surviving and thriving in this scary new world—and more than that, the intellectual tools to help save it."[9] They want their children to graduate school with the capacity to master otherwise disorienting change, and with zest for developing creative responses.

Finally, ever the optimist, I take hope in the possibility our next president might become our Chief Education Officer, our "Learner-in-Chief."[10] Using the bully pulpit, he or she could urge expanding the part played in education by futuristics. The president could emphasize it is low-cost and high yield, a boost to the nation's promotion of life-long learning.

GOING NATIONAL

We need a national steering committee. Made up of highly-placed representatives of America's leading educational organizations (AACTE, AASA, AEE, AFT, CCSSO, CGCS, COSN, EDA, NCTAF, NEA, SIIA, etc.), it can spearhead our futurizing campaign. Build the necessary scaffolding. Help jumpstart the national conversation, and, above all, commit itself to staying on the case.[11] This last attribute is vital, as "a preferred future takes many lifetimes of inspired learning."[12]

Called perhaps Education for Tomorrow (EFT), this creative and dynamic organization (funded by membership organizations) could steadily tackle related challenges. For example:

- It could urge teachers colleges to hire guest futurists and offer required basic courses in futuristics, along with offering subsidies to help with attendant start-up costs;
- It could urge major educational organizations, as backers of the EFT, to include workshops in futuristics at all major gatherings, and add a column boosting the campaign—provided by the steering committee—to its major publications and Web sites;
- It could place informational ads in the popular press explaining to the public why they might support the campaign, and soliciting their suggestions;
- It could promote passage in school districts of a requirement that every student completes an introductory course in futuristics in order to graduate;
- It could create a high-quality Web site that can serve as a clearinghouse for reports from the field of gains and setbacks, and especially of transferable lessons, as the campaign succeeds in opening up more schools to futuristics;

- It could assess and help improve the benchmarks for K–12 use of educational technology proposed in 2008 by the Software & Information Industry Association.[13]
- It could assess and help improve the National Education Technology Plan, now in its third version since its 2005 release by the U.S. Department of Education.[14]
- It could encourage the AFT and NEA to offer workshops in teaching futuristics at regional and national meetings; speakers could be provided at no cost;
- It could hold a national Conference in a different major city every two years (with speakers also invited from abroad) to salute "best practices," and highlight possibilities and perils;
- It could urge attention to futuristics in updates of the 1996 model Standards for School Leaders, and updates of the National Assessment of Educational progress (NEAP); and it could lobby for passage of new federal education legislation—called perhaps, Every Child Helped Ahead—that would include strong, strategic, and lasting support for our futurizing campaign; for example, fund a federal R&D Institute for Educational Futuristics (IEF) at the level of funding for the National Institute of Health.

Naturally, any EFT agenda should revise these starting points as momentum grows, and fresh thinking energizes everyone. When something is both desirable and necessary, it is increasingly politically viable.

Typical of especially tough, and yet also critical efforts the EFT might tackle once it has stability and a track record of success is an impartial search for scientific evidence that bears on the claim futurizing K–12 education *really* pays off. I believe futuristics, when ably conceived and creatively employed, leads to learning successes. I have highlighted such possibilities, but shared no *scientific* evidence, as none as yet exists.[15]

We both know science demands something less squishy than my confidence. If futurizing is as vital a component of a child's formal education as I maintain . . . if its ideas have large and lasting consequence . . . this claim should be verified. Objective evidence is called for—one way or the other—and the EFT should urge outsiders to test the proposition and publicize the findings.

Finally, the EFT should look to a new source of funding, a twenty-first-century generation of relatively young nonconventional donors to education philanthropy. Strong in having controversial ideas about education, in wanting to see change and measurable outcomes, these men and women give nearly $4 billion a year to educational projects, especially if they see them as fundamental game-changing strategies.

Hailed as a "kind of wedge movement into the way we think about education in general,"[16] these new donors want to create environments where the right people and solutions can thrive—as in a high school of the future. Some are close enough to their own K–12 years to appreciate the urgent need to futurize that education.[17] The EFT could linkup with three aggressive human-resource projects already favored by the new donors—New Leaders for New Schools, the New Teacher Project, and Teach for America— and add its futurizing campaign; the combination should win substantial grants.

SUMMARY

Can our goals soon be met? I write in the shadow of the passing on March 18, 2008, of Arthur C. Clarke, the science-fiction/fact writer, who long ago suggested "the only way of finding out the limits of the possible is by going beyond them."[18] Likewise, the world's best-known futurist, Alvin Toffler, urges us to start a national dialogue about what sort of K–12 schooling we really want: "Let's sit down as a culture, as a society, and say, 'Teachers, parents, people outside, how do we completely rethink this?'"[19]

The chances of our pro-future campaign hinge in large part on YOU, and on your many counterparts among the nation's three million teachers, and hundreds of thousands of allies among administrators, office staff, School Board members, parents, and, most especially, concerned students.[20] For as a journalist writing about futuristics points out, "Our enhanced ability to understand the consequences of our acts will make no difference if nobody moves to correct errors."[21]

If you chose to creatively improve on my blueprint, I expect your custom-tailored futurizing program can rapidly earn the appreciation of significant others. And if carefully nurtured, it should go on to earn the long-term continuity it will need to prove its full worth. [22]

If you have gotten this far in this book, you have ideas of your own about how the campaign could be moved along. About what your own school can contribute. About how your school district might take a leadership role here. And about what gains in their "Futures I.Q." could mean for young learners. You understand this is a work in progress, incomplete, but rife with promise.

Time, then, that we got going on it, wouldn't you say?

HIGHLY RECOMMENDED READING

1) *Windows on the Future: Education in the Age of Technology*, by Ted Mc-Cain and Ian Jukes. Thousand Oaks, CA: Corwin Press, 2001. Explores key

trends, new skills needed by students, new roles for teachers, and the need for vision: "We need action beyond our words if we want real change in our schools, and this means we have to stop doing what we are doing now and start doing new things" (128). 2) *The Meaning of the 21ˢᵗ Century: A Vital Blueprint for Ensuring Our Future*, by James Martin. New York: Riverhead Books, 2006. Outlines specific, achievable solutions for solving a wide array of the world's problems. A readable call to arms, and a pragmatic blueprint for change.

NOTES

1. Cleveland, Harlan, as quoted in editorial, "Futurism is not Dead," www.wfs.org/futurism.htm.

2. Saffo, Paul, in Thornburg, David S. "Foreword." In McVann, Ted and Ian Jukes. *Windows on the Future: Education in the Age of Technology*. Thousand Oaks, CA: Corwin Press, 2001, viii.

3. As cited in Dowd, Maureen. "Black, White, & Gray." *New York Times*, March 19, 2008, A19.

4. As many as 62 percent of school systems in 2007 had added an average of three hours of math or reading instruction a week at the expense of time for social studies, art, other subjects. Manzo, Kathleen K. "Analysis Finds Time Stolen From Other Subjects for Math, Reading." *Education Week*, February 27, 2008, 6. See also Dillon, Sam. "Survey Finds Teenagers Ignorant on Basic History and Literature Questions." *New York Times*, February 27, 2008, A16.

5. OECD. *Think Scenarios, Rethink Education*. Paris: Organization for Economic Co-Operation and Development, 2006. See also Hicks, David. *Lessons for the Future: The Missing Dimension in Education*. London: Routledge/Palmer, 2002, and UNESCO. *Toward Knowledge Societies*. New York: UNESCO, 2005.

6. Freed, Eric Corey, "Building in Sustainability," in The Green Media Group. *Greenopia: The Urban Dweller's Guide to Green Living*. Santa Monica, CA: The Green Media Group, 2007, 15.

7. Kelly, Kevin. "Why Do We Still Have Big Questions?" WIRED, February 2007, 124.

8. Brown, Patricia. "For New Wave of 'EcoMoms,' Saving Earth begins at Home." *New York Times*, February 16, 2008, A1 (A1, 12). See also Kristol, William. "Generation Obama? Perhaps Not." *New York Times*, March 17, 2008, A19.

9. Kapp, Diana. "Schools Gone Wild." *San Francisco Magazine*, October 2007, 23.

10. Friedman, Tom, as quoted in "Tom Friedman on Education in the 'Flat World.'" [Interview] *The School Administrator*, February 2008, 16. See the section on the president as learner in Gross, Bertram. *A Great Society?* New York: Basic Books, 1968, 342–348. See also Sisk, Dorothy and Charles E. Whaley. *The Futures Primer for Classroom Teachers*. Unionville, NY: Trillium Press, 1987, 57. "Our primary charge in education today is to develop a perspective which is more future-focused" (3).

11. American Association of Colleges for Teacher Education, American Association of School Administrators, Alliance for Excellent Education, American Federation of Teachers, Council of Chief State School Officers, Council of Great City Schools, Consortium for School Networking, Education Deans Alliance, National Commission on Teaching and America's Future, National Education Association, Software & Information Industry Association.

12. Rhea, 2005, 107.

13. See Trotter, Andrew. "Software Industry Promotes Goals for School Technology." *Education Week*, March 28, 2008, 10.

14. *Ibid*. See also *Education Week*, January 12, 2005, p. 6.

15. The situation of music education is similar, though Futuristics has a clear relationship to immediate policy matters: "It is difficult to translate that conviction [that music has a unique and irreplaceable value] into hard sociological data. Whenever advocates try to build a case for music on utilitarian grounds, they run up against fundamental uncertainties about the ultimate purpose of an art. . . . One problem is that music education lacks a powerful lobby." Ross, Alex. "Learning the Score." *New Yorker*, September 4, 2006, 84 (812–88).

16. Klein, Joel I., Chancellor of the New York City school system, as quoted in Tough, Paul, ed. "How many Billionaires Does It Take to Fix a School System?" *New York Times Magazine*, March 9, 2008, 55 (50–55, 70).

17. Aquirre, Abby. "Easy Come, Easy Go for Idealistic Heirs." *New York Times*, March 8, 2008, ST11.

18. E-mail citation, March 18, 2008. Gerontology Research group; grg@lists.ucla.edu.

19. Toffler, Alvin. "Future School." *Edutopia*, February 2007, 53 (50–53).

20. Writer Daniel Pink notes—"It's such a massively screwed up system that it's inspiring [K–12 educators] are willing to show up every day to push the boulder a little further up the mountain." As quoted in "Tom Friedman on Education in the 'Flat World.'" [Interview] *The School Administrator*, February 2008, 16. (12–18). See also Wallis, Claudia. "How to Make Great Teachers." *Time*, February 25, 2008, 31 (28–34).

21. Hine, Thomas. *Facing Tomorrow: What the Future Has Been, What the Future Can Be*. New York: Knopf, 1991, xii.

22. My blueprint takes controversial stands; for instance, I urge a low-profile "cat's paws" approach, rather than use of a brass band. I discourage a Futures Committee from developing its own forecasts. I urge inclusion of student members. I urge renovation rather than new construction. And I recommend required courses be user-friendly, but also unapologetically demanding. Please e-mail me your disagreements, as I expect I can learn much from them. Do not let them keep you from adapting these ideas, and promoting ever-better use of futuristics in education.

Selected Resources

A 42-page annotated bibliography of futures books in a 2004 book, *Futuring: The Exploration of the Future*, by Edward Cornish, founder of the World Future Society (WFS), is so good as to relieve me of the need to cite many from that pre-2004 literature. Likewise, the annotated bibliography service of the WFS, *Future Survey*, is invaluable for keeping up with the burgeoning literature (it takes note of six hundred books and articles a year). Sixteen especially highly recommended books are highlighted at the close of each chapter, two books each, and are therefore not mentioned below. Please share with me your own recommendations for the articles, books, and websites to cite in the next edition (shostaka@drexel.edu).

BOOKS: FUTURES

Beyond Humanity: CyberEvolution and Future Minds, by Gregory S. Paul and Warl D. Cox. Rockland, MA: Charles River Media, 1996. Explores possibilities after computers have learned to think and are more efficient than humans. Written by an evolutionary biologist and a computer scientist/AI expert. Includes a rare discussion of the future of religion.

Break Through: From the Death of Environmentalism to the Politics of Possibility, by Ted Nordhaus and Michael Shellenberger. Boston: Houghton Mifflin, 2007. Explains why a negative approach ("doomsday discourse") is inferior to an inspiring, positive vision that carries a critique of the current moment within it.

Building the Future, by Jill Loukides and Lawrie Gardner. Washington, DC: World Future Society, 2006. A workbook to accompany *Futuring: The Exploration of the Future*, by Edward Cornish. Rich in chapter outlines, learning objectives, critical thinking questions, activities, self-study questions, etc.

Conversations on the Edge of the Apocalypse: Contemplating the Future with Noam Chomsky, George Carlin, Deepak Chopra, Rupert Sheldrake, and Others, edited by David Jay

Brown. New York: Palgrave Macmillan, 2005. Interviews with visionary thinkers who offer novel insights, intuitions, and paradigms where the future is concerned.

Dimensions of Science Fiction, by William Sims Bainbridge. Cambridge, MA: Harvard University Press, 1986. A pioneering comprehensive quantitative study of audience, effects, methods, and writers: "Science fiction breaks through the walls of ideology, opening eternal doors of transcendence through which the human spirit may fly, out into the universe" (222).

Future Frequencies, by Derek Woodgate with Wayne R. Pethrick. Austin, TX: FringeCore, 2004. Examines how a professional forecasting company operates, and discusses the lessons available for forecasting from provocative cultural figures (progressive culture).

Future Studies: Personal and Global Possibilities, by Charles E. Whaley. New York: Trillium Press, 1984. Discusses how futures studies promotes four goals: 1) Develop the skills and concept necessary to understand complex systems; 2) Develop more sophisticated and positive ways of thinking about possibilities for the future; 3) Understand the nature of change and develop a means for coping with rapid change; 4) Develop abilities that help students identify and understand major issues that will shape their future.

Futuristic Exercises: A Workbook on Emerging Lifestyles and Careers in the 21st Century and Beyond, by S. Norman Feingold. Garrett Park, MD: Garrett Park Press, 1989. This book has 460 engaging and mind-stretching exercises broken down into forty-eight categories, such as creativity, education, lifestyles, war, and work.

Gross National Happiness: Why Happiness Matters for America—and How We can Get More of It, by Arthur C. Brooks. Washington, DC: AEI, 2008. Explores the myths about happiness in America, and finds that secularism, excessive reliance on the state to solve problems, and an addiction to security all promote unhappiness.

Gusher of Lies: The Dangerous Delusions of "Energy Independence" by Robert Bryce. New York: Basic Books, 2008. An attack on the concept of energy independence and the technologies being advanced to achieve it. Goes after one cherished green belief after another, along with the political right.

Infotopia: How Many Minds Produce Knowledge, by Cass R. Sunstein. New York: Oxford, 2006. Offers a "deeply optimistic understanding of the human potential to pool information, and to use that knowledge to improve our lives."

Physics of the Impossible: A Scientific Exploration into the World of Phasers, Force Fields, Teleportation, and Time Travel, by Michio Kaku. New York: Doubleday, 2008. Discusses three types of technology: those not doable today, but possibly so in the foreseeable future; those impossible in the foreseeable future, but do not violate the laws of physics; and those that do violate the laws as we know them today.

Tackling Tomorrow Today, a four-book series edited by Arthur B. Shostak. New York: Chelsea House, 2005. Vol. 1, *Futuristics: Looking Ahead*; Vol. 2, *America: Moving Ahead*; Vol. 3, *Getting Personal: Staying Ahead*; Vol. 4, *Moving Along: Far Ahead*. Original essays written for high-school readers: Constructive, informal, and encouraging. Includes feedback from high schoolers.

The Best that Money Can't Buy: Beyond Politics, Poverty, and War, by Jacque Fresco. Venus, FL: Global Cyber-Visions, 2002. Outstanding example of values-driven Preferable Future advocacy, enriched by stunning artwork and mind stretching thinking. Points to a better world via humane applications of technology and a more appropriate social design.

The Cultural Creatives: How 50 Million People are Changing the World, by Paul H. Ray and Sherry R. Anderson. New York: Three River Press, 2000. Explores arrival of Americans busy creating surprising new cultural solutions, as guided by their own vision for the future. Their self-awareness "will help us all, will help our civilization develop the fresh solutions that we need so urgently now. . . . Visionaries and futurists have been predicting a change of this magnitude for well over two decades" (xii, 5).

The Future Does Not Compute: Transcending the Machines in Our Midst, by Stephen L. Talbott. Sebastopol, CA: O'Reilly & Associates, 1995. Explores our willingness to become "machines." Contends that only in wakefulness can we distinguish ourselves from the automatisms around us: "Computers have led us onto the knife edge, and as our current vertigo already indicates, we cannot long avoid committing ourselves to one side or the other. We will either choose for ourselves, or else receive an unceremonious shove from gathering technological NIUs" (412).

The Future of Everything: The Science of Prediction, by David Orrell. New York: Thunder's Mouth Press, 2007. An unsparing and illuminating account of the difficulties of forecasting: "Even if we cannot predict storms, we can predict our ability to weather them . . . [forecasts] may serve as a compass, point out dangers, and help us navigate an unpredictable world" (348–9).

The Internet Imaginaire, by Patrice Flichy, translated by Liz Carey-Libbrecht. Cambridge, MA: MIT Press, 2007. First published in 2001 in French, this valuable guide discusses two major domains of the technical *imaginaire*: ". . . the utopias and ideologies associated with the elaboration and possibly diffusion of technical devices, and the description of an imaginary virtual society" (13). Ideas are drawn from such Internet seers as de Chardin, William Gibson, George Gilder, Kevin Kelly, Arthur Kroker, Marshall McLuhan, Howard Rheingold, Neal Stephenson, Bruce Sterling, and Alvin Toffler. Flichy ranges far and wide in demonstrating the strategic importance of utopian discourse.

The Next Three Futures, by W. Warren Wagar. Westport, CT: Praeger, 1991. Helpful exploration of how three ideological paradigms within the futures field—the Technoliberal, the Radical, and the Countercultural—play a role in the study of the future.

The Singularity is Near: When Humans Transcend Biology. By Ray Kurzweil. New York: Viking, 2005. Seminal exploration of the long-range union of humans and machines. Our intelligence may become increasingly nonbiological and trillions of times more powerful than it is today, and even death may be turned into a soluble problem. Kurzweil maintains a radically optimistic view of our ultimate destiny.

Viable Utopian Ideas: Shaping a Better World, by Arthur B. Shostak, ed. Armonk, NY: M. E. Sharpe, 2003. Forty-seven original essays that try to clarify preferable futures and detail pragmatic affordable ways to get there from here.

VIVO [Voice-In/Voice-Out]: The Coming Age of Talking Computers, by William Crossman. Oakland, CA: Regent Press, 2004. Path-breaking exploration of a future where a revived oral tradition has replaced our current reliance on writing. VIVO computers may replace all text/written languages in the electronically-developed countries by 2050. Raises the possibility we might be far better off for the transition (www.compspeak2050.org).

What Are You Optimistic About?: Today's Leading Thinkers on Why Things are Good and Getting Better, edited by John Brockman. New York: HarperPerennial, 2007. About 200 short answers to the question, rich in carefully considered optimistic visions of tomorrow.

What's Next: The Experts' Guide, edited by Jane Buckingham, New York: Harper, 2008. Wide-ranging short thought pieces from a diverse assortment of celebrity figures.

365 Ways to Change the World, by Michael Norton. New York: Simon and Schuster. 2007. A year's worth of pragmatic advice on how an individual can make a constructive difference.

BOOKS: EDUCATIONAL FUTURES

A Time to Learn: The Story of One High School's Remarkable Transformation and the People Who Made It Happen, by George H. Wood. New York: Plume, 1999. Nuts-and-bolts account by a principal of a successful renewing, powered by a practical sense of optimism.

Creating the Capacity for Change: How and Why Governors and Legislatures Are Opening a New-Schools Sector in Public Education, by Ted Kolderie. Bethesda, MD: Education Week Press, 2008. Examines the state of K–12 education policy, and offers advice on behalf of achieving real change.

Cyberschools: An Education Renaissance, by Glenn R. Jones. Englewood, CO: Jones Digital Century, 1997. Explores what students and educators need to know about the learning dividends possible from electronic distance education in the knowledge age: "The overlying contribution of cyberschools . . . is that they provide a transfer of power to individuals [that] enables them to transform their own lives. . . ." (163).

Designing Modern Childhoods: History, Space, and the Material Culture of Children, edited by Marta Gutman and Ning de Coninck-Smith. New Brunswick, NJ: Rutgers University Press, 2008. Traces and assesses the specialized architecture (including schools) and objects (including cell phones) that have shaped the private lives of children. Urges reform of government priorities in favor of providing a high-quality environment in early childhood education.

Education for the Twenty-First Century, by William H. Boyer. San Francisco, CA: Caddo Gap Press, 2002. Essays by a pioneer in transformative education. Attention is paid to issues of war and peace, along with alternative visions of the future.

Future Studies in the K–12 Curriculum, by John D. Haas. Silver Spring, MD: Social Science Education Consortium, 1988. While dated where facts are concerned, the manual remains very helpful in its cogency, constructive perspective, and sound guidance.

Hope and Education: The Role of the Utopian Imagination, by David Happin. London: RoutledgeFalmer, 2003. An engaging and mind-stretching case by a British educator for thinking differently and progressively about the future in general and schooling in particular. Urges employ of a "militant optimism of the Will," and makes exemplary use of the Utopian literature.

Leadership and Futuring: Making Visions Happen, by John R. Hoyle. Thousand Oaks, CA: Corwin Press, 2007. Complete with team-building exercises, the book challenges school administrators to think out of the box about links between effective leadership and visioning for the future.

Lies My Teacher Told Me: Everything Your American History Textbook Got Wrong, by James W. Loewen. New York: Touchstone, 1995. Convincing case for reassessing what students are being taught, and opting this time for the truth.

Making the Grade: Reinventing America's Schools, by Tony Wagner. New York: RoutledgeFalmer, 2002. Makes a convincing case for creating the New Village School, and thereby reimagine K–12 education. He urges us to go beyond repair to recreation: "The central task we face is not to *reform* American education, but to *reinvent* it—just as we had to do nearly 100 years ago" (12).

Moderating the Debate: Rationality and the Promise of American Education, by Michael J. Feuer. Cambridge, MA: Harvard Education Press, 2006. Explores the relations between education research, policy, and practice, and proposes ways to improve the relationships in the interest of meaningful reforms. Urges seeking better solutions rather than waiting for the best.

National Differences, Global Similarities: World Culture and the Future of Schooling, by David P. Baker and Gerald K. LeTendre. Stanford, CA: Stanford University Press, 2005. Based on a four-year investigation of K–12 schooling in 47 countries, the authors contend schooling is a worldwide success story: "Into the future, schooling's social power will continue to sustain the kinds of trends we see here, as well as furnish the logic for educational change" (187).

Neohumanist Educational Futures: Liberating the Pedagogical Intellect, edited by Sohail Inayatullah, Marcus Bussey, and Ivana Milojevic. Taipei, Taiwan: Tankang University Press, 2006. Breaks new ground by linking neohumanism (the expansion of humanism to include nature and deep spirituality) with futures thinking and pedagogy. Focuses on human potential rather than on limited quantitative learning. Offers a fresh worldview of a future that honors the inner dimensions of the child.

Shift to the Future: Rethinking Learning with New Technologies in Education, by Nicola Yelland. New York: Routledge, 2007. An Australian Professor of Education explores optimal ways to promote meaningful and useful learning, as aided by cutting-edge technologies.

Smart Machines in Education: The Coming Revolution in Educational Technology, edited by Kenneth D. Forbus and Paul J. Feltovich. Menlo Park, CA: AAAI Press/The MIT Press, 2001. Twelve original chapters that explore the synergy among AI, cognitive science, and education. The book also addresses cultural and political issues involved in the deployment of new educational technologies.

Teaching the Future: A Guide to Future-oriented Education, by Draper L. Kauffman, Jr. Palm Springs, CA: ETC, 1976. A "practical handbook," it emphasizes teaching methods and resources which have been shown to be both effective and flexible."

The Futures Primer for Classroom Teachers, by Dorothy Sisk and C. E. Whaley. New York: Trillium Press, 1987. Contends that "students today, perhaps more than any other time can profit from the experience of future studies to engage their minds and their spirits for the emerging possibilities" (57).

The Future Traveler, by Dianne Draze. Dandy Lion Publications, 1983. A guide for teachers who want "to help students define their relationship with the rest of the world and select the changes that they would like to see happen in their futures" (3).

The Last Word: The Best Commentary and Controversy in American Education., edited by Education Week Press. New York: Jossey-Bass, 2008. Essays from the last 25 years of *Education Week* Commentary.

The Learning Highway: Smart Students and the Net, by Trevor Owen and Ron Owston. Toronto: Key Porter, 1998. Emphasizes how to use the Internet for "understanding and participating in our increasingly competitive and technological world." Features sixteen projects and a postscript of student feedback.

The Scenario Planning Handbook: Developing Strategies in Uncertain Times, by Bill Ralston and Ian Wilson. Mason, OH: Thompson Learning, 2006. Can help school systems change the way they think about and plan for the future. Provides a detailed handbook for developing and using scenarios. Explains the cultural and organizational changes an organization must undertake to maximize the benefits of scenario-based planning.

Think Scenarios, Rethink Education, by Centre for Educational Research and Innovation Paris: OECD, 2006. The latest volume in a valuable series: Schooling for Tomorrow. Scholarly, but still accessible essays by discerning students of futuristics. Twelve chapters and many original essays exploring educational futures overseas.

When the Best is Free: An Educator's Perspective on Open Source Software. By David D. Thornburg. Lake Barrington, IL: The Thornburg Center, 2006. A fine example of a new way of thinking about education in general and educational uses of computers in particular. Explores several powerful open sources software programs that can help schools "stretch their technology budgets while expanding the reach of computers in support of learning."

ARTICLES, JOURNALS, MAGAZINES, ETC.

Edutopia. The indispensable magazine for educators committed to sensible, and yet also cutting-edge innovation. Wide-ranging, reader-friendly, and especially strong in field-proven ideas from teachers.

Future Survey. Monthly abstracts of 50 outstanding articles and books of value to all intent on trying to stay abreast of the tsunami of relevant forecasting literature. Published by the World Future Society.

"Futuristics in K–12 Classrooms," by Arthur B. Shostak. *The School Administrator*, February 2008, 52–54, 56. Makes a detailed case for expanding the use of futuristics in education [predecessor to this book].

Green Teacher: Education for Planet Earth. A quarterly magazine published in Canada with many articles by classroom teachers.

"High Schools for Futurism: Nurturing the Next Generation," by Arthur B. Shostak. *The Futurist*, November–December 2004, 23–27. Explains how we might get there from here. (This book advances the argument four years later).

"Images of a Sustainable Primary School," by Rowena Morrow. In Mack, Timothy C., ed. *Hopes and Visions for the 21st Century*. Washington, DC: World Future Society, 2007, 307–323. Shares a process whereby 8- to 11-year-old Australian children explored their preferred future space at their school: "The students are [now] aware, at all levels, of the impact they can have on the sustainability of the school and what this means in the wider world." (p. 321)

Rethinking Schools. A quarterly magazine written by teachers, parents, and education activists who understand the daily realities of reforming our schools; arguably America's leading grassroots education journal.

The Futurist. Best futures magazine choice for staying abreast of developments; published by the World Future Society.

Yes! Building a Just and Sustainable World. A quarterly magazine published by the Positive Futures Network, Bainbridge Island, WA. Dedicated to making the world a better place.

WEBSITES

www.biosphere.ec.gc.ca—Biosphere Environmental Museum in Montreal offers a free distance learning activity by videoconference to students in grades 8 to 12.

www.curriki.com—A free Web 2.0 application that offers lessons linked to wiki articles; e.g., math activities set within the context of Antarctica, the history and culture of Israel, mobile learning, video production, etc.

www.digitaldirections.org—From the publishers of Education Week, it is designed to help K–12 staff create the right technology solutions for their schools. Provides advice, tips, and tools.

www.earthforce.org—Engages young people in improving their environment and communities through service-learning.

www.elon.edu/e-web/predictions/expertsurveys/default.xhtml—2004–6 surveys on the future.

www.essentialschools.org—Three DVD series and professional development guides to help transform school culture and capture the essence of the Common principles at work.

www.facingthefuture.org—Offers K–4 curriculum on global sustainability. Promotes a learning experience that is simple, local, and personal.

www.GlobalSchoolNet.org—Enables teachers and students to find learning partners worldwide; very cool online projects and teacher tools. Teaches 21st century, information-age skills. Conducts two international student project-design competitions.

www.intel.com/educate—Site of the entries in the annual Intel Science Talent Search, one of America's oldest and most prestigious pre-college science competitions. In 2007–8, over 1,600 students participated.

www.jason.org—Explains how weather forecasters operate; designed for grades 5 to 8, with flexibility to adapt to lower or higher grades. Discusses the use of advanced technologies.

www.listenup.org—"A youth media network that connects youth video producers and their allies to resources, support, and projects in order to develop the field and achieve an authentic youth voice in the mass media."

www.mcreview.com—a source to help teachers keep up to date on the dynamic world of multicultural studies.

www.newvillageschools.org—source for latest information and resources for reinventing American education and creating "new village schools."

www.pmi.org/pmief—The PMI Educational Foundation promotes project management skills and knowledge worldwide to students, nonprofit and community organizations, and society-at-large in order to help them achieve their goals.

www.populationinperspective.org—Material that challenge widely-held myths about power and wealth in the world. Fosters a new sense of global citizenship based not on fear, but on deeper understanding.

www.smartgrowthamerica.com—Research on smart growth issues, including a special program on "smart schools."

www.techlearning.com—Constantly updated advice from school tech coordinators, educators, and administrators. Weekly activities from the Library of Congress and the Exploratorium.

www.teachingforchange.org—Over two hundred books and audiovisual resources on multicultural, and antiracist education.

www.tnty.com/newsletter/futures/lifestyle.html—Valuable distinctive array of short wide-ranging forecasts.

www.rethinkingschools.org—Material that combines theory and practice, while linking classroom issues to broader social policy concerns.

www.wfs.org—World Future Society, complete with a Futures Learning Section.

www.shapingtomorrow.com—British futures source; good coverage of European innovations, including education.

www.sfsf.com.au—Schools for a Sustainable Future.

M.I.T. Repository—Good use—especially in math, science, and technology courses—can be made of the largest Internet site available for video lectures geared to highschoolers, the remarkable M.I.T. collection of over 2,600 audio and video clips from university faculty lectures, as well as assignments and lecture notes. M.I.T. freshmen serve as advisers in choosing resources particularly helpful in preparing teenagers (a status they had only a few months ago) for college-level work. The site's simplicity and clear organization earn it plaudits from high schoolers eager to preview college-level work, albeit many say the material is anything but a cakewalk.

Acknowledgments

Several friends critiqued parts of the manuscript and shared great ideas for strengthening it, not all of which I was wise enough to heed. Their ranks include Tom Abeles, Marc Conforti, Ed Cornish, Michael Marien, Bob Schilling, David Pearce Snyder, and John Renesch. David read the book from start to finish, and shared numerous ideas—for which he has my special thanks. His many suggestions were invaluable.

I am also indebted to Bob Peterson, the editor of the invaluable Rethinking Schools Web site, who sent out my invitation to teachers to share futurizing ideas with me. Very helpful responses came back from Liane Casten, Paula Dance, Alison J. George (whose essay is in this book), H. Andrea Neves, and Katherine Spalding and Kelly Smith (whose essay is in this book). My brother, Stanley Shostak, shared ideas, as did also Robert Merikangas and Ed Trice.

Futurists who have paid special attention to educational futuristics, and warrant particular thanks, include Peter Bishop, Marvin J. Cetron, Harland Cleveland, Joseph F. Coates, Will Crossman, Jim Dator, Christopher J. Dede, Dianne Draze, Jean Houston, Earl C. Joseph, Ian Jukes, Draper L. Kauffman, Jr., Gary Marx, Eleanor Barbiere Masini, Ted McCain, James Morrison, Marsha Lynn Rhea, Billy Rojas, Wendy Schultz, Dorothy Sisk, Richard Slaughter, Stephen F. Steele, Don Tapscott, Alvin and Heidi Toffler, Edith Weiner, and Charles E. Whaley. None, of course, are responsible for faults in my use of their sage counsel.

My editor, Tom Koerner, encouraged this project from the start, was patient and understanding, and never faltered in his belief futurizing was worth bringing to the attention of educators. Editorial Assistant Maera

Winters, assistant production editor Alison Syring, and editor Paul Cacciato all sheparded the production process ably and cordially.

As always before, my wife, Lynn Seng, helped me stay focused, compensated for my lapses in home duties, buoyed my spirits, and in 101 other loving ways, smoothed the path. Words fail me here more than elsewhere . . . but Lynn knows our love for one another makes this all possible.

About the Author

Educated between 1943 and 1954 in public schools in Brooklyn and Queens, New York, Art Shostak earned a B.S. degree at the New York State School of Industrial and Labor Relations at Cornell University (1954–1958). While earning a PhD in Sociology at Princeton (1958–1961), he grew increasingly interested in futuristics. He went on to teach at the Wharton School at the University of Pennsylvania (1961–1967), and then at Drexel University (1967–2003). Between 1975 and 2000, he was also an Adjunct Sociologist at the AFL-CIO George Meany Center for Labor Studies, Silver Spring, Maryland.

Art became a charter member in 1970 of the World Future Society (twenty thousand members in 2008 in over seventy countries). In 1972 he helped create its now-oldest city-level chapter (Philadelphia), and led it for over thirty years. He regularly attended its Annual Meeting, a three-day gathering of two thousand or so forecasters, the largest bloc of whom were, and are today, public school teachers and principals.

Art served for many decades as a consultant on the future with superintendents, principals, teachers, and locals of teachers unions. On in-service days, and especially at the start of a new school year he shared ideas about near future options in K–12 education. In due course he got to advocate K–12 uses of futuristics to audiences at national conferences of the American Federation of Teachers, the National Educational Association, and various national, regional, and local associations of school superintendents, school board members, and PTAs.

At the Annual Meetings of the WFS Art gave papers exploring aspects of the futurizing of education. He also accepted invitations to discuss futurizing pre-college education at Education Conferences in Canada, England, Israel, Japan, South Korea, and Taiwan.

Off campus Art served as co-chair of the board of the Miquon School, outside of Philadelphia, an experimental K–6 school his two sons attended. He also assisted an activist local organization (Citizens Concerned with Public Education) as an assessor of area school quality.

As a writer, Art's 165 articles and 33 books include six books of special relevance: In 2003, he edited Viable *Utopian Ideas: Shaping a Better World* (M. E. Sharpe), and in 2005, he edited a series of four books—Tackling Tomorrow Today—each with original essays written for high school students (Chelsea House). Now, in retirement he enjoys writing, seeing the world with his wife Lynn Seng, and enjoying his grandchildren.

Praise for *Anticipating the School You Want*

"Arthur B. Shostak's new book, *Anticipate the School You Want*, is an extraordinarily timely addition to the literature. The time is certainly right for a practical tome which builds upon the long-recognized need for providing the next generation with the tools to shape their own futures, and Dr. Shostak has provided a cogent and knowledgeable set of guidelines for making that happen. This is not a book for dreamers but for working teachers, with resources, strategies, and expected outcomes. And it does not underestimate the obstacles to changing schools for the better, but instead outlines a strong case for why the teaching of foresight in K–12 programs must be initiated and then expanded. The book is articulate and thoughtful, providing an excellent introduction to foresight and its benefits, as well as well crafted lesson plans and related documentation. In a time when change can be disruptive and confusing, this book shines a light on the potential for innovative improvement within the education system."
— TIMOTHY C. MACK, president, World Future Society

"Arthur B. Shostak's book does two things excellently: it makes an ironclad case for the necessity of integrating futuristics with K–12 education, and it proposes common-sense concrete steps we can take now to begin to make this integration a reality. In my grade book, Shostak gets an A+."
— WILLIAM CROSSMAN, author of *VIVO [Voice-In/Voice-Out]: The Coming Age of Talking Computers*, and faculty at Berkeley City College, Berkeley, California

"Arthur B. Shostak has created an extremely thought-provoking treatise, challenging all to see the future possibilities. He is laying the groundwork for redesigning our educational system to allow our children to be properly prepared for the future. Shame on us if we do not take up his call. Our children deserve nothing less."

—MARK D. CONFORTI, elected member,
Montgomery Township Board of Education, New Jersey

"Arthur B. Shostak has an extraordinary gift: he synthesizes large amounts of information into significant future trends; he makes connections between the present and the future; and he charts understandable paths to make the journey both fruitful and optimistic. Professor Shostak recently helped create an extraordinarily successful strategic planning event with the Montgomery Township community. I recommend his book to all school administrators interested in managing the future."

—SAM STEWART, acting superintendent,
Montgomery Township School System, New Jersey

"Futures Studies should be considered an essential part of education. Arthur B. Shostak lays out a cascade of possibilities for making it happen. At the heart of his book is learning through inquiry . . . with a futuristic twist."

—GARY MARX, president,
Center for Public Outreach, Vienna, Virginia

"Arthur B. Shostak makes a compelling and practical argument for a transition from a linear education model of the 19th and 20th centuries to a synergistic model for the 21st century. The book moves from concept to process to practical strategies with concrete examples that enhance implementation. The "how-to" nature of the work is particularly valuable to anyone looking for one map for the future of education."

—STEPHEN F. STEELE, PhD, professor of sociology and futures studies
at the Institute for the Future of Anne Arundel
Community College, Maryland

"Not since Alvin Toffler's classic anthology *Learning for Tomorrow: the Role of the Future in Education* (written over 30 years ago) have we had such a comprehensive attempt to infuse learning with futuristic thinking. I predict that along with Toffler, Arthur B. Shostak's book will also become a classic in the field, a standard by which 21st-century educators and futurists will measure their own endeavors. Chapter 1 sets the tone, a ruthless definition of what futuristics is and what it is not, and the implications this has for educators. The rest of the book, following on this brilliant opening gambit, does not disappoint. By clearing the rubble of failed futuristic structures of the past

Shostak prepares the ground for a much more robust theoretical and practical edifice. Shostak's fundamental intellectual honesty infuses the entire book with a practical, doable approach rarely found in academe but which is most welcome for those of us who labor in the frontlines of real life educational systems. His proposals for what should be and what could be done are disciplined by a pragmatism of what can be done in the complex educational reality of today. A must read for all those concerned that modern educational systems are becoming increasingly inadequate to the needs of the 21st century."

—Tsvi Bisk, director,
Center for Strategic Futurist Thinking

"Arthur B. Shostak is one of the most creative and innovative futurists that we have. He has developed some powerful ways how to deal with the future learning for our children where they need it most—in the K–12 school system. If America is to have a significant part to play in the future of our globalized world, those who are in charge of the education of the next generation should read and implement what he is suggesting."

—Rabbi, Dr. Moshe Dror, president,
World Network of Religious Futurists

"As a long-time foreign observer and resident of Japan with two children, it seems clear to me that the Japanese education system needs to encourage the kind of "out of the box" thinking and exploration embodied by Arthur B. Shostak's "Future IQ" concept."

—Carl Kay, Tokyo-based consultant and
author of *Saying Yes to Japan*, as well as
vice president of the Harvard Club of Japan

"Arthur B. Shostak calls on schools to recognize the urgency of preparing students for a future where people will need to learn collaboratively how to solve significant global and local challenges. Learning about our future is just as important as learning about our past, and Shostak offers practical advice about how to create space in our educational priorities to bring a greater awareness to the wisdom of both perspectives."

—Marsha Lynne Rhea, Senior Futurist, Institute for Alternative Futures
and author of *Anticipate the World You Want: Learning for
Alternative Senior Futurist, Institute for Alternative Futures* and
Anticipate the World You Want: Learning for Alternative Futures